CURIOSITIES

OF

BRISTOL

AND ITS NEIGHBOURHOOD:

WITH A GUIDE, FOR THE USE OF STRANGERS.

BRISTOL:

M. MATHEWS, BRISTOL DIRECTORY OFFICE.

LONDON: HOULSTON AND STONEMAN.

AND MAY BE HAD OF ALL BOOKSELLERS.

First published by M. Mathews 1854
This edition first published 2010

The History Press
The Mill, Brimscombe Port
Stroud, Gloucestershire, GL5 2QG
www.thehistorypress.co.uk

© Dr J.K.R. Wreford, 1854, 2010

The right of Dr J.K.R. Wreford to be identified as the Author
of this work has been asserted in accordance with the
Copyrights, Designs and Patents Act 1988.

British Library Cataloguing in Publication Data.
A catalogue record for this book is available from the British Library.

ISBN 978 0 7524 5413 9

Typesetting and origination by The History Press
Printed in India, Aegean Offset

PREFACE.

It is with much regret that we have to announce that, circumstances, into which we need not enter, have induced us to suspend, for a time, the publication of this periodical.

We have the satisfaction of knowing, that in the short time during which the work has been in existence, many interesting and valuable papers have appeared in it, which have been the means of throwing light upon some points of our local history and antiquities, and of correcting several errors into which some former writers had fallen.

It may be proper to mention, that the article on the Interior of Bristol Cathedral (p. 14), contains a few mistakes: it was inadvertently admitted into our columns by the gentleman who was the projector of the work, during a period of severe illness, and who—unhappily for his family and his friends—closed his useful career soon after the commencement of the undertaking.

To all those who have assisted us by their contributions and their suggestions, we beg to offer our best acknowledgments.

J. K. R. W.

Bristol, *July*, 1854.

INDEX.

GUIDE BOOK TO THE
CURIOSITIES OF BRISTOL
AND ITS NEIGHBOURHOOD.

PREFATORY NUMBER TO THE "CURIOSITIES OF BRISTOL."　　　　PRICE 1d.

THE CITY OF BRISTOL.

To the brief notice of the origin of Bristol, (" *Curiosities*," p. 1) the following details are here added.

In 1735, the number of houses in this city was 6701; in 1788 they had increased to 8701. The population was at the latter date between 70,000 and 80,000. The manufacture of brass was commenced in 1704; that of zinc in 1743. In 1745, the receipt for one year of wharfage,—a local toll on foreign imports and exports,—was £918: In 1775, £2000. From the year 1750 to 1757 the average net receipts of the Customs at Bristol was £155,189; at Liverpool, £51,136. The net receipt at Bristol in 1764 was £195,000; the number of vessels reported inwards 2353. After the latter date the trade at Bristol began to decline: we find that in 1784, the customs of this city yielded 334,909; those of Liverpool, 648,684.

The reason of the decline of the business at Bristol was owing partly to the local taxation and partly to the springing up of the great manufactories at manufactories at Manchester, Bolton and other cities of the north of England; nearly all their goods were sent through Liverpool.

In 1848, Bristol was made a free port, and since that time a very great improvement has taken place. The revenue shows from the returns a very large increase during the last two or three years, and there seems every probability of continued prosperity.

The population of Bristol, according to the last census, is 137,328. The number of houses, 18,850, including the out parishes of St. Paul's and St. Philip's.

ANCIENT REMAINS.

THE following ancient remains should be visited by the lovers of antiquity. The architectural peculiarities of some are very remarkable and interesting.

REMAINS OF THE CASTLE, in Tower Street, in a house and coach-house on the right hand side.

A PORTION OF THE CITY WALL and a bastion; on the Froom. This can be seen in going from Union Street into the Pithay.

The remains of an ancient tower are to be seen on the Froom, at the back of the central police station.

ST. JOHN'S GATEWAY, under the church of St. John, bottom of Broad Street. The north gate of the city.

TOWER GATE, at the bottom of John Street. One of the smaller entrances to the city.

THE ANCIENT NEW-GATE was removed many years since to Arno's Vale, Brislington.

BUTTRESSES OF ST. JAMES'S PRIORY. Between St. James's Church and the Barton Alley (now called Bond Street).

ENTRANCE GATEWAY OF THE ABBEY of St. Augustine, College Green.

REMAINS OF THE ABBOT'S HOUSE and Bishop's Palace, and entrance thereto, on the south side of the Cathedral. A small but interesting Norman crypt underneath.

DOORWAYS and other remains in the Cloisters of the Cathedral, formerly leading to the Refectory, etc., of the Monastery.

ENTRANCE GATEWAY of St. Bartholomew's Hospital, Christmas Street.

DORMITORY and other remains of the monastery of the Black Friars, situated in "the Friars," Merchant Street.

A few scanty portions of the HOSPITAL OF ST. CATHERINE, Brightbow, Bedminster.

CRYPT under the house long occupied by the Messrs. Stuckey and Co., at the corner of High Street and Wine Street; supposed by some to have been the crypt of a church dedicated to St. Andrew.

NICHE AND FRAGMENT of a winged Lion in a house at the corner of Pipe Lane and Frogmore Street, marking the boundary wall of the Hospital of the Gaunts in that direction.

CHAPEL IN CANYNGES' HOUSE, Redcliffe Street. The modern house in which this interesting relic is preserved, is inhabited by Mr. Jeffries, bookseller.

REMAINS OF THE WEAVERS' HOSPITAL on the east side of Temple Street, under a building formerly the Jews' Synagogue, now used as a school for poor girls.

Some slight remains of the FORT ON BRANDON HILL, may still be seen on the summit of the hill.

PLACES OF WORSHIP.

ACCORDING to the Census of Religious Worship in England, recently published, it appears that there are 119 places of worship in this city. Of these, 42 are occupied by the Church of England. The remaining 77 chapels are divided as follows:—Independents, 19; Particular Baptists, 9; Baptists, (undefined) 1; Society of Friends, 1; Unitarians 2; Moravians, 1; Wesleyan Methodists, 12; Primitive Methodists, 2; Bible Christians, 1; Wesleyan Reformers, 10; Calvinistic Methodists, 1; Plymouth Brethren, 1; Isolated Congregations, 8; Catholics, 6; Latter Day Saints, 2; Jews, 1.

THE CHURCHES.

At page 43 (*Curiosities*) is a list of the ancient churches of Bristol, all of which, with the exception of two or three, are well worthy a visit from the antiquary. For the fullest particulars respecting their styles of architecture, we refer the reader to Mr. Pryce's excellent " Notes on the Ecclesiastical and Monumental Architecture and Sculpture of the Middle Ages in Bristol," published by Lavars, Bridge-street, which is the only work on the subject of the churches of Bristol, on which reliance can be placed.

The following is a list of the modern parish churches, district churches, and chapels of ease within the boundary of the county of Bristol. The architecture of most of them is plain and devoid of taste. Two or three are constructed in a manner belonging to no style of English architecture, and are perfect abortions.

REDLAND CHAPEL—Chapel of ease to Westbury.
ST. PAUL—Portland Square.
DOWRY CHAPEL.
CLIFTON CHURCH, dedicated to St. Andrew.
ST. GEORGE—Great George Street.
TRINITY—Hotwell Road.
ST. PAUL—Bedminster.
TRINITY—End of West Street, St. Philip's
ST. MATTHEW—Kingsdown.
BLIND ASYLUM CHAPEL—top of Park Street.
ST. JOHN THE EVANGELIST — Durdham Down.
ST. BARNABAS—Ashley Road.
ST. LUKE—Near the Cotton Works.
CHRIST CHURCH—Clifton Down.
ST. ANDREW—Montpelier.
ST. SIMON—Baptist Mills.
ST. JUDE—Poyntz Pool.
ST. MATTHIAS—Broad Weir.
ST. PAUL—Victoria Place, Clifton.

A new church is being erected at Bedminster in place of the ancient structure, dedicated to St. John-the-Baptist, which was in so dilapidated a condition, that it became advisable to pull it down.

The foundation stone of another church, to be dedicated to St. Clement, has been laid at the end of Milk Street, in the parish of St. Paul.

At the chapel attached to Barstaple's or Trinity Hospital, Old Market (see " Hospitals," &c., p. 75); the chapel of the Orphan Asylum, Hooks' Mills; the chapel adjoining Forster's Almshouse (see p. 75.); and at Colston's Almshouse, St. Michael's Hill; the service of the Church of England is performed on stated days.

PUBLIC BUILDINGS.

COUNCIL HOUSE.

THE present building was erected 1824—1827, in place of an older structure which had been in existence for a long period (see p. 2.). Here much of the local business of the city is transacted; and the magistrates sit daily in their court. The Council Chamber is a very handsome apartment, and is adorned with many good paintings of eminent men, and with autograph letters of Lord Nelson and others, acknowledging their reception of the freedom of the city.

THE GUILDHALL,
BROAD STREET.

THE present building which stands on the site of a former structure, was opened for public business in 1846. The Assize, in August, the Quarter Sessions, the Tolzey Court, the County Court, and the Court of Bankruptcy are all held here. The statues on the exterior are those of King Edward III., Queen Victoria, Dunning Lord Ashburton, Sir Michael Foster, Edward Colston, and John Whitson.

THE EXCHANGE,
CORN STREET.

THE foundation stone of this handsome building was laid on March 10, 1740. It has been cleaned and repaired twice since that time.

THE POST OFFICE,
CORN STREET,
On the West of the Exchange.

THE COMMERCIAL ROOMS,
CORN STREET,

ADJOINING the West end of the church of St. Werburgh. This edifice was opened in 1811. The London daily and weekly papers, and the provincial journals are taken in here, as well as magazines, &c.

THE CUSTOM HOUSE AND THE EXCISE OFFICE,

are both in Queen Square. The old offices were burnt down at the Riots of 1831, and the present structures erected soon afterwards.

THE MERCHANT VENTURERS' HALL, Corner of King Street, was originally built in 1701. The present front was erected about 1790. The society of Merchant Venturers' was incorporated in the sixth year of the reign of King Edward VI., it is the only one of the twenty-three trading companies now in existence.

These are the most interesting remains easy of access in this city. In some private houses are to be seen very curious staircases, chimney-pieces, etc., and the visitor will notice some curious fragments in most of the streets.

In addition to the houses mentioned p. 78, should be seen,--

ST. PETER'S HOSPITAL, formerly the residence of Thomas Norton, the Alchymist, built about 1400, but greatly altered at a subsequent period. The large room there, is exceedingly handsome, and has some very curious carving.

The Mansion of ROBERT STURMYE, one of the old merchant-princes of Bristol, on the Back, known as the Back Hall. Adjoining it are some remains of Spicer's Hospital.

COLSTON'S HOUSE in Small Street, which has been for the last half century the office of the Bristol Mirror. The large hall is a very handsome apartment; here Charles the First and his two sons were entertained.

In King Street, No. 9, (opposite the seaman's hospital) is the house of John Romsey, Town Clerk of Bristol, in which he entertained JUDGE JEFFERYS, when he visited this city at the period of the Bloody Assize.

PLACES OF AMUSEMENT.

THE THEATRE ROYAL,
KING STREET.

(For an account of the Ancient Theatres in this city, see p. 45.). The present elegant theatre was opened in 1766. It was enlarged and re-decorated in 1853; and was re-opened in September 1853, under the management of Mr. J. H. Chute, who has carried it on with great spirit and judgment. Mr. Chute became lessee at the death of his mother-in-law, Mrs. Macready, who had held it for many years.

The theatre is usually open from September to May or June. We trust that the efficiency of the company and the excellent character of the plays produced there, will insure for it, a large and increased share of the patronage of the public.

ZOOLOGICAL GARDENS,

Durdham-down. The gardens are extensive and well laid out. The zoological stock includes a great variety of the most rare and peculiar of the animal creation. The public are admitted on payment of sixpence each person. The children attending free-schools are admitted on Fridays at twopence each child.

THE ASSEMBLY ROOMS, PRINCE'S STREET. Until the building of the Victoria Rooms, this was the usual place where concerts, etc., were held.

It is a handsome room, and most eminently fitted for music. It is now used for panoramas, conjurers, etc.

THE VICTORIA ROOMS,

CLIFTON, Nearly opposite Tyndall's Park Gate. These handsome rooms, in which all the principal concerts, balls, etc., take place, were built in the year 1840, and were opened, 1842.

THE ROYAL ALBERT ROOMS,

COLLEGE GREEN, are also used for concerts, lectures, and exhibitions of various kinds.

THE BROADMEAD ROOMS.

THE large room has lately been re-decorated, and is now an elegant apartment. Concerts, lectures, etc., are given here; and all the excellent entertainments provided by the Early Closing Association.

THE BRISTOL ACADEMY FOR THE PROMOTION OF THE FINE ARTS,

is at present at No. 18, St. Augustine's Back; a new building will soon, we understand, be erected near the Victoria Rooms. An annual exhibition of the works of the members is held in the rooms of the academy, and lectures are delivered on stated occasions for the instruction of the pupils.

We hope that the city which boasts of a Lawrence, a Baily, a Danby, and a Müller, will not be backward in lending every possible means for the furtherance of the objects of the Academy.

THE BRISTOL ATHENÆUM,
NICHOLAS STREET.

THE new building of this useful and valuable institution is only partly open. It will, we understand, be entirely thrown open in the course of the autumn of this year. In consequence of the want of a proper hall at their late rooms, no lectures have been given for some length of time. They will be resumed after the opening of the building.

THE BRISTOL INSTITUTION,
FOR THE ADVANCEMENT OF SCIENCE, LITERATURE, AND THE ARTS,
AT THE BOTTOM OF PARK STREET.

THIS institution was founded in 1820, and the building was opened in 1823. There is a reading-room, library, museum, a theatre for lectures, etc. Many curious and interesting relics are preserved in the museum. Among the works of sculpture may be seen Baily's statue of Eve at the Fountain, and casts from many of the ancient sculptures. The specimens of reptiles, shells, etc., are very extensive and interesting. Lectures on literary and scientific subjects are now delivered here every Monday evening from October to April.

Strangers may be introduced to the musum and reading-room for a month by a member of the institution.

THE BRISTOL LIBRARY,
IN KING STREET.

THIS institution was founded in 1615, by Mr. Robert Redwood, who bequeathed a house in King Street for a public library. In 1636, some land adjoining was given by Mr. Richard Vickris, at the time Sheriff of Bristol, in order that the library might be enlarged. The library was opened in 1773; it only contained 500 volumes, but the numbers gradually increased in consequence of gifts made by several individuals in this city.

It is much to be desired that this building should be made a Public Library, and we trust that the time is not very far distant when it will be thrown open for the use of the public of this great city, which unhappily has no such institution.

For a full account of the Bristol Library, we refer the reader to Mr. Tovey's very excellent work on the subject.

PUBLIC GROUNDS, SQUARES, ETC.

BRANDON HILL.

No visitor should omit to ascend Brandon Hill. "From this lofty eminence, rising in the midst of the city, is one of the noblest town views upon which the eye can possibly rest. Looking towards Bath, the vast city, spread out upon an undulating ground, lies tranquilly beneath, reeking with the black-and-blue breath of a scattered host of factory chimneys, among which the dark pyramids of the glass-houses loom heavily, and the square towers and pointed spires of the churches, half buried in the smoke, lift their gilded weather-vanes into the sun-light. Right in front, on the eastern verge of the city, and farthest from the eye, a dense and almost impenetrable brown mist marks the grimy and hovel-crowded district of 'The Dings,' where labour and squalor have shaken hands and made a compact together to withstand the opposing forces of civilization and comfort. To the left, the lower town stretches away upon an extensive level, the limits of which are concealed from view by interposing buildings on high ground close at hand. Down deep below, on the right, gleams the pent-up water of the wide 'float,' by which the shipping is brought into the heart of Bristol. The summit of Brandon-hill is a place of

favourite resort; pleasant walks are laid out, and seats are fixed for the accommodation of the citizens. Here on the night of the 30th of October, 1831, might have been seen many an alarmed and anxious group watching the progress of the fires of incendiarism and rapine, while the city below, all but surrendered to the hands of a lawless and drunken crew, resounded with the shouts of demoniac riot and ravage, and the red flames, shooting high into the sky from various quarters at once, proclaimed to all the country for twenty miles around the ruffian rule of the plundering mob. Queen-square lies in front, a little to the left, at the distance of about half a mile."

Descending Brandon-hill on its eastern side, and ascending the opposite height, we reach CLIFTON; which during the last two or three generations, has risen from comparatively a village. Noble streets and handsome mansions have usurped the level down and the abrupt declivities, and on all side the evidences of wealth and architectural taste meet the eye.

CLIFTON DOWN,

Is an extensive piece of open ground centrally situated amid the villas of Clifton. On the side towards ST. VINCENT'S ROCKS, it is bounded by the acclivity on which is the old BRITISH ENCAMPMENT. Within the area of the camp is the CLIFTON OBSERVATORY. All visitors to Clifton should enter the observatory, in which there is an admirable camera obscura, which paints upon its white disk the whole of the surrounding scenery with wondrous truth and vivid colouring. Here also are capital telescopes for the convenience of the visitor, by means of which he may on a clear day take a peep into Wales, and scan any part of the distant horizon: there are various scientific instruments besides, in the use of which an hour or two may be profitably and agreeably employed. But, perhaps, the greatest attraction which the observatory presents to the antiquary is Ghyston Cave, or as it is more frequently called, the GIANT'S CAVE. This is a cavern of some considerable extent, situated, according to the statement of William Wyrcestre, who visited it in 1480, in the heart of the rock at the height of sixty vethym (fathoms) above the bed of the river, and about ninety feet from the summit of the rock. It is said to have been formerly a hermitage, containing a chapel and an oratory. The proprietor of the observatory, which is situated nearly over the cave, has excavated a passage through the solid rock, to which an entrance by a circular flight of steps is obtained from the large telescope-room. There is a fine view from the cave.

DURDHAM DOWN,

Adjoins Clifton-down, and its extensive dimensions renders it a favourite resort for equestrians.

VICTORIA SQUARE

Is situated in the centre of Clifton, and presents, as far as it is completed, architectural features more uniform and handsome than any other in the city. In the ornamental grounds of the centre is the only public fountain yet erected in Bristol.

COLLEGE GREEN,

Extends from the near river, opposite the principal quay, towards Brandon-hill. It is flanked by lofty trees. On the south side is the CATHEDRAL. This edifice is a beautiful and venerable structure, and adds greatly to the picturesque aspect of this portion of the city.

QUEEN SQUARE,

The principal arena of the disgraceful riots of 1831, lies between the old city and the confluence of rivers Froom and Avon which invest the square on three sides. External to the square, on the east, south, and west, are the wharfs, distinguished as the Welsh Back, —The Grove,—The Narrow and the Broad Quays.

PORTLAND SQUARE. BRUNSWICK SQUARE. KING SQUARE.

The three squares above mentioned are on the northern side of the city, in the parish of St. Paul's. The first named is the largest, and in the centre it has an enclosed space laid out with walks and shrubberies.

ST. JAMES'S CHURCHYARD.

In addition to the burying ground is an extensive open space on which the Hay Market is now held, twice a week. On this spot were buried those who fell in Bristol during the Great Plague; and it afterward became a prevalent idea that the ground dared not to be excavated for any purpose, on account of the direful consequences certain to ensue.

THE CEMETERY, ARNO'S VALE,

Is open to the public free of charge. It is extensive and has been laid out with great taste. The chapels are handsome erections; and many of the monuments about the grounds are tasteful and costly structures.

ENDOWED INSTITUTIONS.

THE BRISTOL INFIRMARY.

Established in 1735. Two spacious wards were opened in 1841, which greatly added to the accommodation of the sick and wounded. This institution expends annually between £6000 and £7000 in its ordinary disbursements. It receives, on an average, upwards of 2500 in, and 15,000 out patients; total, about 17,500 per annum. The building contains baths, a lecturing theatre, an operation room—which not unfrequently contains 100 spectators—a valuable library, and an extensive and exceedingly rich museum, bequeathed and endowed by the late Richard Smith, Esq., and a room for the accommodation of the students. The wards contain 245 beds. The Charity is supported by annual subscriptions of two guineas and upwards;— legacies also from a large item in the receipts.

BRISTOL GENERAL HOSPITAL,

Guinea-street,—established in 1832. In-patients to December 1852, 483. Out-patients, 5207.

CITY SCHOOL.
(Queen Elizabeth's Hospital.)

Two hundred boys are maintained and educated. The building is a massive and imposing structure built in the Tudor style, placed on a commanding site on the north-west slope of Brandon-hill.

COLSTON'S HOSPITAL. COLSTON'S SCHOOL.

The former in St. Augustine's Place, for educating and maintaining 100 boys; the latter in Temple Street, for 40 boys. There is a portrait of the founder in the school-room in Temple Street.

RED MAIDS' SCHOOL,

Denmark Street, for educating and maintaining 120 girls.

BISHOP'S COLLEGE,

Park Street, for youths of the higher classes, in connection with the Church of England.

BAPTIST COLLEGE,

Stoke's Croft, for educating young men as ministers, in connection with the Baptist denomination.

THE MUSEUM at the Baptist College contains many rare and valuable relics of historic interest. An inspection of them will be courteously granted to strangers by the gentlemen of the college who have them in charge.

The following may be mentioned:—

Cromwell's likeness—one of two. This original portrait of Oliver Cromwell (painted by Cooper), was left to the Baptist Museum in Bristol, by the Rev. Andrew Cibbard, D.D., who assured John Page, Esq., that he had been offered for it from the Empress of Russia, the sum of 500 guineas.

In the same case a concordance printed in 1673—edited by—Owen, D.D., on the waste leaf is—" John Bunyan, his book."

The life of Francis Spiera—the well known apostate. The work is in Latin, and Bishop Latimer's autograph is on the title.

A Specimen of Bitumen from the Lake of Sodom.

A flagon holding about three quarts. Part of the communion service of the most ancient Baptist congregation in this city, which met at the Friars under the care of —. Hyman, 1645.

An original letter from Oliver Cromwell, to Captain Underwood, dated June 6th, 1645, from Huntingdon; directing the breast-work to be strengthened, and adding,—"desire Col. Fothergill to take care of keeping a strong guard."

Two letters from the same, addressed to Gualter Frost, Esq., given at Whitehall, January 1st, 1654; the other dated 24th of January, 1654. The first directs to pay the salary of the persons enumerated, amounting to £242 13s. 4d. The second directs the payment of salaries amounting to £1000, "of which you are not to fail."

A pair of white lace gloves which belonged to Queen Elizabeth. Tradition states that she left them behind when she visited Bristol.

A piece of embroidered serge, labelled—"A piece of Wycliff's Garment."

BRISTOL ASYLUM FOR THE BLIND.

The object of this institution is to instruct the blind in some useful employment, by which they may be enabled to provide for their maintenance. The principal manufactures are fine and coarse baskets and door mats of various kinds, which are on sale at the Asylum. The blind are also taught reading by the embossed Roman character, singing the organ, pianoforte, etc.

INSTITUTION FOR THE DEAF AND DUMB,

Park Row.

ORPHAN ASYLUM,

Ashley Hill; for receiving destitute girls, qualifying them for servants in respectable families.

NEW ORPHAN HOUSE, ASHLEY DOWN,

For maintaining and educating 300 destitute children, bereaved of both parents. Supported by voluntary contributions.

Another and larger edifice is about to be erected by the founders of the last-named; intended to accommodate 1000 orphans.

ALMS HOUSES.

There are 22 ALMS HOUSES in various parts of the city, each of them for stated numbers of aged inmates; some for males, others for females.

———o———

In addition to the above are many excellent minor charities, public schools, asylums, annual gifts to the poor, and various benevolent societies.

BATHS.

Baths and Wash-Houses, Ropewalk. No. 9, College Green, warm, cold, vapour, etc.

Hotwell House, warm, cold, and vapour. Sion Hill, Clifton, warm and cold. Jacob's Wells, cold. Rennison's Bath, Montpelier. Victoria Baths, East Clifton.

PLACES TO BE SEEN IN THE NEIGHBOURHOOD.

———

GLOUCESTERSHIRE.

———

BERKELEY CASTLE,

About twenty miles from Bristol, now easily accessible by rail-road. This interesting building was founded in the reign of Henry I., and was enlarged in subsequent times. Here the unfortunate Edward II. was murdered, and the room is still shown in which the deed was perpetrated. This is one of the residences of Earl Fitzhardinge.

The church, which is very large, contains a chapel, the place of sepulture of the Berkeley family. The tower stands at some distance from the church; it probably belonged to an older structure.

THORNBURY CASTLE,

Eleven miles from Bristol, was commenced in 1511 by "poor Edward Bohun," Duke of Buckingham, who was beheaded in the reign of Henry VIII.

The Castle was never completed, but what there is, is mostly in good preservation and is very beautiful. A very remarkable echo is to be heard in the court-yard. The church is a very fine structure in the perpendicular style of architecture. It has lately been restored with taste and judgment.

ALMONDSBURY, about six miles from Bristol, should be seen on account of the extensive and beautiful view of the Severn from the hill. The church, some parts of which are very ancient, is worth inspection.

BADMINTON, about sixteen miles from Bristol, the seat of the Duke of Beaufort.

HENBURY.

This beautiful village, about five miles from Bristol, should be seen by every visitor to this city. The church is one of the most picturesque in this neighbourhood, and with the adjoining churchyard is kept in excellent preservation and neatness. We do not know a more perfect churchyard. The Henbury cottages, which are most elegant tasteful buildings, should also be seen.

BLAISE CASTLE,

Henbury, the delightful seat of J. S. Harford, Esq. The castle is modern but very picturesque and the view from it is very beautiful A chapel dedicated to St. Blasius or Blaise formerly stood here. Close by is an ancient encampment.

KINGSWESTON HILL AND PEN POLE HILL, Should be visited for the delightful prospect therefrom. Kingsweston House, the seat of P. W. S. Miles, Esq., was built by Sir John Vanbrugh, the celebrated dramatist. King William III. s'ept here on returning from the Battle of the Boyne.

SEA MILLS, on the river Avon, was anciently a Roman Station. Some writers fix the Station Abona here; others place Abona at Bitton and consider Sea Mills to have been Ad Sabrinam.

STAPLETON, about two miles from Bristol, is a very neat village. Here is the Palace of the Bishop of Gloucester and Bristol. Nearly opposite is the house, formerly occupied by the Rev. John Foster. The church with the exception of the tower, is meagre and ugly in the extreme. It is about to be pulled down (we regret to find with the exception of the chancel) and a new one is to be erected by the generosity of the Bishop.

WESTBURY-ON-TRYM, four miles from Bristol. Here was formerly a college of priests, of which William Canynges, jun., was dean. Some portions are left incorporated in the large house at the bottom of the hill. (See Mr. Pryce's " Memorials of the Canynges' Family," recently published.)

SOMERSETSHIRE.

ABBOT'S LEIGH, four miles from Bristol. (See pp. 33-37.) The noble mansion of William Miles, Esq., M.P., contains a collection of very fine pictures. Persons are liberally allowed to see them every Thursday, by an order which should be obtained some days before at the Counting house of the Messrs. Miles, 61 Queen Square.

ASHTON, is about three miles from Bristol across Bedminster Bridge; going by Rownham Ferry, the distance is only half a mile. This pretty spot was long celebrated for its Strawberry Gardens, which are now closed. The church is an exceedingly elegant building both inside and out, in the perpendicular style of architecture. (See article " Ashton Court and Manor," p. 16.)

Above the village are the remains of Ashton Camp.

BANWELL,

About sixteen miles from Bristol, on the Bristol and Exeter Railway.

The church is one of the most beautiful in Somersetshire. The bone caves at Banwell are the great attraction. They are carefully arranged and preserved, and every attention is shown by Mr. Beard the zealous curator of them.

BEDMINSTER, formerly a village of small dimensions, but now forming part of Bristol, was in ancient times part of the extensive property of the Berkeley family. A few remains of the Hospital of St. Catherine, Brightbow, may be seen near the Police Station. The old church dedicated to St. John-the-Baptist has been recently pulled down ; and a new one, which promises to be among the few good modern churches in Bristol, is in progress of erection.

BRISLINGTON, about two miles and a half from Bristol, is an exceedingly neat and pleasant village, with several elegant mansions. The manor of Brislington was granted by King John to Sir John de la Warre ; one of the family afterwards founded a chapel dedicated to St. Ann, near Brislington. Not a vestige of it remains. The ancient Newgate, one of the city gates of Bristol, was removed to Arno's Vale in this parish, where are also preserved some ancient statues which formerly adorned Lawford's Gate. Brislington church is a very elegant building with a beautiful perpendicular English tower.

BROCKLEY COMBE and its romantic and most beautiful neighbourhood, should be seen by every lover of the picturesque. Brockley is about eight miles from Bristol. Backwell church with its beautiful perpendicular tower will be noticed on the left of the road.

CHEDDAR.

This interesting place is situated about eighteen miles from Bristol. The magnificent cliffs here attract much notice. There is also a very beautiful stalactite cavern which was discovered by Mr. Cox on his own property. Mr. C. has had galleries cut round it, and when it is lighted with candles, the effect is singularly beautiful.

The ancient market cross in the centre of the town is worthy of inspection.

CLEVEDON,

About thirteen miles from Bristol, takes its name from a family of the name of Clevedon, who possessed the manor. It belonged to them from the reign of Henry II., to the reign of Edward III.; it then, in default of heirs male, passed successively into the families of Hogsham, Lovell, and Wake. Sir Thomas Wake inherited the property in the reign of Edward IV. In the reign of Charles the first, Clevedon came into the possession of John Digby, Earl of Bristol, from whom it passed into the possession of the Elton family. Sir Arthur Hallam Elton, Bart., is the present possessor.

CLEVEDON COURT, the residence of the Elton family, is a very interesting old mansion, some portions are of considerable antiquity.

The old church is a very picturesque looking building, portions of it are well worthy inspection. Among the monuments will be noticed one to the memory of the two elder sons of the late Sir Charles A. Elton, who were unhappily drowned near Weston. There are also tablets to the memory of the late Mrs. Hallam, wife of the distinguished historian and sister to Sir Charles Elton, and her two sons—Arthur Henry, and Henry Fitzmaurice. The early death of the former very accomplished young man was the origin of Tennyson's very beautiful poem, "In Memoriam." The inscriptions on the tombs of the Hallam's are exceedingly touching.

At Rose Cottage in the old village of Clevedon, Coleridge resided; and here his gifted but unhappy son, Hartley, was born in 1796.

CADBURY CAMP, an interesting and very perfect specimen of the old camps, is situated near Clevedon.

KEYNSHAM, about five miles from Bristol, on the Great Western Railway, is a neat market town. It was in early times the seat of a priory, founded by William Earl of Gloucester, in 1164. No remains of it are to be seen. The church, of which mention is made as early as 1292, is a capacious and fine structure. Two handsome tombs will be noticed in the chancel.

PORTISHEAD. (See p. 6.) This favourite little watering place is situated at the mouth of the river Avon. The church, particularly the tower, is a handsome building, prettily situated. In going to Portishead by land, the traveller should notice the fine church at Portbury. The tower of the church of St. George, or Easton-in-Gordano, is also worthy inspection.

STANTON-DREW. (See pp. 13, 34, &c.) There is a very interesting barrow at Butcombe about four miles from Stanton-Drew.

WESTON-SUPER-MARE,

On the Bristol Channel, a favourite place of summer resort, is now assuming the air of a town, and has consequently lost much of the attraction it formerly afforded to many; it is no longer the quiet little retired spot that it was twenty years ago. Some pleasant walks may be made thence: to Uphill, where is an old church, now disused; to Kewstoke, where there is an interesting church containing a fine carved pulpit; to Woodspring Priory, etc. At high water the beach is exceedingly pleasant; but the water retires so fast that during the greater part of the day there is little else to be seen but mud and sand.

Adjacent to the town, on the summit of the hill, are the remains of an extensive and remarkable fortified town or encampment. From its great dimensions, the colossal magnitude of its walls and outworks, and the evidence of very high antiquity which are apparent, it is deservedly an object of much interest to archeologists; and considerable light has recently been thrown on vicissitudes which have occurred in its history.

WRINGTON, about ten miles from Bristol, is a neat village agreeably situated. The church is a handsome building. In the churchyard will be seen the grave of Hannah More (who long resided at Barley Wood, near Wrington) and four of her sisters. A monument is to be seen in the church to the memory of Mrs. More; where also is a tablet erected to the memory of the Rev. William Leeves, composer of the music of "Auld Robin Gray." At a house closely adjoining the churchyard, the celebrated John Locke was born. The country around Wrington is very pleasing; and the view of the valley of Congresbury and its pretty church, from the hills above, is very beautiful. A day or two may be well employed in exploring the adjoining country. The woods of Cleve and Brockley are rich in stores of objects of natural history.

Very delightful excursions may be made from Bristol to CHEPSTOW,—(with its fine Castle; the west end of the church, formerly the church of a Priory); the princely domain of Piercefield, a mile from Chepstow; the Wynd Cliff, which embraces a most beautiful prospect; TYNTERNE ABBEY, one of the most picturesque ruins in England, beautifully situated on the Wye; Raglan Castle, etc. The steam-packet to Chepstow sails daily from Bristol.

CAERLEON and CAERWENT, near Newport, with their valuable Roman remains. Both places are now easy of access from Chepstow by the South Wales Railway.

In the summer, pleasant sea trips may be made to the FLAT AND STEEP HOLMES, two singular islands in the Bristol Channel. The former is about eight miles from the Somersetshire coast, nearly opposite Weston-super-Mare; the latter about three miles to the south of the Flat Holmes.

Other places worthy of a visit the traveller will find out after he has seen those that we have mentioned.

MATHEWS'S SCHOOL CATECHISMS.— English History. Geography. Mother's Catechism. Useful Knowledge. Arts and Sciences Old Testament History. New Testament History. English Grammar. Price Two-Pence each.

Upwards of a hundred thousand of these useful little books have been sold.

Mathews, Bristol; Houlston & Stoneman, London; and all Booksellers.

Printed and Published at the Office of the Bristol DIRECTORY, 9, Narrow Wine Street, Bristol by M. Mathews.—August 1, 1853.

CURIOSITIES OF BRISTOL

AND ITS NEIGHBOURHOOD.

No. 1.   SEPTEMBER, 1853.   PRICE ONE PENNY.

TO OUR READERS.

THIS little paper aspires to be a depository for such matters as its title indicates. The Editor has, in leisure moments, had great pleasure in collecting the materials from which the contents of the present sheet has been selected; and he is aware that there are many of his fellow-citizens whose tastes run in the same direction, and who equally with himself desire to see our local fragmentary lore brought together in a concise, but popular and readable form.

Shall an attempt now be made to collect the treasures referred to? Will the gentlemen interested in our object make these pages a medium for bringing to the light of day what is now hidden and scattered?

There is much unwritten tradition floating amongst us. We hope to have an opportunity of sifting from the mass some things curious and interesting. There is our folk-lore too, and our local legends; little has hitherto been done to collect them—yet who is there that has not in his juvenile days listened to them with absorbing interest?—and who would not be pleased to see them in print?

And there are files of dusty newspapers to be waded through; but who will undertake the task? Who will restore to us a host of paragraphs that will serve as links in the chain of local history?

There are also tracts and pamphlets in existence of singular interest—some of ancient date and very scarce. We should like to give extracts from them. Will our curiosity-hunters and book-worms aid us?

Finally: we know there are those in Bristol who will rejoice to sustain an attempt like the present, with their "Notes and Queries." But whether there is a sufficient number of readers remains to be seen. If the number of copies sold should be sufficient to cover the cost of printing, we shall be satisfied; but we cannot afford to sacrifice much beyond editorial labour. If however, the sale should be sufficient to warrant it, we will enlarge the next number to double its present size; namely, eight pages instead of four.

BRISTOL: A FEW WORDS ABOUT ITS ORIGIN.

BRISTOL is one of the most ancient cities in England, and as may be expected, it origin is hid in great obscurity. Tradition says that Brennus the Gaul, who conquered Rome 338 years before Christ, was its founder, and that Belinus, took part in the work. There are two curiously carved statues, said to represent them, on the city side of St. John's Gate, at the foot of Broad Street; they are certainly of great antiquity, which would seem to countenance the tradition. But nothing certain is known of them.

It is, however, pretty evident, that under the name of Caer Odor our British ancestors inhabited a strong fortress on Clifton Down, the remains of which are there to this day. When the Romans invaded this country, the Strong-holds were seized, and greatly improved. Thus, these remains, like many similar works in this country, bear the marks of British and of Roman labour.

There is a strong probability that when the British were dispossessed of their fortress at Clifton, they settled on the little hill between the two rivers (Avon and Froom), and it was called Caer Brito,—the other retaining its name Caer Odor. If, however, this is to be taken as the date of the foundation of our city, it would be about the year of our Lord 50.

Having pitched upon so convenient and commanding a situation, the hill being 40 feet in perpendicular height, with a descent on every side towards the water, they arranged their habitations into four streets, now called High Street, Wine Street, Broad Street, and Corn Street. In process of time, for security and defence, they walled it round, placing a gate at the end of each street, and a church at each corner of the four streets in the centre, where a cross was also erected. The wall, joining and enclosing the whole was embattled at the top, and was about a mile in circuit.

THE TOWN WALL AND GATES.

THE earliest or internal wall, (referred to in the preceding article), and which formed the boundary of the old city, may be easily traced by commencing at the bottom of Corn Street, across which stood St. Leonard's Gate, joining Nicholas Street on one side, and St. Leonard's Lane on the other ; this Lane, where parts of the wall still remain, leads to the foot of Small Street, across which was St. Giles's Gate, with St. Giles's Church over it.—Thence along Bell Lane, and passing on the left the site of St. Lawrence Church, (now Waterman's Shoe Factory) to St. John's Gate,—thence along Tower Lane, passing Blind Gate at St. John's Steep, to the top of the Pithay, in Wine Street (opposite the pump). Here stood Old-gate or Aldgate.— The wall continued thence to Old (or Ella) gate, in Narrow Wine Street, and turned southward at Chequers Lane towards St. Peter's Church, and returned in a westerly direction along Worship Street (right hand side of Bridge Street) to St. Nicholas' Gate which crossed the foot of High Street, and continuing along Nicholas Street, completed its circuit at St. Leonard's Gate, from whence we started.

THE TOLZEY AND COUNCIL HOUSE.

THE Tolzey is a word to which no two persons seem to attach the same meaning. It was originally written *Tholsel*, and was the name given to a colonnade erected in 1550, on the site of what was at an earlier date called the *Counter* (afterwards the Council-house). Here the Mayor and Sheriff used to sit and hear complaints, from 8 till 11, mornings, and from 2 till 5 afternoons. Truly they had more to do in those days than they have now. Perhaps a passage from Ricart's Kalendar will in part explain it. " On St. Nicholas' day the corporation went to St. Nicholas' Church to hear mass. After dinner they assembled at the *Counter*, and while they waited the coming of the Bishop, they amused themselves by playing at dice. It was the business of the town-clerk to find them dice, and he received for every raffle one penny."

" We can imagine (says Evans) the bronze tables of the Exchange *now* so occupied, and Mr. Town-Clerk looking out for his pence with one eye, and for the approach of the Rev. Father with the other."

In the year 1552 a Council House was added to the Tolzey, being built on the site of St. John's Chapel, which formed part of St. Ewen's (or Owen's) Church. There was a Piazza supported by stone pillars ; and under the Piazza were three bronze tables, similar to those in front of the Exchange. In 1704 the Council House was partly rebuilt. In 1824 the present structure was raised on the site of the old one, and St. Ewen's Church.

The Tolzey or Colonnade was partly re-built in 1662, and taken down in 1782.

THE BRONZE PILLARS IN FRONT OF THE EXCHANGE.

THESE pieces of antiquity have occupied their present position since 1771. They had previously stood in front of the Council House. Their history is curious.

Pillar number one is that next to All Saints Church. Although it was originally moulded in bold relief, it is now become illegible by the constant wear it has had as a resting place for the baskets and burdens of errand-boys and porters. It is evidently very much older than either of the others, and most probably, is one of three which stood under the "shed" at the Tolzey in 1550.

Pillar number two bears the following inscription in a ring on the face.—" This Post is the gift of Master Robert Kitchin, Merchant, some time Maior and Alderman of this city, who dec. 1 Septemb. 1594." On the garter beneath are the words,—" His executors were fower of his Servants, John Barker, Matthew Haviland, Abel Kitchin, Aldermen of this city, and John Rowborow, Sherif. 1630.

Pillar number three contains on a gartar below the face, the following inscription.— " Thomas Hobson of Bristol made me, anno 1625. Nicholas Crisp of London gave me to this honourable city, in rememberance of God's mercy in Anno Domini 1625. N. C." In a ring on the face are the words,—" Praise the Lord O my soule, and forget not all his benefits. He saved my life from destruction and...... to his mercy and lovingkindness. Praise...." The remainder is worn out.

Pillar number four stands next the Post-office. On the ring of the surface is inscribed the words,—" A. D. 1631. This is the guift of Mr. White of Bristoll, Merchant, brother unto Dr. Thos. White, a famous benefactor to this Citie." Six lines in verse, and a shield, with armourial bearings, engraven in the centre of the table, are obliterated. On the garter round the exterior, — " The church of the living God is the pillar and ground of the truth.—So was the work of the pillars finished."

Theological puns abounded at that period.

Our Local Legends.

BRANDON HILL AND ITS LEGENDS.

BRANDON Hill commands one of the noblest city views upon which the eye can possible rest. To the left the vast city spread out on undulating ground lies beneath you, the square towers and pointed spires of the churches lifting their gilded weather-vanes into the sun-light. Beyond and in front are scattered a host of factory chimneys, pointing out the dingy, smoky neighbourhood of St.

Philip's. Down below, on the right, gleams the pent-up waters of the float. And there at a little distance off, lies the unfortunate Demerara — launched to become a wreck before she had voyaged a mile.

The hill is 250 feet in perpendicular height, of a conic form, and is peculiarly interesting from its historical associations.

Ascend to the summit, and you may stand on the very spot where dwelt for centuries the "Hermit of St. Brendan,"—or rather a succession of hermits. It appears that in the year 1351 a chapel and hermitage were erected and permission was granted by the Bishop of Worcester, to a female, one Lucy of New-church, to shut herself up from the world, and become its solitary inhabitant. Other Hermits wasted their lives there, down to the days of the Reformation. One of them, Reginald Taillor is mentioned in 1403, as the "poor Hermit of the Chapel of St. Brendan." The Hermitage having been swept away by Henry VIII., we find some twenty-five years afterwards, (in 1565,) Mr. Read, the town-clerk, engaged in erecting a windmill on its ruins. Somehow or other, the hill now got into private hands, and it was a vexed question down to 1625, when it was bought of Mr. Somebody (name unknown), of Clifton, by the Corporation ; the conditions being, that it be well laid out, and the hedges well prepared and maintained, so as to admit of the drying of clothes by the townswomen, for ever.

The Fort, the remains of which are still to seen, was built by the magistrates, at the suggestion of Charles I., in 1642, during the civil war.

THE SHOT TOWER AND WATTS'S FOLLY.

The manufacture of Shot as now practised, is remarkable, not only for the details of the method employed, but also for the circumstances connected with the invention and the inventor.

A plumber of the name of William Watts, a worthy citizen, was blest with a wife given to dreaming,—at length she dreamed to some advantage. Dix tells us in his humourous *Local Legends* that she awoke from her slumbers early one morning, and arousing her spouse after considerable difficulty, got him to lend an ear to the story of her dream. She had seen in her vision molten lead poured from a great height into a cistern of water, and the drops thus so suddenly cooled retained their perfect roundness,—a quality greatly desired, but till that hour unattained.

She demanded of Mr. W. that a trial of the plan should come off forthwith, and

> Promised she would shew
> How shot could best be made.

The experiment was tried from the tower of Redcliff Church, and proved eminently successful. So, without a moment's delay—

> A tower was built for making shot
> It stood on Redcliff Hill ;
> And, as I'm certain it was not
> Remov'd, it stands there still—
> An old square tower.—Far, far below
> Its base was dug a well,
> Which all may see who wish to know
> If truth the muse doth tell.
> Still from the summit of that tower.
> The molten lead falls, like a shower
> Of shining silver rain,
> Into the water far below,
> Which cools it suddenly, and lo !
> Small shot it doth remain.

Mr. Watts obtained his patent in 1782, and not long after sold it, with his stock-in-trade to the firm of Walker & Co. for the sum of 10,000*l.* Unfortunately for Mr. Watts, and his suddenly acquired wealth, he projected the formation of Windsor Terrace. He spent the whole of the money in making excavations and foundation walls ! There they remained for years afterwards, monuments of miscalculation and folly !

The property passed from the hands of poor Watts ; but how he and Mrs. Watts fared in after years, tradition sayeth not.

But the curious stranger asks, where is Windsor Terrace ? Let him treat himself to a walk beside the Avon so far as Mr. Bolton's Saloon, at the Hotwell House, and he will see the memorable fabric on high, far above his head, or (to quote again from Dix)—

> If he, from Rownham Ferry boat,
> Just upwards casts his eye,
> A *Terrace*, WINDSOR called, will note,
> Between him and the sky.
> Bright with the sunshine, can it raise
> One thought of melancholy ?
> Alas ! another name betrays
> *Its* history—" WATTS's FOLLY !"
> For Mr. Watts retired from trade,
> To build it, resolution made ;
> And found to his chagrin,
> That cash a great deal faster went
> When 'twas on " brick and mortar" spent,
> Than ever it came in.
> On mere *foundations* went his all,
> And WATTS's FOLLY still we call
> That luckless spot of ground.

Notes and Queries on Local Matters.

THE CASTLE BANK.

The very curious building at the top of High street, known as Stuckey's Bank was build in Amsterdam ; and consisting of an elaborate frame-work of wood, it was taken to pieces and brought to Bristol in a ship, together with two others. All three are mentioned as being in existence in 1733 ; but of the date of their erection, and where the other two were situated we are not informed.

ST. JAMES'S FAIR.

The earliest mention of this Fair is in the year 1174. William Earl of Gloster gave the profits to the Priory of St. James. The Prior began to receive his rents for the " pales " in 1374. The "standings" are mentioned in 1687 as yielding eighty pounds, received by the churchwardens. The Fair was suppressed in 1837 on account of its demoralizing effects.

THE COUNTY OF BRISTOL.

Bristol was separated from the counties of Gloster and Somerset in the year 1373 by a charter of Edward III, and made a county of itself.

ORIGIN OF " FLARE UP."

In Mackey's *History of Popular Delusions* it is stated that this phrase was first used at the Bristol Riots in 1831, by the mob,—when the fires were said to "flare up." The use of the expression spread through the nation like wild-fire.

PAY DOWN ON THE NAIL.

We have heard it stated that this phrase first originated in Bristol, when it was common for the merchants to buy and sell at the Bronze Pillars (Exchange)—the pillars being commonly called " *Nails.*"

HUNTING THE DUCK.

Bathurst Basin was formerly a mill-pond belonging to Treen Mill, which stood near to the spot now well known as the landing-place of the Newport and Cardiff Steamers. In the year 1247 the sport of hunting the duck being very popular among the magistrates and other worshipful citizens, the Corporation got the pond from the Abbot of St. Augustine's : they gave him for it, a piece of ground called Chaunter's close, near the Marsh. The site of the Close is indicated by the Alms house and Cooper's hall, King street.

DEPTH OF WELLS.

There are several ancient wells in Bristol, such as those of St. Peter's Pump, Wine Street Pump, the Pithay Pump, &c. What are their several depths—and the average depth of other wells in Bristol ? Can any one inform us, with any other particulars on the same subject ? We have seen a curious account of some wells in Surrey, where there are many of the depth of 600 and even 700 feet.

LAWFORD'S GATE.

Although this gate has been taken down ever since 1768, it is still common to hear the neighbourhood called " outside the gate." It crossed the Old Market Street, at the Dial Alms House. The earliest mention of this gate occurs in 1324, when it was kept by one William Corbet, who had a house there for his services. It was rebuilt in 1395.

PARISH REGISTERS.

It would be a great advantage to the genealogists and archæologists, and indeed the general public, if the the abolition of fees could be extended to our parish Registers. Why not permit free access to these documents at stated times ? Can a fee be *legally* demanded for making search ? If so, how much ? and by whom ?

NOTES ON STREETS.

Wine Street was originally Wynch Street. So far back the year 819 it was thus named, being the chief road to Wynchcombe, (Glostershire) which was then the chief city of Mercia, and court of the King.

Corn Street was spoken of as Old Corn Street, as early as 1200.

The Barton, St. James's. The Barton farm is mentioned as early as 1086.

The Gate in Barrs Lane is mentioned in 1129, beside which was a " pound," and two " great barns."

THE TOWN WALL.—It would be interesting to know " the present difference, in feet, of the *level* of the streets immediately within the walls, and those immediately without the walls." We do not recollct that the subject has been noticed by either of our historians. Will some friend make a survey, and forward particulars for our next ?

THE CITY LIBRARY.—We have perused with much pleasure, Mr. Tovey's book on this subject, and we heartily thank him on behalf the public for this service. We do hope the citizens will not let the matter drop, and that the issue will be—a Free Library for the People.

OUR HISTORICAL AUTHORITIES.— We have made free use of " Barrett's History," " Sayer's Memoirs," and " Evans's Chron. History."

Printed and Published at the Office of the Bristol DIRECTORY, 9 Narrow Wine Street, Bristol, by M. Mathews.—September 1, 1853.

CURIOSITIES OF BRISTOL

AND ITS NEIGHBOURHOOD.

No. 2.   OCTOBER, 1853.   PRICE ONE PENNY.

THE BRISTOL RIOTS OF 1831.

FIRST ARTICLE.

THE memorable riots of 1831, it is well known, arose out of political causes.

Whenever such convulsions take place in a community, they will almost always be traceable to one cause, namely, an unnatural state of society, arising from misgovernment. Hence it is not difficult to understand how, at that period, the openly corrupt character of our political and civic institutions on the one hand, and the constant excitement of the mind of the populace by the agitation of the Reform Bill, on the other, generated throughout the country by a very natural process, an uneasy, undefined desire for vengeance, especially among the less educated classes. In our own city this feeling at length found vent in acts of open violence and frightful disaster.

Sir Charles Wetherell, the Recorder of Bristol, it appears, had rendered himself obnoxious to the promoters of the reform bill by his strenuous opposition to it in the House of Commons. It is very likely, however, that this would have passed unnoticed, and it was believed that he might have performed his duties in Bristol without any manifestation of dislike, had he not declared in the House, in rather contemptuous terms, that the citizens of Bristol were quite indifferent to reform. The consequence was, that resentment prevailed extensively, and that, when in the exercise of his judicial functions he visited this city in April, 1831, a large party went out to Totterdown, with a view to give him a convincing proof of his error.

As his carriage reared the spot where they were assembled, he was assailed with the most vehement hisses and groans. We shall never forget (says an eye witness) the start and look of surprise which he gave when the unexpected sound struck his ear.

Ominous as the reception seemed, Sir Charles left the city without personal violence being offered him; and from his subsequent conduct, it is evident that he thought he had seen the worst of a Bristol mob. His assertions were repeated in the House of Commons, the citizens were again annoyed, and many expressed their mind in no measured terms.

Discrimination and forbearance not being the characteristic virtues of a mob, a repetition of groans and hisses was naturally to be expected on the public entry into Bristol of Sir Charles Wetherell at his next visit. The authorities had therefore sworn in a large number of hired bludgeon-men as special constables, called out the constables of the various parishes, and sent a deputation to the Home Secretary, to request the aid of soldiers. These steps, together with the sanction of some injudicious party demonstrations, only made matters worse, and increased the excitement in the public mind.

The day appointed for opening the commission of assize was Saturday, October 29th,—a day that will ever form a mournful episode in our chronological calendar.

It was about ten o'clock in the morning when the special constables passed down High-street on their way to Totterdown. At this hour the town presented a scene of more than ordinary animation. As the streets became more crowded, the shutters of the various shops were closed, while many persons were to be seen hastily proceeding on their way to Temple-gate. Still there were no manifestations of disturbance: many of the populace, it is true, deprecated the display of constabulary force which had just been exhibited, and many inveighed against the impolicy of having troops within call, considering such measures rather as incentives to violence, than as calculated to repress it; but it was hoped and believed that no necessity would arise for either being called into action.

On arriving at Totterdown, the special constables halted near the Blue Bowl, between which and the iron bridge about 2000 of the populace had assembled; there were also very many persons along the New Cut, particularly in the direction of the Cattle Market, prompted by curiosity to view the troops. Among the number there were some whose appearance and conduct betokened that they were fit agents for works of violence. These, judging from their exterior, belonged to that class whose subsistence depending chiefly on the opportunities afforded for rapine and plunder, renders them inimical to a well ordered system of government. This was the state of the multitude when a chariot, drawn by four greys, advancing at a rapid rate along Arno's Vale, announced the arrival of the Recorder.

In an instant he was at Totterdown, and was received by the populace with the most astounding yells, groans, and hisses. A few seconds elapsed while he was handed into the Sheriff's carriage, after which the procession, including the usual attendance of officers connected with the Corporation, mounted on horseback with favours in their hats, and preceded by trumpeters, moved on towards the city. For the better protection of Sir Charles's person, two gentlemen on horseback rode close by the carriage doors. On arriving at Hill's-Bridge, four or five stones were thrown, some of them striking the carriage in which the Recorder was seated. This circumstance, however, beyond the casting of anxious glances towards the direction whence they proceeded, occasioned no movement on the part of the constables, whose attention seemed exclusively directed to the safety of their charge.

By the time the procession had reached Temple-gate, the crowd, which had collected to an immense number, literally choked up the road, and retarded it on its way; the demonstrations of feeling became more and more deafening, and occasionally a stone or other missile was hurled in the direction of the Recorder. On coming within sight of Bristol Bridge, he was saluted with the most unequivocal and opprobrious marks of displeasure from the individuals who had there posted themselves to witness his arrival, and who occupied the footpaths as well as the balustrades. As he passed over it, and on his way up High-street, his carriage was again assailed with stones. At length the cavalcade arrived at the Guildhall, in Broad-street; but the pressure was so great that some minutes elapsed ere it was judged prudent for Sir Charles to alight. He was, however, handed out in safety, and immediately proceeded to take his station on the bench. The doors of the Hall were then thrown open to the populace, and, in a few minutes, the area was completely choked up.

The usual forms for opening the commission now commenced, by reading the Charter; but the noise and confusion occasioned considerable interruption. With a view to allay the uproar, some constables were sent into the body of the hall, among the people, who then adopted a different species of annoyance, by coughing, which at length they ended in a general burst of indignation.

In this manner the usual preliminaries were gone through, ending by the adjournment of the Court, by Sir Charles, till eight o'clock on Monday morning. The Recorder then withdrew from the bench, and the populace, after some further marks of their displeasure towards the learned Judge, gave three cheers for the King, and retired into the street.

A TRIP TO PORTSHEAD.

EXCURSIONS to the neighbourhood of Portshead have of late become highly popular; and justly so; for, in addition to the pleasures of the voyage down the Avon, the scenery in this vicinity is truly delightful, especially on the side of the hill towards the Bristol Channel. Steam packets make the to and fro passage almost daily, during the summer months, affording every facility for visitors, or such as desire a day's relaxation among the woods, cliffs, and curiosities of this interesting place.

Portshead, in some old records, is called Portchester. The present name is evidently derived (as Rutter remarks) from its situation —the head of the port—being one of the horns of the port of Kingroad. The following extracts are from a pleasing little volume just issued—the Handbook to Portshead, by J. N. Duck. Bristol: Evans and Abbott. 1s.

"A considerable portion of the village is below the level of the water at high spring-tides, on which account an embankment has been made, following the line of coast from the mouth of the Avon to the mill. At this spot, in the autumn of 1848, the embankment gave way, inundating a large portion of the village, and doing much damage.

PORTSHEAD POINT.

"On account of the numerous sand-banks on the Monmouthshire coast, the strongest current and the deepest water flows near our shore, and to take advantage of these, vessels are obliged to steer rather close to the land. At the battery point this is more especially the case. There the rocks on the northern side are nearly precipitous, thus enabling a vessel of large size to float within a few hundred yards of them. On the 26th of June, 1581, the St. Dominic, a ship laden with spices, was wrecked on this point, and twenty-seven men were lost.

"During the late war, a small battery was erected a few yards from the ancient fort. This battery, which has long since been dismantled and unoccupied, mounted four long guns. They were removed about the year 1815. Their site, however, is easily distinguishable."

The semicircular mounds within the boundary wall will show where the guns stood, and a careful examination will discover the sockets in which the gun swivels turned. The property now belongs to J. A. Gordon, Esq., but "to what base uses we may return," This fort, once a strong garrison, and a place of great consequence, has been converted into (O tempora, O mores!) a beer-shop.

"The fort was besieged in 1645. Sir Thomas Fairfax having on the 28th of August raised 2000 men in Somersetshire, they joined a part of his army, and took the fort after a siege of four days, with six pieces of ordnance, a demi-culverin, and two hundred arms; thirty-six of the garrison had leave to return to their houses; the rest had run away before."

SITE OF BRISTOL CATHEDRAL, COLLEGE GREEN.

THE ground on which this edifice stands is invested with peculiar interest, from its being the place where Austin, or Augustine, the missionary, from Rome, preached to our idolatrous Saxon forefathers, and where he held his celebrated conference with the British bishops, in 603. The spot was called, from that event, Augustine's Oak, (whose locality is known in our day as College-green,) and the monastery afterwards erected here, received its name as a memorial of the transaction. Jordan, one of the companions of Augustine, also preached here. College-green is described by an old writer as a large green place, shaded by a double row of trees, with a pulpit of stone, and a chapel wherein Jordan was buried. The exact site of this chapel cannot now be ascertained, but it appears to have been standing as late as the year 1492. In 1486, when King Henry VII., on his visit to Bristol, went in procession about the "great Greene," it was called the sanctuary: the annals add that the Bishop of Worcester preached in the pulpit in the middle of the Green, to a great audience of the Mayor and Burgesses and their wives, and many people of the country. For a series of years it was the common burying-ground, or cemetery to the Monastery, and the House of the Gaunts, and, like other consecrated ground in Popish countries, invested with the privilege of sanctuary, until abolished by royal order, in the year 1495, previously to which the handicraftsmen, who took refuge in the precincts of the Monastery, occupied it as a ropewalk.

THE CORPORATION OF BRISTOL AND THEIR QUARRELSOME BISHOP.

IN 1608 occurred a very curious quarrel between the Corporation of Bristol and the Bishop. It appears that the Mayor and Council-men had built a costly gallery on the north side of the College, or Cathedral Church, in College-green, near where the pulpit now stands. They also made some fine seats, on the ground under the gallery, for their wives. The Bishop, Dr. Thornborough, not having been consulted in the matter, took great offence, and pulled it down, alleging that the College was his, and no others had any authority therein without his leave. The Mayor and Aldermen demanded aid of the Dean and Prebends in vain, for they equivocated, and joined with the Bishop, at which the Mayor and Council disdaining, refused to go to the College at Easter, and other times, as they used to do, and undertook of themselves on their own authority to furnish our city with learned Divines, despising the Bishop and Clergy for their abuse of power; so the lectures at the College for a time were little frequented, for every Sabbath-day we had at least six sermons preached in our City.

Note here, by the way, that the Bishop, Dean, and Prebends, however, supposed that the Mayor and Council ought, of duty and custom, to come to the College at Easter; but they were deceived, and our Council knew well what they had to do.

The King, however, ordered the Bishop to put up the gallery in its former place, at his own cost; but he rebuilt it only two or three feet above the ground, and placed the pulpit on the lower pillar, next the clock-house. When the Bishop went to London, the King rebuked him for this ungracious perversion of his Majesty's commands; so that he stayed at Dorchester, and "would not come to Bristol for shame and disgrace."

Bristol Worthies.

JOHN SIMMONS, THE BRISTOL PAINTER.

JOHN SIMMONS was born at Nailsea, in Somersetshire, near Bristol, either in the year 1714 or 1715. His parents died in his infancy. He manifested a fondness for drawing when a boy, and expressed his wishes to be a painter. His friends doubtless thought they had gratified his inclination, by placing him an apprentice to a house and ship painter in this city. His master died before the expiration of his apprenticeship, but he continued to serve the widow, whose circumstances requiring assistance, he would frequently give her the money which he earned by working after the usual hours. She ever afterward expressed the strongest regard for him, in consequence of the kindness of his conduct towards her. Though his employment at this time did not afford him the means of indulging his inclination for drawing, his attachment to it continued to increase: and he frequently passed the greater part of the night in cultivating this talent. On the expiration of his apprenticeship, he commenced business as a house and sign painter in Small-street, from whence he removed to Broad-street; afterward

CURIOSITIES OF BRISTOL.

to the house since occupied by Mr. Shiercliffe, opposite the Drawbridge, and lastly to Bridge-street. For some years he held the office of city painter, and carried on his business with very considerable success, especially as a sign painter. It is well known that the use of sign boards was not at that time confined to public-houses, but was very generally adopted by tradesmen, and that they were usually hung out before the house in as projecting a manner as possible, and with the most showy embellishments. The pictorial talent of the country met with little employment except in this way; and so much interest did these productions excite, that in 1762, an exhibition of signs was opened in Bow-street, Covent-garden, and a catalogue was published, containing the names of the painters. The public, however, experienced so much inconvenience from the manner in which signs extended over the pavement and into the street, that an Act passed for their removal. This regulation was enforced in Bristol, in 1765, and was the cause of such a disuse of them, that Simmons declared it occasioned him a loss of £500 a year.

When Hogarth's paintings were fixed in Redcliff Church, Simmons executed the four niches under them, containing the scriptural narration of the subjects. There is a traditionary story, that as soon as Hogarth arrived at Bristol, in passing through Redcliff-street, the sign of the Angel attracted his attention, and on being informed that it was painted by Simmons of Bristol, he said, "Then they need not have sent for me." The following anecdote was related by a relative of Mr. Simmons, and authenticates the opinion which Hogarth is said to have entertained of Simmons's talents. They had been walking together about the city, when Hogarth stood for some time contemplating a sign board; and on Simmons asking him why he noticed it, Hogarth replied, "I am sure you painted it, for there is no one else here that could."

Simmons afterwards painted the Annunciation, for the altar-piece of All-Saints' Church. He painted the altar-piece of St. John's, at Devizes, the subject of which is the Resurrection; and an altar-piece was also painted by him for one of the West India islands.

During this period Simmons painted several portraits, and among them an excellent one of Ferguson the astronomer. This extraordinary man frequently delivered lectures in in this city, on which occasions he was the constant tea table visitor of his friend Simmons. It is said this portrait was twice exhibited in London, and obtained considerable notice. Mr. Simmons was invited to dine with the Academicians—introduced to them individually, and particular marks of attention were shown him. On this occasion he was strongly advised to remove to the metropolis, as presenting a fair prospect of benefiting himself. But his old habits and connexions were not easily to be given up, and he had not courage enough to make the sacrifice.

There are portraits by him still in this city, of some of its then public characters. The Rev. Bernard Fosket, Baptist minister, at Broadmead, sat to him, from whose portrait an engraving was taken. Also Burgum the pewterer, and Cruger the M.P. He painted a strong likeness of rather an extraordinary pauper, then known in Bristol by the name of Black John, who is represented as he always appeared, with a round slouched hat, a haulier's frock, a long beard, and a long square stick. When he came to sit for his picture, Simmons told him to go down stairs and wash his face; this he did without cleaning his hands, which induced the painter to give them in the picture their usual appearance. He also painted one of Tom Bennett, another Bristol mendicant. Simmons finished a portrait of Morgan Davis, who then kept the Beaufort Arms, Petty France. This innkeeper was remarkable for his corpulency—he weighed twenty-four stone. The picture was exhibited at the Royal Academy, and obtained for Simmons the prize for that year. He also painted a head of the celebrated Emanuel Collins. The original was in the possession of Mr. Cocking, who was first a schoolmaster in Corn-street, and subsequently printer of Felix Farley's Bristol Journal in Small-street.

It can hardly be necessary, however, to observe, that he did not meet with sufficient employment. Knowing this to be the case, about four years before he was obliged to relinquish business, ten of his fellow-citizens agreed among themselves to sit to him for their portraits, at ten guineas each. The names of these friends were, Mr. Windey, Mr. Hughes, Mr. Burges, and Mr. Murray, attornies; Mr. Joseph Hinton and Mr. T. Dyer, linen merchants; Mr. George Winter, wine merchant; Mr. Robertson, Mr. Richard Tombs, and Mr. W. Tombs, a lad, who was painted with a spaniel. He also painted a large piece, consisting of the Daubeny family.

In the year 1777, he experienced a paralytic seizure, which rendered him wholly incapable of pursuing his business; and for some time previous to his decease, he was so debilitated in body and mind as not to know his own family. A portrait of him was painted by Beech.

In 1778, the pictures he possessed were sold by auction at the West India Coffee-house.

Simmons died the 18th January, 1780, aged 65 years, and was buried in Redcliff churchyard. His life appears to have been characterised by those dispositions which render their possessor void of offence. Of social habits, unassuming manners, and simple and undiguised intentions, he presented none of those points and projections of character which so often interfere with the convenience and obstruct the designs of our associates. His mind never having been occupied by the collisions of interest, was unqualified for the pursuit of gain. As a painter, Simmons's productions evince that his abilities, if fostered by patronage, might have been matured to excellence.

SIR JOHN DUDDLESTONE.

THE remains of this gentleman, with those of his lady, lie buried in All-Saints' Church. He was an eminent tobacco merchant, and had the honour of entertaining Prince George of Denmark, when he privately visited this city. This circumstance gave rise to the well known story, in which Sir John is described as a boddice maker, and his lady as the wearer of a blue apron. Sir John being of the "True Blue," or "Tory" party, it is very probable the tale had a political origin (see a subsequent page of this work). The name of Sir John Duddlestone stands at the head of a list of trustees to Colston's Hospital, in St. Augustine's-place, on its establishment by the founder.

Our Local Legends.

MOTHER PUGSLEY'S WELL, NINE-TREE HILL.

Mother Pugsley! who does not remember thy well,
 With its waters so cool and so clear;
But how few can the tale of thy constancy tell,
 Unto few do thy sorrows appear.—Dix.

WHEN we were children,—we mean those of us who are now men and women, and have children of our own—one of the favourite spots for a morning or evening's ramble was Conduit Close, on Nine-tree hill. Aye, we can well remember with what glee we scampered to and fro upon its daisied turf. We would not call it Conduit Close, we chose its more suggestive name of Mother Pugsley's Field.

Yes, in those days of our sunny youth, we often wandered there—

 "As happy as happy could be,
With schoolboy companions, merry and free,
Chasing the bee and the butterfly gay,
And sporting, like them, through the long summer day."

We were fond of the marvellous. We had heard the story of Dame Pugsley—it was a mystery to us, for those who told the tale never answered all our questions respecting the old lady. And so, when we stood by the venerable fountain, called after her name, and looked on the two stone basins, the one holding water whose HEALING virtues were undisputed—the other supplying the crystal liquid in its highest purity for domestic use—we almost persuaded ourselves that here was enchanted ground, a spot within the region of fairy-land.

And now, since we have reached man's estate, and being by no means satisfied with the tale our nursemaids told us, we confess we have searched in books for further light, but they tell us nothing new; so on this subject we are but little wiser than we were then. But lest the story should be lost to our children—for the fountain has been demolished, and the field itself overwhelmed by an invasion of brick and mortar—let us at least tell all we know.

Come with us then to the top of Nine-tree hill. Now mark this spot in Somerset street, beside No. 1, Fremantle square, here stood Prior's Fort.—Now look across to the rising ground at Montpelier, and there, bowered in elm trees, is Fairfax farm—right in front stood the Battery.

Now walk along Fremantle road, and stop at Spring Villa, for in the middle of the front yard of this house, about 40 feet from the top of the hill and 12 from the side, is the spot where stood "Dame Pugsley's Well," which for nearly 200 years, that is, from 1645 to 1835, was daily visited for the cure of disease of the eyes.

On Wednesday, September 10th, 1645, at two o'clock in the morning, commenced the siege of Bristol; and at this locality raged the conflict of war, which continued till daylight, between the soldiers of Cromwell and the soldiers of King Charles. Cromwell's men occupied Montpelier, but the King's men held Prior Fort. Many of the King's soldiers fell that day, and among them was a young man aged 25, whose name was Pugsley,—He had only lately married a young and blooming lady, two years younger than himself. Pugsley was an officer under Prince Rupert, and during the siege he received his death as he walked within the wall, by a shell or shot thrown probably by a morter from the redoubt on Montpelier. He fell at a spot which was for many years marked by a monumental tablet in the boundary wall of the garden, now belonging to Mr. Vine's Boarding School. At the time of the siege, the whole of this field and some of the surrounding land belonged to the young officer—and he was buried with military honours beneath the turf stained with his blood.

His widow, young and beautiful as she was, had many offers of marriage, but she resisted every importunity to change her condition, and chose to mourn in forlorn solitude the loss of him for whom she cherished undying affection, till she passed her eightieth year.

Tradition tells us that she spent much of her life at the fountain, and when there came those whose disorders needed the healing virtues of the water, she was there like a ministering angel to assist or advise them. It is said too that she was extremely fond of children, and very large was the juvenile circle who regarded her with special kindliness. And many a one in after life could tell some little incident which gave them pleasure; some gift of sweetmeats, or some fond embrace, or some loving words. And it is these characteristics of the good woman more perhaps than anything else, that made the spring so famous; for it was not the people of Bristol alone that believed in the healing virtues of the magic "eye water," but many who came great distances, declared that they derived great benefit from its use.

There is a melancholy chapter in the history of humanity, and every day our Asylums bear mournful evidence of cases resembling this, of the beautiful, the virtuous, and the benevolent becoming the prey of disappointed hopes and crushed affections—and when we observe their remarkable effects on contemplative minds, we shall not be surprised to learn that from the first distracted hour of her widowhood, to the end of her long life, Mrs. Pugsley regarded death as most desirable. "To me, (said she,) it will be the hour of RE-UNION, the hour of release from a long captivity that separates me from the object of my earthly love." We can honour such a character however peculiar, and charitably believe that no sentiment of religion was wanting in this view of her destiny.

On August 4th, 1700, Gammar Pugsley died, leaving in her will money to buy bread for sixteen poor women, inmates of St. Nicholas Alms House in King street, for ever. A sixpenny and ninepenny loaf at Easter, and a twopenny loaf on Twelfth' day. She left also directions respecting her funeral. Whether they were strictly followed we cannot say, but she was buried in the eastern manner, without a coffin. Her shroud was her "wedding garment," the dress she wore on her marriage day. Her winding sheet was her wedding sheet. The corpse was borne on a bier through the streets of the city, two young girls going before it and strewing herbs and flowers on the path, and a musician in front playing on a violin; at the same time the bells of St. Nicholas ringing a merry peal as the procession passed under St. Nicholas Gate.

The body was carried to the field which bore her name, and overshadowed by the nine elm trees, buried in the grave which contained all that was dear to her. There were no special mourners, but she was committed to the dust in presence of ten thousand spectators. The strangeness of the sight no doubt brought some thoughtless ones to the spot, but many came that understood her personal peculiarities, and admired the goodness of her character, and so dropt a sacred tear in memory of departed worth.

Great changes have been made in this neighbourhood within the memory of "the oldest inhabitant;" the nine elm trees became decayed, and were burnt down by mischievous boys; the boundary wall and monumental tablet have been removed, the grave of Mr. and Mrs. Pugsley has been disturbed, and their bones found imbedded in a large quantity of ashes,—"dust to dust, ashes to ashes." Every vestige of Prior's Fort and the walls thence to Lawford's Gate on the one side, and Colston Fort back of the Montague on the other, have disappeared; and the wondrous well of two sources and two stone basins, that to the right hand for eye water, and that to the left hand for tea water, became a nuisance from the multitude of ragged urchins who, with more picturesqueness than propriety, resorted thither to lave their nude proportions; and the stone basins, into the glassy bosom of whose waters "one generation after another had cast their waxing and waning shadows, as if human life were but a flitting image in a fountain," were removed; a well was dug a few yards from the spot as a reservoir for the waters, and a channel constructed to conduct them thither. In the progress of this work, Mr. Hucker, the builder, discovered the double source to be but a myth—an antique fiction—for the birthplace of the waters was near. From Kingsdown parade on the one side, and Colston Fort on the other, was a gradual slope towards the brow of the steep on which the well was situated, at the head of that deep glen through which the waters of the well flowed, was a break in the strata, and from beneath a table of pervious rock, about three feet in thickness, lying upon a subsoil of impervious clay, issued the unceasing stream.

Near the site of the well has been found in great abundance a peculiar spar, known in commerce as sulphate of strontia; nitrate of strontia gives the brilliant red light often exhibited in displays of fireworks.

There is an ancient stone tank in the garden of Mr. Vines, from which it is highly probable the defenders of Prior's Fort drew their supplies of water.

SAINT CONGAR THE HERMIT OF CONGRESBURY.

THE village of Congresbury derives its name, according to ancient legends, from Saint Congar, a religious hermit, and son of one of the Eastern emperors, who stole away privately, in the dress of a beggar, from the Imperial Court of Constantinople, in order to avoid an arrangement made by his parents for his being married to a young princess whom he did not love. First of all he wandered through Italy, then through France, and at length came to Britain; and finding this spot, which belonged to the Saxon King Ina, exactly suited to his wishes, being surrounded with water, reeds, and woods, he settled upon it, built himself a habitation, and afterwards a chapel, which he dedicated to the Holy Trinity. King Ina gave Saint Congar the little territory around his cell, wherein he instituted twelve canons. Having settled all matters relating to his priory, he set out on a pilgrimage to Jerusalem, where he died. His body was brought back to Congresbury, and there buried.

Some of the young folks tell the first portion of this story to their papas and mamas by way of a caution.

The Manor of Congresbury belongs to the Bristol Board of Charities, as governors of one of the noblest of our institutions, the City School, commonly called Queen Elizabeth's Hospital.

Folk Lore.

THE PINNACLE PULPIT.

At Flax Bourton, a hamlet in Somersetshire, about six miles from Bristol, the people have a legend with which they amuse children and strangers, by gravely assuring them that the Clergyman, at stated periods, ascends and preaches upon a pinnacle of the church tower. On explanation, this proves to be literally true. Many years ago one of the pinnacles was blown down, which, instead of being replaced, was cut into supports for the present pulpit. This story reminds us of one current in Bristol respecting

KING WILLIAM III. IN QUEEN SQUARE.

It assures us that when the metallic monarch hears the clock of St. Mary Redcliff strike one, he dismounts from his horse, descends from the pedestal, makes his obeisance, and then returns to his seat. Another version is, that both horse and king descend from the pedestal and take a gallop *round* the *square!*

Notes and Queries on Local Matters.

ORIGIN OF THE " BLANKET."

An extensive woollen manufactory was established in Tucker-street (Bath-street) in the year 1340. The proprietors were three brothers—Edward, Edmund, and Thomas Blanket. They were enterprising, skilful, and successful men, and were the first to manufacture the useful article of bed-furniture which has immortalised their name—*the* BLANKET.

Thomas Blanket was one of the bailiffs in 1341, and Edward Blanket was member in Parliament for Bristol in the year 1362—time of Edward III.

NOTES ON THE NEIGHBOURHOOD.

Ashton (Somersetshire, three miles from Bristol), was anciently called Easton, from its eastern situation from Portbury, which was the most important place on this side of the river.

Ashton Dando is the name of a tything in the parish of Ashton, which derives its name from the De Anlo family, who once owned the Manor of Long Ashton—Dando being a corruption of De Anlo.

Ashton Lyons is the name of another tything, derived from the family of De Lyons, who were descended from a native of Lyons, and a follower of William the Conqueror.

Ashton Philips, and *Ashton Theynes,* were manors held by families of note so named. The Theyne family were probably descended from one of three Saxon Thanes, who held Ashton previous to the Conquest.

HOSPITALS AT TEMPLE GATE.

The Swan Public-house, in Temple-street, marks the spot where stood a house of charity, or hospital, founded by John Spycer, probably a brother of Richard Spycer, who was three times mayor—in 1353, 1354, and 1371. It adjoined Temple-gate. There was a similar house on the opposite side of the street, the site of which is now an extensive manufactory of agricultural implements—firm of Fowler and Fry.

LAWFORD'S GATE.

At the entrance to Bull-Paunch Lane, is a stone 22 inches by 11, which marks the City-bounds, and also indicates the site of Lawford's Gate. It is embedded in the ground, level with the pitching, at a distance of five feet from the corner of the house occupied by Mr. Day, confectioner.

LEANING TOWER.

The curious old tower of Puxton Church overhangs its base considerably towards the west. No records exist respecting it, but it is quite probable it has been in that situation upwards of 500 years. Puxton adjoins Congresbury, and is 11½ miles from Bristol.

NOTES ON STREETS AND LANES.

Limekiln Lane was called Cow Lane down to the time of the Commonwealth.

Stephen Street was called Fisher Lane previous to the building of Clare street. The fish-market was held here.

Baldwin Street, was so called from a large house build about 1070 by Harding, and named in honour of Baldwin, Earl of Flanders. Hassall's Leather Warehouse now occupies its site. Portions of the walls remain.

The Pithay was anciently called Aylward's Street, after Aylward, warden of Bristol Castle in 930.

Small Street is said to derive its name from Smallaricus, fourth warden of the Castle.

Quay Street was in 1210 called Jewrie lane, being inhabited by Jews. They had a Synagogue in Small Street.

TO CORRESPONDENTS.

K. W. is thanked for his valuable papers. We shall make use of them in our next. In the mean time we beg to bespeak further favours.

New & Old. A correspondent under this signature, says that " the greatest curiosity of Bristol is the characteristics of Bristolians themselves." He asks why, " with the finest roadstead and safest anchorage in the world, do we sit, with folded arms, on our banks of mud, while less favoured places are outstripping us in the race of progress ? "—with several questions of a like nature. There is considerable point in your communication, but to answer your queries would fill a volume. The subject might with propriety be discussed in the columns of a newspaper; it is, however, scarcely within range of our rifle.

Proteus. Your " Walks about Bristol " will be admissible, provided you bear in mind that " brevity is the soul of wit."

J. E. next month. E. L. ditto. T. We will think of it.

CURIOSITIES OF BRISTOL
AND ITS NEIGHBOURHOOD.

No. 3.   NOVEMBER, 1853.   PRICE ONE PENNY.

A PILGRIMAGE TO THE DRUIDICAL TEMPLE AT STANTON DREW.

ONE bright morning in June, I rose almost with the sun, to carry out a project I had settled on some months previously, namely, a pilgrimage to the DruidicalStones at Stanton Drew. Being duly equipped, with staff in hand, and note-book in pocket—(to which should be added a paper bag, with Nattriss's name printed thereon, which a pair of dark eyes had stealthily conveyed into my pocket,) I started from Bristol, and at the end of two hours, I found myself at Pensford, having performed the journey of six miles at a leisurely pace.

Here I met a country-man, whom I accosted familiarly—will you tell me the way to Stanton Drew ?

Ees I will. You go past the mill, and, keep strait a'ter the stream, then turn to y'er left an' then to y'er right. Then ax anybody you do zee, an' you'l zoon vind it out.

What is the distance.

How var is it, do ye mean ? Why that's the very virst thing I ever larnt. Han't ye heard tell of these rhyme,—

Stanton Drew,
One mile from Pensford—two from Chew.

I thanked him for his information, and bidding him good morning, I pursued my journey. I need not stay to detail the pleasures of my walk, as my object is to describe briefly what I saw, and what I have learnt respecting these antiquities.

Stanton Drew is a small parish, and lies seven miles south of Bristol. The name is held to mean the Stone Town of the Druids. The learned Dr. Stukeley is of opinion that these remains are more ancient than Avebury or Stonehenge. The temple consists of three circles, a large central circle, and two smaller ones, composed of ponderous stones ; besides these there are some detached masses difficult to account for. The greater number of the stones are of magnesian limestone, such as is used for mending the roads, and for which

purpose some of them have been entirely destroyed,—for this ruthless work was long carried on ; some are of the quality called red sand-stones, and others of breccia, composed of pebbles and grit, firmly cemented together. The largest and smallest circles are both situated in a field called Stone Close. The other circle is in an orchard 150 yards to the south-west of the large one, and is called the Lunar Temple

The great circle measures about 126 yards in diameter, it is situated in a vale within about a hundred yards of the river Chew, from which it is separated by some rising ground. Fourteen stones only are now apparent ; five of which stand erect in their places, eight others are evidently buried just below the surface ; whilst the position of five more is indicated in dry summers by the withering of the turf over them. It is impossible to say how many stones originally formed the circle. Seyer makes the number twenty seven ; but Dr. Musgrave says there were thirty two. Others affirm that the number was thirty, correspond-ing with the days of the month. The stones vary in size ; the largest measuring nine feet in height, and twenty two in circumference. The entrance to this circle was on the eastern side, where lie two large stones ; opposite these are five stones placed in two rows.

At the distance of forty yards to the north-east, and within the Stone Close, is the smallest circle, of seven stones, corresponding with the days of the week. It is 32 yards in diameter, the stones forming it being very large, and of far superior finish to the others. Some retain their erect position, the others lie high above the ground. There is a group of seven stones at a short distance on the eastern side, which seem to have formed an avenue leading to this circle.

The lunar temple, we have referred to is so called because it consists of twelve stones, which most probably had reference to the months of the year. The circle is forty yards in diameter, and occupies the summit of a low

hill or knoll. The stones were placed on the
edges ; portions of ten remain, some lying
prostrate, others standing erect, and a few
buried below the surface.

At a distance of 157 yards from the lunar
temple, and near the parish church, on a low
eminence, are three great flat stones, placed in
a triangular position. These stones form what
is called the Cove, enclosing a space of about
ten feet wide by eight deep. Here it is supposed the Druids sat and administered justice
to the neighbouring tribes. But they were
not only judges, but priests and legislators ;
and it is almost certain the village of Stanton
Drew was in some sense a metropolis or seat
of government. Julius Cæser says, " They
are the ministers of sacred things ; they have
the charge of the sacrifice. Young men resort
to them for instruction. It is they that determine disputes, whether of the state or individuals ; they punish crime, and settle the
boundaries of lands."

As to the date of the erection of these stupendous works, it is impossible to speak with
certainty. As Aubrey says "they are so
exceedingly old that no books do reach them."
Whatever be their date, it is certainly very
remote, and corresponds with the circles,
cromlechs, and other monuments of the highest
antiquity, both in Britain, and other parts of
the world. Such erections are found in Jersey,
France, Germany, and Portugal ; in India,
Persia, and Palestine,—and here we are reminded of the record in Holy Writ, of the
stones taken by Joshua, out of the bed of the
Jordan, and set up in Gilgal—which name
signifies a circle. Gilgal, it will be remembered
was a place of sacred rites, and of legislative
acts.

Bowles states as his opinion, that Stanton
Drew like Avebury, was dedicated to the
Greatest Teacher, the one God, called _Thoth._

Thoth was an astronomer, and the grandson
of Ham, the son of Noah, his ideas of the one
God, were derived according to the same hy-
pothesis, from patriarchal tradition. On account of his knowledge of the heavenly bodies
and the religious instruction he gave his people,
his memory was venerated, and he at length
became an object of worship. The _Thoth_ of
the Phenicians, the Egyptian _Taxut,_ and the
Teut of the Druids.

A GLANCE AT THE INTERIOR OF
BRISTOL CATHEDRAL.

THE external of the Bristol Cathedral, it is
true, does not assume that imposing aspect
which so strikingly characterises most of our
English Cathedrals; it may not present such
a stately pile of masonry as to prove a very
conspicuous object among the surrounding
buildings; but on entering the interior by the
north door we are struck with the air of

majestic grandeur produced by the four
massive piers that support the tower; then
of the chancel, two side aisles, and cross-aisle ;
glancing round we perceive the uniform height
of the portion of the nave yet standing, this
gives a feeling of unusual space, and the effect
must have been magnificent, when the other
portion of the nave,—said to have extended
150 feet westward—was in existence. The
vaulting is light and elegant, and some of the
bosses are extremely grotesque in character.
In what is called the elder Lady Chapel, at
the north side of the church, there is a device
which has received a good deal of attention :
while the Shepherd sleeps, the Wolf is devour-
ing the Sheep—a Ram mean-while is playing
a sort of fiddle with a remarkably long bow.
It is a curious fact that the invention of the
fiddlestick is dated centuries after the building
of this church. The chapel is evidently the
oldest portion of the building ; and no doubt
formed a part of the original Abbey, built by
Fitzhardinge, whose tomb it contains. Our
historians seem uncertain as to when, or how,
the nave was destroyed ; there is a tradition
however that it was demolished by some of
Henry VIII's commissioners, and the materials
sold, before it was decided to convert it into a
cathedral.

Of the ill usage the place has received, a
writer in "the Land we Live In" thus
speaks :—

" The interior suffered much damage during
the cival wars, many fine windows were
destroyed, and several of the ancient monuments were, unfortunately, greatly injured,
and those which have survived the two revolutions, religious and political, are now slowly
succumbing under the hands of barbarous
deans. [The writer should have exempted the
present and late dean, who have shown every
disposition to repair the misdeeds of their
predecessors.] The slovenly yellow-wash
brush has been smeared over monuments as
well as walls ; and cross-legged crusaders—
many of whom sleep here their stoney sleep—
mitred abbots and knights, who once lay in
all the splendour of coloured and gilded
armour, now alike repose in garments of
yellow-wash, put on one over the other, until
the original features beneath them are almost
obscured. There is one little chapel in which
particular havoc has been committed—the
chapel of the Newtons—containing several
altar-tombs, effigies upon some of which have
been entirely destroyed. The others, once so
quaint with colour and heraldic embellishments, have now been reduced by the Vandals
of the place to buff coats, and hose of the com-
monest ochre. Upon one of these tombs—

that of Sir Henry Newton, who died in 1599—there is an epitaph, written with such a fine martial tramp, that we cannot forbear giving it :—

' Gourney, Hampton, Cradock, Newton last,
Held on the measure of that ancient line
Of Barons' blood ; full seventy years he past,
And did in peace his sacred soul resign.
His church he loved ; he loved to feed the poor;
Such love assures a life that dies no more.'

Sir Isaac Newton belonged to this family, whose seat, Barr's court, was situated at Hanham, only a few miles from Bristol : it is now a barn ; the garden, once so quaint and beautiful, is reduced to a common field, an outline of the fish-pond is yet traceable within it. The only remnant of this baronial hall to be seen is the coat of arms, let into a building now used as a cowhouse. *Sic transit !* "

THE BRISTOL RIOTS OF 1831.

SECOND ARTICLE.

THE Recorder had, during the formality of opening the Commission, made some observations calculated to further irritate the excited assembly ; his remarks, now that they were conveyed by them to the crowd in the street, were repeated with great bitterness.—Considerable agitation became apparent. Parties of low characters were seen hurrying backward and forward between Broad Street and Small Street, lest Sir Charles should escape by the private entrance of the Guildhall in the latter Street.

In half an hour, he made his appearance at the front of the Hall, and entered the Mayor's Carriage. The demonstrations of the mob however, went no farther than a tremendous volley of yells mingled with cries of " Reform." At this moment, Broad Street, and indeed, the whole line of route to the Mansion House, in Queen Square, was filled with a dense mass of people. As the carriage passed along, nothing but hisses and groans, mingled with expressions of contempt could have met his ear. There was, however, no violence ; and nothing transpired indicative of danger to his person, or to the peace of the city, until he arrived at the Mansion House ; when just as he was about to alight, a number of stones struck the carriage, breaking some glass ; but Sir Charles entered the Mansion House without receiving the slightest injury.

The proceedings which now immediately followed, have been generally regarded as those which led to the violence of the mob. The special constables, instead of acting upon the instructions given them by the Mayor, Chas. Pinney, Esq., that they should perform their duty with the utmost precaution and forbearance, rushed pell-mell among the people, and seizing a man, at random, dragged him before the Magistrates, as one who had thrown stones at the Recorder; whether or not they were able to identify the offenders it is impossible to determine ; it will be admitted that their ability to do so must have been very doubtful. At all events this was the general belief ; and correct or not, did not fail to produce a dire effect on the gathered throng. Had they even stopped here, matters might have gone no further ; but elated with their success, they sallied forth, and in a short time had secured some five or six persons after a most ill-judged fashion ; using their staves most unmercifully and indiscriminately. One of the victims was carried by the people to the Infirmary, with a fractured scull.

Up to this point, it must be confessed, the mob were guiltless of any decided outrage ; and it is much to be regretted that the magistrates did not now personally employ persuasive means to disperse them. Had they gone among them, as was done under very similar circumstances, when a former recorder, Sir Vicary Gibbs, roused the ire of the multitude, doubtless they would have been listened to—as was Mr. Willcox, the Mayor on the occasion referred to. He stood in front of the Mansion House, for hours together, and his persuasive, conciliatory words were attended with the happiest results. But in this case, the special constables did as they list, no magistrate undertaking to direct or regulate their proceedings.

The multitude now consisted of many thousand persons ; and when the constables had been engaged in the way described some ten or fifteen minutes a cry was raised " To the Back"—"To the Back." A large body at once proceeded to the piles of faggots, heaped up there for fire-wood, and in a few minutes hundreds returned to the scene, armed with sticks, and bent on mischief; they were however mostly soon disarmed, and the sticks strewed upon the ground. This was about 1 o'clock in the afternoon ; and had the advantage now gained been prudently followed up, the strife would no doubt have ceased.—Instead of which, one and another would sally forth single handed amongst the mob, on which a scuffle would ensue, ending in further excitement, and progressive exasperation.

As the afternoon advanced, symptoms of violence increased ; sticks were hurled at the constables, and missiles at the windows of the Mansion house at frequent intervals.—And when, at four o'clock, the shades of night closed on the scene, nearly every pane of glass was demolished, and the destruction of the building seemed inevitable.

At this critical moment, when many of the constables had been ordered to retire to their homes for refreshment, and the rioters had become so elated with their exploits as to consider themselves masters of the field, Mr. Pinney, the Mayor, supported by several aldermen, came to the front of the Mansion-house, and attempted to address them, but in vain. His remonstrances were offered in the kindest manner—and the sentiments he uttered did honor to him,—but it was too late. During his address he was assailed by a shower of stones and brick bats; he persevered, however, for some time, amid imminent peril. At length after repeatedly assuring them that he had no wish to read the riot-act, which would place them all in the position of felons, he exhorted them to go home. So far from being influenced by the chief magistrate, they now rushed upon the few constables present; disarmed them, and beat them severely. One was actually chased into the float, and was with great difficulty rescued from a watery grave. Another was compelled to hurl his staff at the Mansion House windows, as a condition of release.

There being now no influence that could curb the mob, nor impediment to hinder the work of destruction, they commenced a general and simultaneous attack on every part of the Mansion House. In a few moments the partly demolished windows and sashes were shivered to atoms; the shutters beaten in pieces; the doors forced; and every article on the ground floor, broken up. Tables, chairs, sideboards, mirrors, chimney glasses—in fact everything that the desperadoes could lay their hands on was destroyed. The iron palisades in front of the house, together with the curb-stones in which they were set, were torn up, and furnished many a furious villan with a formidable weapon. Even the young trees were pulled up by the roots and converted into instruments of destruction;—and the dwarf walls were pulled down to provide brick-bats. At the same time a large quantity of straw and combustibles were brought, with which to fire the whole premises. This was the time selected by Sir Charles to make his escape; which he did,—not without danger and difficulty,—over the roofs of the adjoining houses. Having disguised himself he was not observed; nor was it known except to a few till the next day, when he had left the city, what had become of him. It is clear, that if he had made his appearance in the square he would have been murdered. At this very time one party had arranged themselves all round the building to prevent his egress, and whose vigilence it is a marvel he escaped; another party were attempting to barricade the avenues leading into the square, as they were expecting the troops. For this purpose a number of large planks and other timber, had been brought from the Back and Quay. In order more effectually to carry on their diabolical work, they took the precaution of putting out the gas-lights, by climbing the pillars. Every preparation had been already made, as it afterward appeared, to set fire to the Mansion house, and it was only saved from conflagration by the accidental difficulty of obtaining a light, for lucifer matches were not in common use in those days.

The state of matters within the Mansion House at this juncture it is impossible to record without a smile. The attack of the mob caused such dismay among the domestics that they fled for their lives, leaving their culinary operations, which were proceeding on a large scale for the intended feast, in the most ludicrous confusion. At the blazing fires the joints were turning upon the spits, without a boy to baste them. The saucepans and kettles were boiling and steaming furiously, and no cook was there to save their savoury contents from destruction.

But seriously, if one were disposed to sympathise with those who were disappointed of a good dinner, it is difficult to understand how they could coolly calculate on enjoying their sumptuous meal, surrounded as they had been throughout the day, by circumstances of such excitement and danger.

At six o'clock, a troop of the 14th regiment of cavalry arrived, and soon after they were joined by a troop of the third dragoon guards. Their arrival was the signal for renewing the reform cry, as the soldiers as well as the king were considered to sympathise with it, and they were received with the most enthusiastic cheering from all quarters; and the thousands who had posted themselves on the walls and other elevated situations, waved their hats without manifesting the least symptom of fear or sense of danger. The troops however effectually restrained all further attack upon the Mansion-House that evening, and continued to parade the square and adjoining streets, the people constantly greeting them with cheers for the King and Reform.

HISTORY OF ASHTON COURT AND MANOR.

THE late extraordinary trial of Smyth v Smyth, in reference to this property, having excited an unusual degree of attention, we give a few historical particulars from Rutter.

About two miles from Bristol, adjoining the road from that city to Weston, is a castellated lodge and entrance gateway, leading to the seat of the late Sir John Smyth, Bart. It presents an extensive front, situated on a gentle eminence, in the centre of a luxuriantly wooded park, which was originally enclosed and planted by Thomas de Lyons, in 1391, under a licence granted by Richard II., and who from that time added the name of Ashton to the family appellation. The most ancient part of this mansion was erected by the Ashton Lyons, who resided in it, and whose arms and devices continue conspicuous on many parts of it. At the back part of the mansion still remains the ancient gateway leading from the park into the outer court, in which the Gothic windows, battlements, and projecting buttresses, are preserved, and it continues to be called the Castle Court. A low doorway, between two lofty turrets, forms the entrance into the second, or inner court, which contains the offices.

The front is one hundred and fifty feet in length, and contains several spacious apartments, which command a fine and pleasing prospect. This front was erected in 1634, by Inigo Jones, who was employed to modernize the ancient edifice, and to convert it into a regular quadrangular pile of building ; but whose plan, from the unsettled state of public affairs, was never completed.

The manor of Ashton was given at the conquest to the bishop of Coutances ; in the reign of Henry I, it was possessed by Adam de Heyron ; by his daughter it came to the de Alno family ; it was subsequently possessed by the de Lyons family ; from them it was conveyed in 1454, to Richard Choke of Stanton Drew, the eminent Lord Chief Justice of England ; his grandson sold the manor in 1506 to Sir Giles Daubrey, Knt. In 1511 it was conveyed to Sir Thomas Arundell, Knt ; who sold it in 1545 to John Smyth, Esq. of Aylburton, Glostershire, who was mayor and sheriff of Bristol, and in whose family it still continues.

The present Heir to the Smyth Estates, is Greville Smyth, a youth of about 17. His guardian, "receiver in Chancery to the Ashton Court Estates" is Arthur Edwin Way, Esq.

A FEW WORDS ABOUT THE PORTRAIT OF CHATTERTON.

THE Life of Chatterton by Dix, is embellished with a portrait of Thomas Chatterton ; its authenticity however has been disputed in an able article that appeared some years since in the Gentlemen's Magazine, written by the late Richard Smith, Esq., Surgeon, of this city. It shows that the Portrait in Mr. Dix's work, which is a copy of a painting in the possession of Geo. Weare Braikenridge, Esq. is not a portrait of Chatterton, but a portrait of a lad of the name of Morris, the son of a Portrait Painter. The article written by Mr. Smith contains a copy of a letter from Mr. Burge in which the proof is given that the portrait is not a likeness of Chatterton.

The following is the Letter referred to : —
Sugar House, Back St. Nov. 23, 1837.
My Dear Miller,

For a wonder I did not come to Town yesterday or I would have replied to your note by the bearer, you therein ask me to state what I know concerning the portrait of Chatterton, lately published by Mr. Dix, I will tell you. About thirty five years ago, I became impressed with the notion that I had a taste for pictures, and fancied, like all so impressed, that I had only to rummage brokers' shops, to possess myself of gems and hidden treasures without number ; which illusion a little practical knowledge soon "dismissed with costs." It happened that a gentleman in whose house I then resided, (being at that time a batchelor,) became also touched with the same mania, and in one of his peregrinations picked up the picture you mention, at a broker's, in Castle Ditch, at a house now the Castle and Ball Tavern. The broker's name was Beer ; at the back of the portrait was written with a brush, — "F. Morris aged 13." As well as I can recollect, the gentleman who purchased it, in a playful mood, said "this portrait will do for Chatterton," and immediately placed the name of Chatterton over that of F. Morris. What became of it afterwards, or how it came into the hands of the present possessor, I am quite ignorant of. While in the hands of the gentleman above mentioned, I showed it to Mr. Stewart, the portrait painter who recognized it at once as the portrait of young Morris, the son of Morris the Portrait Painter. This is all I know, and you are at liberty to make what use you please of it.

I am yours truly, GEO. BURGE.

Mr. Smith adds, that Mr. Miller sent the above to the Rev. John Eagles, who gave the letter to him.—The above, I consider, fully proves that the Portrait in Mr. Dix's Life of Chatterton is not a likeness of Chatterton. Therefore there is no evidence that there is in existence a Portrait of Thomas Chatterton, the "Marvellous Boy, who Perished in his Pride." J. D. L.

Bristol Worthies.

OUR VENERABLE TOPOGRAPHER, WILLIAM WYCESTRE.

WILLIAM of Worcester, or more correctly William Wycestre is a name of frequent occurrence in connexion with the topography and antiquities of Bristol. And as we shall have occasionally to refer to the labours of this remarkable man, a brief sketch of his life will probably prove useful and interesting to our readers.

William Wycestre was born in the year 1415. His Father was a worthy burgess of Bristol, and carried on the business of a white-tawer, skinner, and glover, on Saint James's Back. His Mother's name was Botoner. She was of an opulent family settled at Coventry ;

two members of which are said to have built
the Church of the Holy Trinity.

He received his education at Hart Hall,
Oxford, where he was a student four years.
He then became a retainer of Sir John Fastolf,
of Caistre Castle, in the County of Norfolk.
To this gentleman in process of time, he
became secretary, physician, and finally his
executor.

After this he appears to have assumed the name
of W. *Botoner*, called Wycestre, preferring his
mother's name to that of his father.

When he was somewhat advanced in life, we
find him settled in Bristol, and having a house
and garden, near the entrance gate of Saint
Philip's Church-yard. These and some other
estates are described as the property of W.
Wycestre. Here he cultivated medical herbs,
and practised as a physician. One of his
favorite pursuits, was most diligently to survey
his native City— and this he did by way of relaxation and amusement. His investigations
were most minute, and his measurements and
observations were daily written into his note
book, apparently with the utmost attention to
the details. It is quite clear however that
his figures are not always to be depended on,
and there are several discrepancies in his own
manuscript : For example, the measurements
of Bristol Bridge are given with eight several
variations. These may be accounted for by
assuming that he measured from various start-
ing points, of which he takes no notice ; these
defects, are of course, calculated to depreciate
the value of his statements as an authority.

At the same time, when it is remembered
that the manuscripts he left to posterity, consisted of loose unrevised memoranda, and
evidently intended for the foundation of a complete work—we cannot but highly esteem the
labours of our venerable topographer ; more
especially when it is considered that they were
performed in the fifteenth century.

We quote the following observations from
Dallaway, to whom we are chiefly indebted
for the materials of the foregoing sketch.

"The pretensions of William Wycestre, to
learning, as it was professed among the few
erudite ecclesiastics, may be subject to several
considerations of abatement. But his love of
learning was at all times superior to his acquirements, and his industry in copying many
MSS., is sufficiently proved by those which
are still extant. Nor can we say of those which
treat of science only, that he did not in some
degree, make them his own. As to his historical
collections, and the memoranda which he made
of what was passing in his own times, he must,
in candour, be allowed all the merit which, in
such times, was due to any layman, who dedicated his leisure to literary pursuit. Several
historical anecdotes of the reigns of Henry V.
and VI., are not to be found elsewhere, which
came within his own knowledge."

It is supposed, from evidence founded on his
notes, that W. Wycestre died about the year
1484.

A LIST OF EMINENT PERSONS
CONNECTED WITH BRISTOL.

UNDER this title, we purpose in our next
number, to give the first portion of a list,
alphabetically arranged, of individuals who
have been in any degree associated with Bristol,
and who may have contributed by their talents,
research, inventions, enterprize, industry, reforms, or benevolence to the advancement of
society.

We have such a list in a forward state, but
are unwilling to put it to press until we have
had the aid of all who are disposed to help
us. We now ask for such aid, in order that
the list may be as complete as possible. We
select at random the following, which will
show the amount and kind of information
required.

Colston Edward, Philanthropist and Merchant,
a name of which Bristol is justly proud —
born in Temple Street ; died 1721, aged
85 ; buried in All Saints' Church.

Foster Nathaniel, D. D. born in Bristol ; a
profound scholar and linguist; died in 1757,
aged 41 ; buried in the Cathedral.

Hume David, the historian, when a young
man, was for some months a merchant's
clerk in Bristol. 1734.

Southey Robert, LL.D. poet laureate, born
at No. 11 Wine Street, Bristol ; poet, scholar,
antiquary, critic, and historian ; died 1843,
aged 69.

Our Local Legends.

THE DUCKING STOOL ON THE
WEIR.

THE progress of Society in civilization and
refinement, of late years, has been marked by
the extinction of many brutal customs. The
spectacles of bull baiting and cock fighting as
public sports have passed away, and with
them, that class of punishments for minor
offences, which ministered to the depraved
tastes of the vicious. About a century ago
it was not uncommon to place a heavy weight
on the breast of persons refusing to plead in
courts of justice ; some had their thumbs tied
together with whip-cord, so tight, that the
pain might compel them to plead. Burning
the hands was another punishment much in
vogue, and indeed, was not made unlawful
till the reign of George IV.

But among the most troublesome characters,
though not the most dangerous, then as now,
were scolding wives and drunken husbands.
But more pains were taken, it would seem, to
cure the women than the men. We do read, it

is true, of the magistrates of Newcastle, providing a drunkard's cloak—that is, a tub turned bottom upwards, with a hole for his head, and holes on each side for his hands, which he was obliged to wear through the streets. Brawling women and scolds (perhaps not without reason in many cases,) however, *must* be put down, and many an ingenious brain was racked to find a successful cure. Hence the Brank, a sugarloaf-shaped cap made of hoop-iron, with a cross at the top, and a flat piece projecting inward to lay on the tongue. Into this cage the head was thrust, pad-locked behind, and the poor wretch led by a string through the streets. The whirligig too, was a common punishment, it was in appearance like a squirrel-cage set upright. The delinquent was put into this and whirled round until she became exceedingly sick.

But the Ducking stool or tumbrel, of all others, seems to have been the most popular with the multitude, on account of the sport it afforded. Its virtues as an instrument of torture for reforming the termagant, we very much doubt—and as to its influence on the minds and morals of the people, it was, as a public teacher, anything but successful in elevating and improving them.

Such a machine, existed in the Frome on the Weir, just under the castle walls, probably two hundred years; the last remains of it were removed about the year 1785. It consisted of an upright post, across which was placed a beam turning on a swivel, with a chair at one end of it, in which the unfortunate scold was properly placed; the end was then turned to the stream and let down into it. And this was repeated once, twice, thrice, or as often as the tender mercies of the crowd or operator would permit.

The last instance upon record, of a person indicted for a scold in this city, was in the year 1718, when Edward Mountjoy, Mayor, authorized its ministration in due form.

Dix in his humorous legend thus introduces the complainant,—

Young Mr. Blake had a house full of strife,
  And the cause of the rows was
THE TONGUE OF HIS WIFE!

He then describes Mrs. Blake,—

Barbara Blake was both pretty and young,
She had only one fault, BUT it lay in her tongue!
Her eyes they were blue, and her curls were of gold,
A stranger would never have thought her a scold.

And considering these, and some other recommendatory qualities which he has described it would scarcely be believed that poor Blake (who by the way must have been a very gentle spirit,) had to endure, day after day, month after month, and year after year, volleys of abuse from her unruly member. At length

Young Mr. Blake one evening sat,
  His feet on the fender, beating rat-tat;

Each hand in his pocket, up to the wrist;
On his visage a serio-comical twist.
    We shall presently find
    He had made up his mind
No more to be henpecked—no more to submit
To his wife, and only what she thought was fit.

He had often passed the ugly old post on the weir—he hated the sight of it—but then—what *could* he do, and meeting the Mayor's Officer then and there, he laid his case before him. Our Officer nowise loath, soon set the matter agoing. The Ducking Stool was repaired, and here are the results,—

In " seventeen hundred and eighteen,"
  Mountjoy was Bristol's mayor;
Then, on the Weir, might have been seen
  The city ducking chair.
Above the waters of the Frome
  The awful apparatus
Frowned, like a monitor of gloom,
  Just by the castle-gate house.
A high pole, and a transverse beam,
  Which turned ten times a minute,
Upon its pivot o'er the stream,
  Turned with its chair;—hark! there's a scream!
Poor Barbara Blake is in it!

The crowd below, vociferate and shout their approval of the disgusting sport, and it is repeated; but now

Her breath is almost spent,
  Her frame with cold is shivering,
And *not* to Blake's astonishment,
  With voice all meek and quivering,
She promises, that if unhung,
  She'll ever after " hold her tongue,"
From that month when the year is young,
  E'en until dim December.
So to " THE HOUSE " was she returned,
  It was a *quiet house*, I've learned,
  E'er since they chaired the member.
(In a parenthesis I truly
  Agree with Paul that 'twas unruly,)
And 'tis declared that Mr. B.
  Ne'er made one slight objection
  To *her* return.
And ever after Mistress Blake
Sailed only in her husband's wake;
  Remembering her late wet condition,
  No more she led the " opposition."

The record informs us, that as soon as Mountjoy's civic year expired, Blake brought an action against him for assault and battery, in behalf of Mrs. B. before Sir Peter King, at the Guildhall—and actually recovered damages—such damages, (our historian insinuates,) that the Ex-mayor could not endure the mention of *cold duck* ever after. Query, was this species of discipline the origin of the endearing term *my duck*?

Folk Lore.

THE BUILDING OF REDCLIFF CHURCH.

One of our most familiar traditions informs us that Redcliff Church was built when workmen earned a penny a day. The stone was obtained from Dundry Hill, and conveyed from the quarries to the Church after a very novel fashion. The labourers formed a line in single file, standing six feet apart for the whole distance of five miles, and passed on the stones by handing from one to another, and so on to the next, at a pretty rapid rate. And thus the stupendous fabric was completed.

OUR GHOST STORIES.

The folk lore of Durdham Down is rather in the ghost line. There is one story current of a lady ghost who is "doomed for a certain time to walk" "Redland Road," and that she has already frightened several persons "out of their wits."

Some of the folk at the Mardyke, in the Hotwell Road, have a story of a lady ghost who has troubled them for years past by driving her carriage along the tops of walls, through windows and doors; and even on the tops of houses.

Notes and Queries on Local Matters.

OLD WINDOW ON THE WEIR.

The stone work of a small Gothic Window may be seen in the wall of Griffiths's Timber Yard, on the Narrow Weir. It is believed to be the remains of a religious edifice of about the year 1267—Whatever it was, it belongs to that period.

ORIGIN OF "KINGSWOOD."

Kingswood was anciently called the wood of Furzes (1227.) It was a chase for several successive Kings; hence its name. The forester who had the care of it in the time of Edward II. received from the constable of Bristol Castle the wages of seven-pence half-penny a day.

NOTES ON STREETS AND LANES.

Rosemary Street, was formerly Rosemary Lane. In William Wycestre's time, it was Rush Lane—at a still earlier date it was called Irish Mead.

Host Street, was originally Hore Street. Derived probably from William Hore, who was Mayor of Bristol in 1312, and resided in this street; it was afterwards corrupted into Horse Street; and now it stands corrected because the Host was carried in procession through it. This reason however, is a poor one; for whenever the ceremony was required it was for a dying person, and therefore was carried to any part of the city.

Marsh Street, formerly Skadpull (or Scapefulle) street, contained capacious and first rate timber-frame houses, as may be supposed from the appearance of a few that still remain. The wealthiest merchants and mariners of the city resided here on account of its contiguity to the Quay.

Nelson Street, from St. John's Gate to Bridewell Street, was formerly called Hauliers' Lane. In the time of Edward III, it was called Grope Lane. There was also a lane at Oxford, and another at Coventry so called. They were so narrow that two persons could not pass through them abreast.

Orchard Street was so named because it occupied the site of the Orchard and Garden of the Hospital of the Gaunts or "College of Good-men." The Chapel of that institution is now the Mayor's Chapel, College Green.

Culver Street, takes its name from having been built on the site of a "Culver" or Pidgeon house, belonging to the Hospital of the Gaunts.

NOTICE TO OUR READERS.

Number One is now reprinted, and in the hands of the Booksellers. We regret to have disappointed many friends, but we had no reason to anticipate so large a sale for our "Curiosities." It is the first instance, we believe, in this city, of a work of this description being safely established at the first number.

Among various friendly suggestions we have received, is one which we are encouraged to hope will meet the approval of most of our readers, the occasional embellishment of our little work with well executed illustrations. We find we can enlist such pictorial aid as will greatly add to the interest of some of our articles—and we expect to be able to reproduce some scarce, curious, and highly valuable maps, and ancient and modern views of great local interest.—And this can be accomplished at the charge of a halfpenny for each additional sheet—and in some few cases at the rate of a penny.

In accordance with this proposal we shall "feel our way" next month by supplying a ground plan of the remains at Stanton Drew, and a sectional view of Pen Park Hole, at a half-penny extra.

. Communications to the Editor to be forwarded to the Office of the BRISTOL DIRECTORY, 9, Narrow Wine-street.

Advertisements to be sent to M. BINGHAM, 9, Broad-street, by the 10th of the month.

A quarto edition of this work, printed on superior paper, price Twopence each. Either edition can be sent, post free, on receipt of an extra stamp.

Published in London, by Houlston & Stoneman, 65, Paternoster Row, and may be obtained through any bookseller in the United Kingdom.

Printed and Published at the Office of the Bristol DIRECTORY, 9 Narrow Wine Street, Bristol, by M. Mathews.—November 1, 1852.

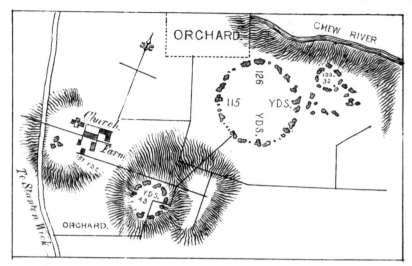

DRUIDICAL TEMPLE AT STANTON DREW.

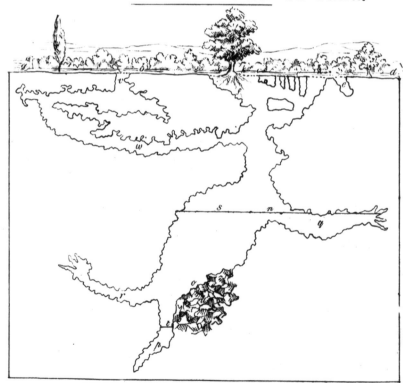

SECTION OF PEN PARK HOLE.

a b c d Surface of the earth–e a small cavern–f the great mouth of the cavern–i the ash tree at the mouth–k l m n o p. descent to the bottom–q the Western cavity–r. the Eastern cavity–s. surface of water at its highest stage–t. ditto. at its lowest stage–u. rubbish–v descent into the Eastern tunnel–w. passage communicating with the great cavern–x. channel by which the water flows out

CURIOSITIES OF BRISTOL
AND ITS NEIGHBOURHOOD.

No. 4.   DECEMBER, 1853.   THREE HALF PENCE.

PEN PARK HOLE AND ITS TRAGIC ASSOCIATIONS.

For a period of two hundred years Pen Park Hole has been an object of considerable curiosity among all classes in this neighbourhood. In the reign of Charles II it was regarded by many with a degree of superstition and terror unknown in the present day; indeed the cavern was confidently believed to be the abode of evil spirits, who haunted its dark chambers with undisputed sway. There were not wanting those who declared they had heard noises of the most doleful and terrific character, issuing from its mouth; these statements, therefore, very naturally, awakened general curiosity, and instances are related of persons who, indulging in a love of the marvellous, dwelt on these statements until very painful results followed.

Pen Park Hole is distant from Bristol about four miles, and is situated in the corner of a field, in the parish of Westbury-upon-Trym. Its notoriety in Bristol is derived chiefly from the melancholy fate of Mr. Newnham, a clergyman, who in 1775, fell into this dismal abyss, after which sad event some thousands of persons visited the spot.

The cavern has been described by George Symes Catcott, who, in a curious pamphlet, printed in Bristol in 1792, portrays its dreary recesses with painful minuteness. Our author descended into the cavern in company with Mr. White, a surveyor, who made a sectional drawing, which was afterwards transferred to copper, and from which we have made the copy accompanying the present number.

The opening to the cavern was formerly protected by a hedge and bushes, to prevent accident, but it is now more effectually guarded by a wall, which completely hides it from view. Within the enclosure thus formed a gloomy chasm presents itself. " At the mouth (says Mr. Catcott) the depth is apparently small, and there is an impending rock, but a little lower down it extends on every side, quite out of sight, into the frightful gloom. If a stone be thrown, it will be heard for some time, dashing against the rocks it meets with, till at last it is lost by plunging into a vast depth of water." We think we shall be best consulting the tastes of our readers by omitting Mr. Catcott's further description of the cavern, which occupies several pages, referring them to the plate as a more ready method of getting an accurate idea of it. We therefore proceed at once to the tragical incidents with which it is associated.

The unfortunate clergyman already referred to, the Rev. Thomas Newnham, was a minor canon of Bristol Cathedral, and the son of a banker of this city. It appears that he had made an appointment with a young lady, to whom he was engaged, and with two other friends, to visit the cavern, on Friday, 17th of March, 1775; and desiring, if possible, to fathom its depth, he provided himself with a line and plummet. On the morning of the same day, Mr. Newnham had undertaken to conduct divine service at Clifton church, and the four friends proceeded thither together. It will be seen, on reference to the Common Prayer-book, that the 88th Psalm occurs as a portion of the service for that day, and contains the following remarkable passages :—

" Let my prayer enter into thy presence : for my soul is full of trouble, and my life draweth nigh unto the grave. I am counted as one of them that go down into the pit. Free among the dead, like the slain that lie in the grave, who are out of remembrance and are cut away from thy hand. Thou hast laid me in the lowest pit; in a place of darkness and in the deep. Thy wrath lieth hard upon me, and thou hast afflicted me with all thy waves. Thou hast put away mine acquaintance far from me, and made me to be abhorred of them. I am so fast in prison ; that I cannot get forth. Lord why castest thou off my soul ? why hidest thou thy face from me ?

my lovers and friends hast thou taken away from me; and hid mine acquaintance out of my sight."

Whatever was the impression made by this psalm on the minds of these four friends, nothing occurred during their journey after the service, to indicate any apprehension of the fearful catastrophe which took place so soon afterwards.

On arriving at the spot, the excursionists at once examined the aperture; then Mr. Newnham proceeded along the slope with a cautious step, unwinding his line as he went, and was in the act of passing it down the perpendicular, when feeling the ground moist beneath his feet, he attempted to strengthen his position by taking hold of a root projecting from an ash tree growing over the opening. The twig broke off, and with it he instantly disappeared, and was precipitated into the dark abyss. The fearful splash which re-echoed through the cavern too vividly told his fate to his terror-stricken friends. They called, but there was no answer, save the echo of their own voices, and then all was still as death—silent as the grave.

Vigorous efforts were soon made for re-covering the body: a scaffolding, with ropes and pullies, was erected at the mouth, and searching parties went down with torches daily, for three weeks, without success. The hat of the unfortunate gentleman was at length brought up; it served to urge a more determined search for a week longer, but every effort proved fruitless; a general impression was that the body had floated away by a submarine channel communicating with the Severn, and was carried out to sea.

The subject was passing away from the public mind, when a singular circumstance brought it once more before the world:—A wager of five pounds had been accepted by Mr. Tucker of the Custom-house, that he would descend into Pen-park-hole. In fulfilment of his engagement he did so, accompanied by a workman, with lights. The latter happening to throw a stone into the water, observed that it made no splash, having fallen on a floating object. After looking attentively, its form became visible—it was the missing body. It was drawn up and conveyed to Pen-park-house, having been in the water thirty-nine days.

The remains of the unfortunate gentleman were conveyed thence, followed by his mourning friends, to Westbury church, on Thursday, April 27th, 1775, the day on which he would have entered his twenty-sixth year.

It is a singular fact, that so far back as 1669, an accidental circumstance invested this cavern with a marvellous interest. A Captain Stermey, with the view of contributing towards some philosophical inquiries under discussion by the Royal Society, undertook an exploration. He says, in the philosophical transactions, that "a mine man and myself lowered ourselves by ropes 150 feet, till we came to a river 120 feet broad and 50 feet deep." Giving other particulars, he thus concludes:—"The miner man went by a ladder, and had just lost sight of me, when he called out cheerfully, saying he had found a rich mine; but his joy was quickly turned into amazement, and he returned, almost frightened to death, by the sight of an evil spirit, which we cannot persuade him but he saw, and so for that reason he will go there no more." It would seem by this extract that the captain treated the matter very coolly: but strange as it may appear, four days after his exploration he was taken ill of a fever and died. The tale spread and gathered strength, and it was declared to be confirmed by the death of Captain Stermey. The mining man asserted that the captain died of fright, and made use of the circumstance to confirm his own version of the story; which from its singular character, and the credence given to ghost stories by almost all persons at that period, became a subject of conversation and wonder far and wide.

Pen-park-hole is a natural cavern; and it is probable that it was worked for lead ore at a very remote period. An attempt, it is said, was recently made to turn its mineral wealth to account, and some rich ore was found, but it did not prove profitable, and was therefore abandoned.

THOMAS BEDDOES, M.D.
THE EMINENT PHYSICIAN.

DOCTOR BEDDOES of this city was one of the most distinguished physicians of his day, not only on account of his own eminent abilities, but also from the training he gave to the famous philosopher he afterwards introduced to the world, Sir Humphry Davy. Beddoes was born at Shriffnal, in Shropshire, where his father carried on the business of a tanner.

At an early age he manifested abilities, which induced his father to promote his education, with a view to qualify him for some profession. An accident, requiring the aid of a surgeon, which befel his grandfather, determined the youth to study medicine.

In 1773, having reached the age of 18, he was placed under the care of the Rev. S. Dickenson, rector of Plym-hill; and three years afterwards he entered at Pembroke College, Oxford, where he soon became distinguished for his learning and his acquaintance with languages, both ancient and modern—in the latter he was entirely self-taught. During his stay at the University he devoted considerable attention to chemistry and geology. The recent discoveries of Black and Priestley, in relation to the different gases, had directed the attention of men of science more especially to these subjects, and Beddoes fully participated in the interest which they excited. He very soon formed high expectations of the uses of these discoveries, especially in the treatment of diseases; and ever afterwards was encouraged to trust greatly to pneumatic medicine.

Arrived at the age of 21 years, he took his bachelor's degree, and proceeded to London, to study medicine, under the celebrated Sheldon. He soon afterwards removed to Edinburgh, where he was greatly distinguished among the students, and was associated with Dr. Cullen in translating works on electricity. He subsequently visited France, where he became acquainted with Lavoisier and other celebrated chemists. On his return home he was appointed reader in chemistry to the University of Oxford. In his views respecting geology he embraced the theory of Hutton, and was a decided believer in the existence of a central fire.

At the age of 32 he resigned his connexion with Oxford, and took up his abode in Shropshire devoting himself to authorship. His publications at this time prove his great industry, as well as the particular direction of his thoughts. They almost all refer to the theory of curing diseases by breathing a medicated atmosphere. In order that these views might have the full benefit of experimental tests, Dr. Beddoes, in conjunction with some other gentlemen, established a pneumatic hospital in Dowry-square, Hotwells, in 1798. The progress of the institution was closely watched by many scientific men throughout the kingdom, but it was found, after some months' careful and anxious solicitude on the part of the hopeful founder, that the results were far from equalling his expectations. It was therefore abandoned, after existing but a few years. The undertaking, however, was by no means useless; for the experiments arising out of its daily practice, led to the splendid discoveries of Humphry Davy. Although not more than twenty years old, the chemical laboratory of the hospital had been placed under his superintendence: and his first work—issued in 1799 from this institution, entitled "Experimental Essays on Heat, Light, and the Combinations of Light," in which his first discoveries are given—shows in a striking point of view, how much science is indebted to the brief existence of the Pneumatic Hospital.

In a life of Dr. Beddoes, published by his friend Dr. Stock (London, 1810, 1 vol. 4to.) those peculiarities of character which are not usually known to the world, are pleasingly portrayed. "He was (says his biographer) an extremely amiable man, who had only truth for his object, and the good of his fellow-creatures as the end of all his efforts." He was extremely enthusiastic in whatever he undertook; but the ardour of his imagination sometimes prevented him from examining carefully his data, or forming the most correct conclusions.

The zeal and astonishing industry of Dr. Beddoes are displayed in the large number of his publications.

Entertaining great expectations of the perfect liberty of human nature, his ardent disposition led him, in the early part of his career, to adopt, in some degree, the views of the partizans of the French Revolution. He was therefore not unfrequently engaged in debating on the political topics of the day, in which he was always the advocate of the more advanced sentiments of the period. Among his chief works are an "Essay on Consumption," (1779) a "Translation on Natural History," (1784) "Chemical Experiments and Opinions," (1790) "History of Isaac Jenkins," a work intended to check drunkenness, (1793) "Essays Moral and Medical, 3 vols. (1802) "Essay on Fear," (1807) with several others of less note, which he continued to publish in rapid succession till 1808, when, in consequence of a disease of the heart, he died, in December of that year, at the age of forty-eight. He was interred in the church of St. Paul, Portland square.

Dr. Beddoes married, in 1794, Miss Anna Maria Edgeworth, a sister of the celebrated authoress; she died in 1824, leaving four children—Thomas Lovell, the poet, who died in 1849; Charles Henry; Anna Frances Emily; and Mary Eliza, who died in 1833.

THE BRISTOL RIOTS OF 1831.

THIRD ARTICLE.

IMMEDIATELY on the arrival of the troops in Queen-square, at six o'clock on Saturday evening, the magistrates gave orders to Colonel Brereton to "clear the streets," but did not suggest the *means* to be employed. The Col. on the other hand, would not take on himself the responsibility of firing among the people or cutting them down, consequently their number increased rather than diminished

About nine o'clock an order was given to "draw swords;" here was at least the appearance of preparing for action, and this position was maintained, without the least effect, till twelve, when another order was issued for employing coercive means. An attack on the mob was the result, the military using the backs and sides of their swords.

It was about this time that a party of rioters left the square, and proceeded to attack the Council-house; they began by smashing the windows, and endeavouring to force the doors. Information of this new outrage speedily reached the Mansion-house, whence an emphatic order to *charge* was instantly given to the troops. The scene now became one of the greatest confusion; the people fled in all directions, and in many cases were pursued to the very outskirts of the city. Those of them who had assembled at the Council-house were also soon scattered; large numbers, however, taking refuge in the numerous courts and alleys of Broad-street and Wine-street, from whence they assailed the troops with stones, one of which, thrown from the top of the Pithay, struck a soldier, and so irritated him, that he turned round and shot a man, named Stephen Bush, dead upon the spot. The feeling of friendliness with which the mob had hitherto regarded the soldiers, was now changed into hatred. It was rumoured that the soldier had dismounted and followed Bush into a corner. This however was not true, but its effect on the people was to intensify their feeling of antipathy. During the charge many were severely wounded by sabre cuts, and one man subsequently died at the Infirmary. The mob was however most completely dispersed, and by one o'clock the streets were perfectly quiet.

Sunday morning dawned on the city with its usual tranquillity, with the exception that some scores of persons sauntered about the square. No danger being apprehended, at eight o'clock orders were given to the troops to withdraw for refreshment, as they had now been on duty more than twenty-four hours. Strange to say, they had scarcely disappeared, when a party of desperadoes entered the Mansion-house, and speedily ransacked every room from the cellar to the attic. The wearing apparel, table linen, china, and other articles of value, were utterly destroyed. The handsome furniture was hurled from the windows to the ground and broken to atoms. The Mayor and Major Mackworth, who had remained on the premises up to this time, were now obliged to fly from their vengeance by a perilous scramble over the tops of the adjoining houses.

But another, and a most deplorable cause of danger, now began to show itself: during the sacking of the Mansion-house the wine cellars received especial attention from the visitors. Here were three thousand six hundred bottles of wine in the hands of an excited mob. The scenes which followed beggar description: hundreds, of both sexes and of all ages, greedily swallowed the intoxicating draught, and rushed hither and thither, regardless of danger, and bent upon mischief, until, overcome by their excesses, they lay by scores upon the ground in a state of drunken insensibility—some to awake no more. Not only in the square were these disgusting scenes to be witnessed, but in many of the central streets it was the same.

There was a strong public feeling among the mass of well conducted persons respecting the Corporation: who considered that they gave too much attention to class interests, irrespective of the public good, and this feeling was now not a little increased by the consideration that the scenes of debauchery around them had their origin in an improper use of the public money, one proof of which was the enormous stores of wine which that body had laid up for the obvious purpose of self-indulgence. In the course of the morning the troops were recalled, and some skirmishes took place on St. Augustine's-back, in which one man was killed and seven or eight were wounded.

The Mayor, driven from the Mansion-house, repaired to the Guildhall, where he issued a number of notices to the citizens, requesting their immediate attendance. They assembled in a considerable body, but returned home, after a long and fruitless discussion, the magistrates having resolved on nothing definite for restoring order.

THE BRIDEWELL.

About one o'clock a small party of desperate fellows, having been assured by a gentleman at the Mansion-house, that Sir Charles Wetherell had left the city, the ringleader coolly replied, "Then we have nothing more to do here; we'll now go to the Bridewell and get out the prisoners taken up last night, and then we can go to the jail and get out the prisoners he came to try." They departed to the Bridewell; the doors were at once assailed with sledge hammers, and an entrance gained. Mr. Evans, the keeper, had just sat down to a dinner, which he was not to be permitted to finish, for the prisoners were at once set free, and the prison set on fire. The outer gates, too, ponderous as they were, were removed from their hinges and thrown over the bridge into the river. All this was accomplished in less than an hour. The party then proceeded, with an air of triumphant confidence, through the very heart of the city, towards the

NEW GAOL ON THE CUT.

Here they were joined by an additional body of rioters; besides these, there were many thousands of lookers on, posted along the New Cut, on the opposite side of the river, and indeed on every spot commanding a view of the gaol. This edifice (built about 30 years previously) was surrounded by a high wall, and the entrance protected by a double set of gates, the inner ones being of massive iron. This apparently inaccessible building was, however, entered. By means of sledge hammers, iron bars, and other instruments, the doors were forced from their hinges, locks and bolts were destroyed, the cells were thrown open, and all the prisoners, amounting to 175 in number, were set at liberty. At the same moment the Governor's house was entered, the furniture broken to pieces, and the fragments thrown into the float. The prison van and the gallows apparatus were also dragged out and launched into the water, the whole of which was speedily carried away by the ebbing tide, the multitude testifying their approval of the deed by rending the air with their shouts of exultation. During these proceedings, some of the magistrates made a fruitless attempt to interfere, but they were driven off by a shower of stones. A detachment of Dragoons also came up, and were hailed by the crowd with great enthusiasm, which the soldiers acknowledged by lifting their caps, and then departed. Mr. Herapath went into the gaol, and addressed the rioters, for half an hour, and was listened to by some with respectful attention, but with the majority it was of no avail; they intimated that they would next destroy the dock gates, and then the banks. This last piece of information induced Mr. Herapath to proceed to the Council-house, where he found some of the aldermen, before whom he laid some plans calculated to allay the further progress of the destroyers. They were, however, rejected.

Our Local Legends.

LLEWELLYN'S BRIDE,

A LEGEND OF BRISTOL CASTLE.

WHO would suppose when passing down Queen street, "in the castle," that any spot in that sombre looking thoroughfare had given birth, as is supposed by many, to the device which has been represented on the Arms of Bristol for six hundred years?—or, who could believe that such a dull, matter-of-fact locality, could father a romance that even the young ladies of the nineteenth century can read with interest? But so it is. And we have the story and the locality, according to many, engraven on our City Seals to this day.

King Edward I, had occupied the throne of England just three years, when it happened that while he was keeping court in his castle, at Bristol, a vessel with a remarkable cargo arrived in the Port. Bristol Castle was at this time (1275) one of the largest and strongest fortresses in the kingdom. It was approached from the river by a creek and water-gate; and the entrance to this same creek is still to be seen in Queen Street. It was the "secret port" of the castle. The open port of the town was near the church of St. Mary-le-Port, where Bridge-street now stands, formerly called Worship-street, and where the king had his custom-house and store-houses for wool and wine. Having stated these preliminary matters, we now proceed with our story. A large ship, coming from France, and bound for the coast of Wales, but which by stress of weather had been driven about in the Bristol Channel for some time, and become disabled, was observed labouring at the mouth of the Avon. She was discovered by four pilots, or pill-men, who dwelt in that neighbourhood, and in their small ships kept a constant watch upon the channel. The strange ship excited the greatest astonishment, not only on account of its size, which they were little used to see, but also because of its furniture and rigging. They suspected, too, that there must be persons of great consequence on board. The pilots, in those days not being over scrupulous in points of honour and honesty where there was any chance of gaining a prize or booty, induced the discomfited voyagers, who were without food, by their plausible statements of certain safety, to sail up the river to the port, where they might refit; which, in their distressed situation, they were only too glad to do. They were piloted in safety, not only into the town port, but past it, and into the secret port of the castle. They perceived when too late, that they had fallen into the hands of their bitterest enemy.

It was now discovered that these illustrious but unfortunate strangers were no other than Elenor, the betrothed lady of Llewellin, Prince of North Wales, the beautiful daughter of Simon de Montfort, the great Earl of Leicester, and her suite. The treachery of the pilots had thrown into the hands of the King a prize that must inevitably involve the two nations in a sanguinary war. Here were, beside those already mentioned, Almeric de Montfort, brother of the illustrious bride, her ladies-in-waiting, knights, and priests, together with the crew of the ship. The vessel also contained the marriage portion of the bride, valuable jewels, rich robes, the manufacture of foreign countries, and other splendid furniture; all this was surrendered into the hands of King Edward himself.

The lady—it must be told to the honour of the king—was treated with all the courtesy and consideration which her situation permitted, as a fast prisoner in the Castle of Bristol. The same attention was also shown to her ladies-in-waiting: but the men—nobles, knights, priests, and mariners, were dealt with according to the savage barbarity peculiar to those early times.

The reason for this behaviour on the part of the king, is to be attributed to the political events of the times. It will be remembered, that not long before this event, Llewellin and the Earl of Launceston had leagued together, and with 30,000 men had overrun the lands of several of the barons who were of the king's party. Edward, however, forced them back into the mountains of Wales; but their patriotic spirit was not to be quelled in this way; nor could it be accomplished, till a more potent power than the sword was brought to bear upon them, namely, the power of love.

It was not long after that Elenor became a prisoner in Bristol Castle, in the way we have described; and now Llewellin was summoned by Edward, to do homage and pay a ransom for his bride of £50,000; at first Llewellin refused to do either, demanding his consort to be given up to him. At this Edward at once proceeded to levy war on the unfortunate prince: he drove him and his army into the fastnesses of the Welsh mountains, when after enduring horrors equal to those consequent on a siege, they were obliged to yield to the power of the English king. Llewellin did homage before Edward, paid the ransom money, and pledged himself to a further sum of one thousand pounds a year during his lifetime, gave up a portion of his territory, and endured many personal insults; and all this he willingly endured for the love he bore to the lady of his choice, Elenor de Montfort.

This story is told, with some slight variations, in Peter Langtoft's Chronicles of England. The following extract, from a metrical version of it by Robert de Brunne, is interesting, as showing the style in which these old chronicles were put into verse :—

" The next yere followand of Edward coronment ;
Leulyn of Walsland, into France he sent
De Montfort's doughter to wedde, her frendes all
    consent,
Almerike her ledde to schyp, now ere hir want
Now they sail and row to Wales to Lewellynes,
A burgeys of Bristowe chargyd was with wines
He overtoke there schyp, withens hir were ?
Hii said with King Philipp to Wales wold hir fare.
What did this burgeys ? disturbed his wending
The may and hir hernesse did lede unto the King ;
The mayden Edwarde toke als he was full courteis,
In safety did hir loke and thankid the burgeys,
When Lewlyne hard say to warre sone be began,
For tene he wend to die, that taken was his leman."

This incident has, as we have above said, been supposed by many to have been the origin of the device on the city seal. Others however,—and among them, J. G. Nichols, Esq. F.S.A., a gentleman of great authority on such subjects,—have altogether denied the probability of such a foundation; alleging that the intricate and awkward entrance to the city, was sufficient reason for the device being employed.

HENRY THE 7TH AND HIS FINE.

It is related that when King Henry the 7th came to Bristol in the year 1490, he made every one of the commons of Bristol, who was worth £200, pay twenty shillings because the wives of the townsmen went about dressed too sumptuously.

Bristol Worthies.

ALDWORTH Robert, merchant and alderman; a benefactor to the city; he resided in the house, now St. Peter's Hospital; died in 1634; buried in St. Peter's Church.

BUSH Paul B.A. first Bishop of Bristol; distinguished for his theological attainments and medical knowledge; died 1558, buried in the Cathedral.

BAILEY E. H. R.A. an eminent sculptor, born in Bristol 1788.

BARRETT Wm. F.S.A. surgeon, author of the History and Antiquities of Bristol; died 1789; buried in St. Mary Redcliff Church.

BIRD Edward, R.A. an eminent Bristol artist; painter to the Princess Charlotte; born at Wolverhampton; died November 2, 1819; aged 47; buried in the Cloisters, Cathedral.

BEDDOES Thomas, M.D. a distinguished physician, chemist, and philanthropist; and author of many valuable works; born in Shropshire; died December 1808, aged 48; buried in St. Paul's Church, Portland square.

BEDDOES Thomas Lovell, poet and dramatist, born at 3 Rodney place, Clifton, (son of the foregoing,) died 1849.

BIDDULPH Rev. Thomas Tregenna, M. A. author and divine; died in 1838 aged 76; he was incumbent of St. James's 38 years.

BLANKET Edward, Edmund, and Thomas; weavers in Tucker street in 1340; inventors of the Blanket. Edward was M. P. for Bristol in 1362.

BOWDICH Thomas Edward, African traveller and naturalist; born in the house now occupied by Messrs. Godwin, No. 1, Clare street; died January 10, 1824.

BUNDY James, philanthropist, he visited the dungeons of Newgate in Castle Mill street, more than 30 years; he is also said to have visited forty thousand sick persons; died March 20, 1818, aged 68.

BURKE Edmund, orator, philosopher, and statesman; M. P. for Bristol from 1774 to 1780; died July 9, 1797, aged 67.

BUTLER Joseph, D.C.L. bishop of Bristol afterwards of Durham; author of the "Analogy of Religion"; a man of great powers of mind; was brought up a dissenter; died in 1752, aged 60; buried in Bristol Cathedral.

BURTON Simon De, the reputed founder of the original Church of St. Mary Redcliff in 1293; he was five times mayor, of Bristol.

BOTONOR William, called Wycestre, [see Wycestre.]

BRENNUS and BELLINUS, two British Kings; the reputed founders of Bristol B.C. 388.

BUDGETT Samuel, a "successful merchant" and philanthropist; died May 1851, aged 59.

Folk Lore.

THE BURKING PANIC.

SOME five and twenty or thirty years ago, the most exciting consternation prevailed amongst the juvenile population, in consequence of a belief that many persons were nightly burked and carried off to the doctors for dissection. The Burking process was described to be as follows: A man came in front of his victim and suddenly covered his mouth with a pitch-plaster, preventing the possibility of giving any alarm by cries for help. Young persons generally could not be prevailed on to go, after dark, into the neighbourhood of the Old Market, Tyndall's Park, or the unlighted suburbs, which were said to be the localities in which these villanies were practised. We do not think, however, that there is one authentic case in relation to Bristol. The method certainly was adopted in Edinburgh, and the murderer, one Burke, from whom it takes its name, soon forfeited his life at the gallows.

ROASTING THE BIBLE.

THERE is a tradition still current in Bristol in reference to a society of Infidels who met weekly in the parish of St. Philip, some forty years since, who among other acts of impiety resolved to roast the Bible, which was done with some ceremony. To mark their contempt for that book they basted it with beer! It is said that every member is now dead, and that in most, if not in all cases, their hour of dissolution was attended by circumstances of peculiar horror.

SPRING-HEEL JACK.

SPRING-HEEL Jack is, we believe, one of the most, if not the most, celebrated of Bristol's imaginary beings—one of the "Wandering Jew" species—we can hardly call him a ghost. He has been known for several generations past in Bristol and "all the country round," as a very tall, lanky, elastic, grave, and mischievous personage. It is said that he could leap twenty yards at a bound. Some have insinuated that he has kidnapped children. Others have declared that he never did, but left kidnapping to the gipsies. We have heard him called Spring-hill Jack because, said our authority, he used to frequent the steps at Spring-hill, but we are inclined to think this a modern innovation, intended to reduce the importance of this personage by limiting his influence to one locality. However, it must be admitted that he has been very little seen of late years: some say he has been "laid in the Red Sea;" but our opinion is that he has perished from the blasting progress of public enlightenment.

FOREST OF DEAN.

OUR Gloucestershire neighbours who dwell in the vicinity of the forest, have a favourite proverb which runs thus—

"Happy is the eye
Betwixt the Severn and the Wye."

The point of which appears to be, an allusion to the productivness of the soil, and to the mineral riches of the district. Foresters may often be heard to boast—that their county could do without all the rest of England, "for we can raise every thing we want."

THE BISHOP OF BATH AND WELLS.

THE very handsome gas-pillar, with three lights, erected at Totterdown at the angle formed by the junction of the Bath and Wells Roads, is usually designated "the Bishop of Bath and Wells," on account of its supposed resemblance to a Bishop, with his arms outstretched and his fingers pointing in the direction of the two cities,—who, it is said, on being asked which of the two he would accept as his diocess, answered in the cockney accent "Both," His patron being uncertain, whether he meant Bath or Both, very handsomely presented him with Bath and Wells. And so the two cities have been united in one diocess ever since.

Notes and Queries on Local Matters.

ANCIENT CHARTERS.

The corporation of Axbridge have preserved their ancient Charters with remarkable care. Among them is an ancient M. S. evidently written about the fifteenth century purporting to have been compiled from the ancient Charter granted by Edward the Confessor, whose life was preserved while hunting. There is some blunder here, for Dunstan was dead before this king was born. The story relates to Edward the Martyr, who was murdered as he sat on his horse, at the age of seventeen, by order of his stepmother, Elfrida, while partaking of her hospitality at the door of Corfe Castle.

CURIOUS CUSTOM at CONGRESBURY.

IN the parish of Congresbury, and the adjoining one of Puxton, were two large tracks of common land, called East and West Dolemoors (the Saxon word *dol* means a portion,) which were occupied from time immemorial, till within a few years, in the following remarkable manner :—The land was divided into single acres, each bearing a peculiar mark, cut in the turf, such as a horn, an ox, a horse, a cross, an oven, &c. On the Saturday before Old Midsummer day, the several proprietors of contiguous estates, or their tenants, assembled on these commons, with a number of apples, marked with similar figures on the rind. These were distributed by a boy, one to each of the commoners, from a bag. At the close of the distribution, each person departed to the allotment marked with the figure corresponding to the one upon his apple, and took possession of that piece of land for the ensuing year. Four acres were reserved to pay the expenses of a feast, at the house of the overseer of the Dolemoors where the evening was spent in festivities, unhappily not of an elevating character.

NOTES ON STREETS AND LANES.

THE north side of Bridge-street includes the sites of Worship-street, Maryport-street, and the Shambles, or Bocher-row. Stand at the foot of the steps leading from Maryport-churchyard to Bridge-street, and you may realise the spot as it appeared in the olden time. At this spot on which you stand was the Mary-port; to your left was Worship-street, with the Custom-house and the King's warehouses, for wool and wine, at an early period, in fact as early as Edward the first. To your right, reaching from the site of Mr. Prickett's house, were the Shambles, or Bocher's-row, reaching to St. Nicholas-church. The whole of these places fronted the river, and were considerably below the present level, a south side of Bridge-street not at that time having been erected.

MARY-PORT CHURCH-YARD.

An old Mooring Post stood in the ground near the north door of the Church, down to 1750, when it was removed. Some large gothic arched cellars which ran back to the church-yard, were also found, in pulling down the Shambles, where the merchants of Worship Street, deposited their Merchandise on being landed at the Mary-port, which was near the present steps leading from Bridge Street into the Church-yard.

TOBIAS MATHEW.

THIS divine, a native of Bristol, received his education at Oxford: he afterwards rose to be Dean, and subsequently Bishop of Durham; and lastly was raised to the Archbishoprick of York, in the magnificent Cathedral of which city he was interred. He was remarkable for the very large amount of sermons which he preached. While Dean of Durham he preached 721; while Bishop 550; and after he was made Archbishop, 721—altogether the very large number of 1992 ! None of these were ever printed: his only publication was a Latin sermon against Campian, a convert to Catholicism. He died in 1628, aged 82 years.

THE CITY LIBRARY.

This institution, which before long we most earnestly hope to see thrown open as a free library for the citizens of Bristol, was erected in 1614. The founders of it were Dr. Mathew, the prolific preacher, (the subject of the foregoing article), and Robert Redwood.—Richard Williams, Vicar of St. Leonard's, was the first keeper thereof.

THE FIRST MAP OF BRISTOL.

The earliest engraved Map of Bristol that can be traced, was published in the year 1575, and is called "A Map of the City of Bristowe, by George Hoefnagle."

CURIOSITIES OF BRISTOL
AND ITS NEIGHBOURHOOD.

No. 5.   JANUARY, 1854.   PRICE ONE PENNY.

THE BRISTOL FRATRICIDE.

AN ACCOUNT OF THE MURDER OF SIR JOHN DINELY GOODERE.

IN the year 1741, a murder of the most daring and atrocious description, was perpetrated near our city. The murderer was an officer of distinction in the Royal Navy, and his victim was a baronet—his only brother. Before detailing the dreadful story, it will be advisable to give a brief account of the family of Goodere.

Edward Goodere, Esq., of Burhope, in the county of Hereford, M. P. for Evesham, and afterwards for Herefordshire, was created a baronet in 1707. He married Eleanor, only daughter and heiress of Sir Edward Dinely, Knight, and had by her two sons and one daughter. The elder of these sons, who succeeded his father as second baronet, was the unfortunate Sir J. Dinely Goodere, the murderd ; the murderer was the younger son, Capt. Samuel Goodere. (The daughter Eleanor, their sister, was married to Samuel Foote, Esq., of Truro, M.P. for Tiverton, by whom she had, with other issue, John Foote, who assumed the name of Dinely, as heir to his uncle. Another son of Mr. and Mrs. Foote, was Samuel Foote, the celebrated wit and dramatist.) Sir John dying without issue, his brother succeeded him, as third baronet; he was at the time of his committing the murder captain of the Ruby man-of-war, and had distinguished himself greatly at the capture of St. Sebastian, Ferral, and St. Antonio. He was married to Miss Elizabeth Watts, of Monmouthshire, and had issue, whom we shall have occasion to mention presently.

It seems that these two brothers had lived on terms little short of hatred for many years ; and as the Captain came frequently to Bristol, (his vessel lying at Kingroad) he thought it would be an excellent opportunity to gratify his evil passion on his relative, and thereby to inherit his title. He therefore engaged one of his seamen, Matthew Mahony, an Irishman, to seize him and bear him to his barge, which was lying at the Hotwells, and thence to take him to his ship, which, as we have above stated, was lying at the mouth of the river. We shall give what occurred at this time from the confession which Mahony made, and principally in his own words:—

" About the 29th of November, I, Matthew Mahony was pressed from a protection on board H.M.S. Ruby, then lying in Kingroad. I could not get my wages from the captain of my ship, 'The Charles,' James Mervin, master. On which account I was obliged to importune with the captain of the man-of-war to permit me to go ashore, in order to enter a prosecution for my wages, and so to return on board the Ruby. Some time after I came ashore, the captain of the man-of-war, Mr. Goodere, sent for me to his lodgings in Prince Street, and acquainted me that he wanted to have a man taken, that had done him and his family a great deal of injury ; at which I asked him on what account he was to be taken, or who he was? Mr. Goodere answered that he was a great rogue, and was at law with him, and ruining his family ; that as he was bred a seaman he would press him, and have him on board. Sometime after he sent for me again, and took me along with him to Mr. Smith's, in the College Green, (the house two doors from St. Augustine's church,) and repeated the above all the way we went. I staid without the door till the Captain returned. This was about fourteen days before the unhappy affair. This day he told me he was going to Bath the Monday following, and I should go along with him, for that his brother was there lying sick, which was the man he wanted to take; for he was bred a seaman, and was the greatest villain upon earth ; that he went by the name of Sir John Dinely, but that he was not worth twenty shillings. * * * Saturday night the Captain came up to town, and sent for me, desiring me and the other men to be in readiness the next morning and come to him ; accordingly we did, when he bade us keep a good look out, for Sir John was to dine at Mr. Berrow's in Peter Street. In the afternoon, I and the privateer's men walked up that way, and in some time we saw Sir John come out of Mr. Berrow's ; on which, we followed at a distance till he came to College Green, when he went into Mr. Smith's, and we went into the White Hart. Shortly after, the barge crew came in likewise, and in a little time we saw the Captain go into Mr. Smith's after his brother," [it seems, from what transpired at the trial, that the two brothers had gone to Mr. Smith's to effect a reconciliation ; they there shook hands, previously to which, Captain Goodere, on entering, went forwards, and hypocritically kissed his brother !] "and there we watched, by his orders, till his brother came out, and as he came down towards the College Green Coffee-house, we rushed out, and at the bottom of the hill one of the privateer's men stept up to him, and told him that a gentleman wanted to speak to him a little ways off. With that he walked freely a little, and seeing nobody he thought could have any business with him, did not care to go further, on which we forced him along ; and the Captain coming up, ordered us to make speed, and hasten him along. As we were hurrying him along, he cried out—' Murder! Murder! Is there no one that will relieve me ?' We then made a great noise to drown his cries : and if any one inquired who he was, his brother would answer ' He's a crazy man, never mind him.' With that four men took him up, and forced him into the barge, which lay near the Hotwell. After which Sir John sat down, and seeing somebody ashore he thought took notice of him, cried out, 'Pray tell Mr. Jarrit Smith in College Green, Sir John Dinely, is gone on board the man of-war !' On which the barge put off. Then he spoke to his brother, 'Sam' says he, ' what is it you mean by this? Where are you carrying me to ? You'll dearly suffer for this. 'Tis a little hard you should use me so, when I might have thrown you into gaol, and let you rot there. I have been too good natured to you.'

"Then Sir John said to the Barge's crew, 'Gentlemen, this is my youngest brother, a cowardly rascal as any in England,' telling him, ' If I was to meet you on the high seas with a Spanish man-of-war of twenty guns, and you with your British fifty-gun ship, I would desire no better sport, I would make you [befoul] yourself.' The Captain replied, ' Curst cows have short horns, we must give liberty to a mad-man to say what he will' ; and to the best of my knowledge the Captain bid him leave off his noise, and make his peace with God that night. To which he replied, ' Sam, you are going to murder me, and your best way is to knock me on the head, and heave me over-board, or get your fellows to do it, and afterwards go ashore and hang yourself ; you had as good do it first as last.'

"The Captain in the discourse told him, ' He had got him out of the lion's mouth,' (meaning the lawyer's hands) 'and would take care he should not spend his estate.'" He then bid the men row away, and they continued their bickering all the way to the mouth of the river, near which the Ruby was lying.

(*To be concluded in our next.*)

THE BRISTOL RIOTS OF 1831.
(FOURTH ARTICLE.)

THE next objects of destruction were the toll-houses, which were, comparatively speaking, trifles, and were very soon reduced to ruins. Having demolished these, the

GLOUCESTER COUNTY PRISON,

at Lawford's Gate, was the next scene of destruction The same method of attack was here employed as on the other large buildings ; sledge-hammers and crow-bars soon did their work, and the prisoners therein confined were set at liberty. They then set fire to the building, which was ere long reduced to a mass of ruins. At the same time one party of the rioters were engaged in destroying this prison, another party proceeded to the Bridewell, to accomplish its demolition, as upon the first attack, only one wing had been partially destroyed. Not more than a score of men remained here, and yet, strange to say, no effort was made on the part of the authorities to preserve the remaining portion of the building from destruction.

But so it was, and the advantageous moment was lost when the outrage might have been stopped. A greater number of rioters returning, flushed with success, they very soon completed the destruction of the premises. At this time, about half-past eight, the reflection in the sky from the three burning prisons was awfully grand. A small body of men at the same time proceeded to the Lock-up House for debtors, in Tailors' Court, Broad Street, kept by Ponting, the sheriff's officer, and demanded the liberation of the prisoners confined there. This was speedily conceded to them and they departed without doing injury to the premises. The terror entertained by many gentlemen was so very great that they removed the plates from their doors, and took other precautions to prevent their houses, and also their persons, from being recognised.

So confident had the rioters become, on account of the great success their measures had met with, that small parties now departed one one way and one another, in quest of objects to destroy. Accordingly, one small detachment began the work of destruction at

THE BISHOP'S PALACE,

where, having gained admittance, they broke into the wine cellars, and then proceeded to destroy the valuable furniture; the work of demolition was a little stayed by the spirited intervention of a few gentlemen, who managed to separate the rioters, and for a time preserved the premises; three of the ringleaders they succeeded in taking, and confined them in one of the cellars. At the same time the crowd outside was rapidly increasing, and assumed an aspect which threatened a recommencement of the assault. A detachment of the 3rd Dragoons, who were quartered at the Horse-bazaar, were then called out for the protection of the Palace, and the other soldiers who still continued in the square were also withdrawn for the same purpose; this last was an unfortunate step, as the events will show.

THE MANSION HOUSE.

At the time of the departure of the military from Queen Square the number of the crowd was not very considerable; it was, however, gradually increasing, and it was easy to perceive that many among them were most eager to finish the destruction of the Mansion House, so soon as a favourable moment offered. The scenes in the wine cellars were still to be seen, and the liquors were handed about in plenty among the crowd. The soldiers being gone, and the number of the rioters having considerably increased, the work of burning the Mansion House was commenced. A fire was lighted in one of the kitchens which was underneath the banqueting-room, and it was soon in a mass of flame. Without waiting until the fire would spread of its own accord from floor to floor, they proceeded to the several apartments and fired them one after another, so that in a very few minutes the whole building was in flames.

As a proof of the great speed with which this was done, it may be mentioned, that the troops had scarcely arrived at the Bishop's Palace when they were told, by the glare of the flames, what had taken place. Finding the Palace in a state of tolerable security, they returned to the Mansion House in hopes of being in time to stay any further mischief. They had barely returned to the Square, when looking back in the direction whence they had come, they saw by the reflection in that direction, that that building had also fallen a prey to their vengeance; thus in hopes of saving both buildings, the destruction of each was facilitated. In a short time after their arrival in the Square, the roof, together with the front of the Mansion House came down upon the pavement with a tremendous crash.

Bristol Worthies.

BROUGHTON Thomas, D.D., one of the original writers in the "Encyclopædia Britannica," and compiler of a "Dictionary of all Religions." Vicar of Bedminster, &c. Died, 1774. Buried in Redcliff Church.

BURKHEAD Henry, dramatist, a merchant in Bristol in the reign of Charles I.

CABOT John, an eminent navigator, lived in Baldwin Street; he probably was with his son, —

CABOT Sebastian, the great navigator, when, in 1497, he discovered the continent of America; he subsequently made other highly important discoveries.

CANYNGES William, Six times mayor of Bristol; M.P. for Bristol, 1364, 1384; died 1398.

CANYNGES William, jun., grandson of the above, born in Bristol. Five times mayor; and M.P. 1451, 1455. Died 1474. Buried in Redcliff church.

CARR John, founder of the City School. Buried in the Mayor's Chapel.

CARPENTER Lant, LL.D., born at Kidderminster, 1780; from 1817 until 1840 one of the ministers of Lewin's Mead Chapel; resided at 2 Great George Street; author of many highly-esteemed theological and other works. Died, 1840.

CHILD William, Mus. Doc., born in Bristol about 1607.

COLSTON Edward, born in Temple Street, 1636; died at Mortlake, in Surrey, 1721, buried in All Saints' church, Bristol.

CHATTERTON Thomas, born in the parish of Redcliff, 1752, died in London, 1770.

COLERIDGE, S. T., poet, lived for a short time with Southey and Lovell, at 48 College Street; in 1795 he was living on Redcliff Hill; he afterwards resided at Clevedon, in a "pretty cot" still standing. In 1795 he lectured at the Plume of Feathers, Wine Street, and the Assembly Coffee House; in 1814 at the White Lion. Died at Highgate, 1834.

COLERIDGE Hartley, son of the above, born at Clevedon, (in the cottage above referred to) 1796. Died near Grasmere, 1849.

CANNE Rev. —, an eminent puritan divine, founder of the first Baptist church in Bristol, 1640.

COTTLE Joseph, author, bookseller, and publisher of the early works of Coleridge, Southey, Wordsworth, etc. His shop (since burnt down) was 49 High street. Resided, No. 1, Carlton place, Bedminster; and afterwards at Firfield house, Knowle; where he died June 7th, 1853.

DALLAWAY Rev. James, M.A., F.S.A., etc., antiquary and man of letters.; vicar of Leatherhead, in Surrey; born in the parish of St. Philip, Bristol; died at Leatherhead, 1834.

JOHN WHITSON.

JOHN WHITSON the benevolent founder of the Red Maids School and other charities in this city and elsewhere, was born in the year 1557, of obscure parents, at Clearwell, in the parish of Newland, Gloucestershire. Nothing certain can be stated as to where he received his education, but probably it was at some school in the neighbourhood. Tradition says that he experienced severe treatment from the person in the country with whom he was placed. He left and came to Bristol. Here he entered the service of a wine-cooper in Nicholas street, in a low capacity. However, at length, through his diligence and honesty, he became the chief clerk in his master's counting-house, and had the entire management of the business for the widow, who approving of his conduct in due time rewarded him with her hand. He now commenced business for himself, and became an eminent merchant, and was chosen a member of the corporation. The place of his residence was in Nicholas street. He was married three times, and his family consisted of two daughters, who preceded him to the grave, and one step daughter, a child by his first wife's former husband. In 1603 he filled the office of mayor, and again in 1615; and was also member in four parliaments, for this city. At length becoming fatigued with public life, he retired from the noise and bustle of the world to prepare himself for a future state. About this time he composed the "Pious Meditations, or the Aged Christian's Final Farewell to the World and its Vanities," which has passed through several editions. As he had acquired his fortune by industry, he much lamented the profligacy of his nephews, who as he had no children living became his heirs.

He one day overheard a conversation in an adjoining room between them. the subject of which was, what they intended to do with their *uncle's* large fortune; they agreed that when they came into the possession of it they would act very differently from him, and *spend it like gentlemen*. The old gentleman hearing this, burst in upon them, and with an honest indignation told them, that, since he heard from their own mouths their resolution with respect to his fortune, and as he had oftentimes remonstrated with them on the impropriety of their conduct he had come to the conclusion of leaving his fortune for charitable uses, which he accordingly did, and on the 22nd of March, 1627, he made his will, and left the bulk of his property, after the death of his wife, for benevolent purposes, the principal of which is the school in Denmark street, originally for 40 girls to be clothed, educated, and maintained; but through the increase in the value of the estates, the number is now augmented to 120. He died in the beginning of the year 1629, in the 72nd year of his age. His death was supposed to have been hastened by an injury he received by a fall from his horse.. He was buried on the 9th of March, 1629, in the church of St. Nicholas, where also his three wives and daughters lie interred. The anniversary of this excellent man is celebrated on the 19th day of November in each year, when the mayor and some members of the corporation and charity trustees, with the children of the Red Maids and City Schools attend the church of St. Nicholas, on which occasion an appropriate sermon is preached.   J. D. L.

[The reason of Whiston's memory being celebrated on November 19th, is, that that day was his birth day, and also because on the same day of that month he had escaped from the hands of an assassin. In addition to the excellent foundation – the Red Maids' School, he provided for £52 to be distributed yearly among fifty-two poor honest married women in child-birth, twenty of whom are appropriated by the mayoress for the time being, and thirty-two by the charity trustees. To the schoolmaster of Queen Elizabeth's Free Grammar School, (held in the Lady Chapel of Redcliff Church) £9. 2. 6 yearly. £500 to be lent to free burgesses, in sums of £50 and £20, for seven years. £20 for exhibitions at the university of Oxford or Cambridge to be given to two scholars educated at the Grammar School. These are the chief of the charities of Whitson, several more of lesser amount need not be mentioned here.]—ED.

DUNDRY CHURCH.

EVERY Bristolian knows Dundry Tower by sight at a distance, very few know it by closer inspection, nor are they aware that lofty-looking object towards which the eye is anxiously directed in stormy and uncertain weather, is one of the richest and most beautiful examples of the Perpendicular style of English architecture. It was erected in 1482. The church (dedicated to St. Michael) to which this noble tower is appended, is in many parts of more ancient date than the tower. It is however a mean and uninteresting-looking structure. There is an Early English lancet window, and some specimens of the succeeding styles of architecture; but they are not of sufficient beauty and importance to warrant much attention being bestowed on them. The tower indeed is quite enough to absorb the attention of the antiquary for some length of time. The view from the summit is of immense extent, including Bristol with its numerous towers and spires; Clifton, with its crescents seemingly hanging on the sides of the hills, and, below, the picturesque St. Vincent's Rocks and Leigh Woods. Farther to the west is seen Ashton Court, and beyond, "Severn's ample waters" appear in the distance, bounded by the Welsh coast. To the south the eye ranges over Alfred's Tower and the richly-wooded domain of Stourhead,—where, among other objects, are preserved our ancient Civic High Cross, and also the cross which formerly surmounted Peter's Pump.—Also, Knole hill, near Warminster, with the plantations of Longleat, belonging to the Marquis of Bath, and those of the Duke of Somerset at Maiden Bradley; beyond which are the high downs of Wilts and Dorset. Besides these and other more distant objects there are to be seen numerous villages and churches, scattered among the luxuriant vallies below.

The principal monuments in the church are those to the memory of William Symes, gent, and several of his successors; and of members of the families of Tibbot, Haythorne, and Baker, of Alwick Court. The visitor will also notice a memorial of one William Jones, of Bishport, of whom it is said, "that his natural abilities unaided by academical education, enabled him to refute, with uncommon sagacity, the slavish systems of usurped authority over the rights, the consciences, or the reason of mankind"!

The height of Dundry hill above the level of the sea, is 729 feet. The height of the church tower is 100 feet.

"Dundry" is derived from two Erse words signifying a hill of oaks; from which it is to be presumed that there was an abundance of those trees in former times.

In the churchyard is a cross, with a tall shaft having an ornamented head, in good preservation, fixed on a high pedestal, on five rows of steps. There is also to be seen on the south side a very massive stone of about five feet cubic measure, called the Money Stone, and on it the poor of the parish have been paid from time immemorial.

The manor of Dundry was formerly united to that of Chew Magna, and held by the Bishop of Bath and Wells, for a period of five hundred years, until the time of Edward VI, when it was alienated from the Church, and given to the Duke of Somerset, on whose attainder it reverted to the Crown; it has since passed through several hands. The living is a curacy annexed to Chew Magna.

ABBOT'S LEIGH
AND ITS ASSOCIATIONS.

THE pretty village of Abbot's Leigh, independently of its natural attractions, is very interesting, as being one of the many places in which Charles the Second found refuge, after the disastrous defeat at Worcester. The possessor of Leigh Court, (where Charles was concealed) at that time was Mr., afterwards Sir George Norton, Knight.

Abbot's Leigh was a manor belonging to the Abbots of St. Augustine's Abbey, Bristol, and after the dissolution of religious houses, was given to Paul Bush, the first Bishop of Bristol, who in 1548 surrendered it to the king; he was allowed to keep it until his death however, and then the reversion of the estate was granted to Sir George Norton, Knt. who after

the death of Bush, in 1551, took possession of it. He was the great-great-great-grandfather of the loyal Sir George Norton, to whom we now turn. As he left no representatives in his own name, the estate went to his nephew John Trenchard*, the son of his sister Ellen and William Trenchard. He also died without issue, and the property descended to his nephew Robert Hippisley, (who assumed the name of Trenchard in addition to that of Hippisley) the son of his sister Frances and John Hippisley. He was succeeded by his son John William Hippisley Trenchard, of Cutteridge and Abbot's Leigh, and died in 1801, having devised his estates to two of his nephews, sons of his sister Ellen, by different husbands. It was then that the estate was purchased by the late P. J. Miles, Esq. who, we are sorry to state, entirely pulled down the old Leigh Court, the place of Charles's refuge, and erected at some distance from it the present Leigh Court.

The church of Abbot's Leigh, dedicated to the Holy Trinity, is an exceedingly pretty and tastefully built church. With the exception of the tower, chancel, and some monuments, it was in 1848 destroyed by fire. It has been re-built as much like the old structure as possible, and is one of the best restorations we know. The principal monuments are those to the memory of Sir George Norton, and some of his descendants; and one recently erected to the memory of the late P. J. Miles, Esq., who represented the city of Bristol in Parliament, from 1835 to 1837.

We need scarcely say that the most interesting of the monuments is that to the memory of Sir George Norton; it is a handsome marble monument, and stands against the north wall of the chancel. It bears the following inscription : –

" Near this place lies the body of Sr. George Norton of Abbot's Leigh in ye County of Somerset, son of Sr. George Norton of the same place. So eminently loyal in hazarding both his life and fortune by concealing in his house the sacred person of our late most

---

* This gentleman, born in 1662, a barrister by profession, and a commissioner for the forfeited estates in Ireland, gained great reputation by his political writings. In 1698, he published in connection with Mr. Moyles, a well-known pamphlet, entitled " An Argument, shewing that a standing army is inconsistent with a free government, and absolutely destructive to the constitution of the English Monarchy." It attracted much attention, and contributed greatly by the conviction it carried, to the procuring a majority in the parliament which obliged the king to send home his Dutch guards, and to reduce his army. He was also the author of other pamphlets; but his most distinguished works were " Cato's Letters," and " The Independent Whig." The object at which the former pointed was the administration in state; the latter was directed against the heirarchy of the church. They both appeared in 1720. Mr. Trenchard was M.P. for Taunton, and was a leading member of the House of Commons.

Gratious Sovereign King Charles yᵉ Second till he could provide means for his escape into France.

And by his pious and virtuous Lady Dame Frances Norton this monument is erected to his memory.

He dyed the xxvith day of April, MDCCXV. in the LXVIIth year of his age.

He married Frances the daughter of Ralph Freke of Harrington in the County of Wilts Esq. By whom he had issue three children George, Grace, and Elizabeth, the first and last dyed young. Grace married as the monument in this church expresseth."

The daughter, Grace, alluded to at the end of the above inscription, was married to Sir Richard Gethin, Bart., of Gethinsgrott, in she died in 1697, aged 21 years, and was buried in Westminster Abbey.

In our next number we hope to give an account of Charles the Second's escape to Leigh, and what occurred whilst he was a fugitive there.

REMARKS ON DRUIDICAL REMAINS IN THE NEIGHBOURHOOD OF BRISTOL, THEIR ORIGIN, AND THE PURPOSE OF THEIR ERECTION.

BY GEORGE PRYCE.

'Tis said that here
The Druid wander'd. Haply have these hills
With shouts ferocious, and the mingled shriek,
Resounded, when to Jupiter unblamed
The human hecatomb. The frantic seer
Here built his sacred circle."

N. T. CARRINGTON.

In an endeavour to ascertain any particulars relating to the origin of such stone erections as those to which the following remarks have reference – the people by whom they were raised, and the rites and ceremonies observed in connection with them – our inquiries will be found to conduct us back over a space of not less than thirty centuries in the world's history. Such an investigation, however apocryphal it may appear at the outset, is not to be regarded as one of mere curiosity and idle speculation, but rather of critical importance to those who, in the pursuit of historical and philosophical truth, delight to contemplate the rude dwellers in our sea-girt isle, from the period when the simple natives in their primitive occupations peopled its hills, vallies, and plains with an artless, unsophisticated race – through every phase of human progress, tracing step by step as he proceeds in the path of improvement, the advancement of knowledge ; the onward march of civilization ; and the gradual expansion of the human intellect.

The stone erections of antiquity, especially those which relate to ancient Britain may be regarded as belonging to the highest class of archæology, that is, they were raised in the remotest times, and in the very infancy of society, by a people whose political existence has long ceased to influence mankind. Their prototype is to be found in the oldest volume in the world ; and from that alone we derive our earliest information upon this antiquated subject ; for with the solitary exception of that of the Hebrews as recorded by Moses, an impenetrable obscurity overshadows the early history of every other nation – each having its beginning in the myths of heathen creation.

The priesthood of every ancient nation exercised a potent influence over the minds of the deluded votaries of superstition. It was so in the East from whence the Druidical institution in Britain derived its origin ; for Asia was undoubtedly the great parent of this kind of idolatry. A marked affinity, too, between the Druids of these islands and the sacred orders amongst the Asiatics of remote ages, is also observable ; and this resemblance has long been a settled point in the world of antiquaries. The Druids were in fact the Wise Men of the West from a very early period ; their relation to the Brahmins of India has been very learnedly argued by Maurice ; and, with the exception of the name, Keysler has shewn them to be of one and the same character with the oriental Dervish. Their close analogy to the Magi of Persia seems to be pointed out by Pliny, who denominates the Druids the *Magi* of the Gauls and Britons ;- in short our British Druid swayed as powerful an authority over the minds of our ancestors, as did either of the above-named sacred orders over the p ople of eastern countries ; and in this respect they will bear comparison with the Magicians of Egypt, the Chaldeans or Soothsayers of Assyria ; the Curetes of Greece ; and others of the greatest antiquity, whose common origin may be traced to the earliest recorded patriarchal priests after the Flood.

As this resemblance between so many of the priesthoods of Eastern origin with that of Britain is of too general a character to be accounted for by, or resolved into, any accidental concurrence of circumstances in those early ages, many learned men have endeavoured to ascertain how the opinions, usages, and ceremonials, religious as well as political, of countries in the remote East, could have found their way into the far West. The subject is, however, one of conjecture only ; and as no record of the event exists, we can but adopt the opinion of the most judicious writers in ascribing the peopling of this island to the Gauls ; for from that country its first inhabitants seem to have passed over to these shores ; and it has been thought by some authors that the nomadic tribes soon after the Flood, in consequence of the rapid increase of the human family, and the continued necessity of obtaining fresh pastures for their greatly extended possessions in flocks and herds, spread themselves not only over oriental countries, but had even reached and settled in Britain in the comparatively short space of two centuries after the deluge. Be this as it may, there is sufficient circumstantial evidence (as we shall see) to show that these islands must have been known to the Asiatics in the time of Moses—that is to say 1500 years before the Christian era; at which time, no doubt, the method of constructing what are still known as Druidical Temples was first introduced into Britain; and with it also the peculiar rites of worship appertaining to them.

The Druids, or priests, who ministered in holy things among the ancient inhabitants of this island, appear to have composed a sort of religious hierarchy, under the superintendence of one high-priest, or Arch-Druid. With them were associated two other classes of officials; the first were the Bards—the historical and metrical genealogists and philosophers of the nation; the second were the Faids, Vates, or religious poets and presumptive prophets of the association, whose duties were confined to the composition of hymns which they chanted on solemn occasions in honour of the gods. They also delivered such revelations to the people as impressed them with reverence and awe for their pretended converse with the Deity. To the priestly power every other institution was tributary; for the Druid not only officiated at the altar, but he also filled the highest civil dignity in the state, next to the sovereign. He was supreme both in religion and law; the dispenser of all spiritual government, and the arbiter in all judicial proceedings. In this two-fold capacity he had been preceded by the practice of the patriarchal ages; from whence, as we shall see, much of precept as well as of practice was derived by the druids of subsequent times.

It is not improbable that the secret belief of the Druids was in One God, the great Creator of the universe; and they sought to over-awe their superstitious followers by a belief that divine communications were made to man through themselves, his ministers. As in all systems of idolatry objects of sense were chosen to represent the invisible Supreme, so the Druids set up a variety of divinities as worthy the worship of their infatuated disciples; among which none were more distinguished for the adoration paid to them than the Sun and Moon and the Host of Heaven. Streams, too, were deified by them, and became fitting objects of devotional rites; princes, renowned for their warlike achievements were, after death, raised to the rank of gods; and so numerous were the delusions practised by this potent priesthood for the amusement of their followers, that the homage paid to the Great First Cause of all, ultimately degenerated into the worship of the mere creations of fancy, with all the accumulated horrors, sanguinary rites, and abominable ceremonies of human immolation.

The great luminary of the heavens, had from the very first ages of the world been the visible representation of the Creator; and to him adoration had been paid as to the noblest symbol in the universe of that unknown God, to whom the Athenians raised an altar in the days of the apostle Paul. The patriarch Job, who is believed to have been contemporary with Jacob, thus refers to this practice, "If I beheld the sun when it shined, or the moon walking in brightness; and my heart hath been secretly enticed, or my mouth hath kissed my hand: this also were an iniquity to be punished by the judge: for I should have denied the God that is above." (Job, xxxi, 26, 27, 28.) Thus was the sun the chief object of adoration among the ancients, but particularly so with the Sabeans, the people to whom the verses just quoted have special reference. He was regarded as a special emanation from God, because through his agency the whole of nature became tributary to the wants of man. His name throughout all Asia was Bel or Baal, and by that designation he was known in Britain. To his honour circular stone temples were erected, of which Stanton Drew is an example; and as the worship of the sun was the basis of Asiatic superstition, so it became at a subsequent, though still very early period, the religion of the British Isles.

(To be continued.)

RELIGIOUS HOUSES OF BRISTOL

FOUNDED

BEFORE THE REFORMATION.

I. MONASTIC INSTITUTIONS.

PRIORY OF ST. JAMES, founded 1130, by Robert Earl of Gloucester, and occupied by monks of the order of St. Benedict. The church of the Priory is now the parish church of St. James.

ABBEY OF ST. AUGUSTINE, founded about 1142 by Robert Fitzharding. Inhabited by monks of the order of St. Augustine, as modified by St. Victor. The church of the monastery was converted into a cathedral by Henry VIII.

PRIORY OF ST. PHILIP.—The original church of St. Philip is supposed on very plausible grounds, to have been the church of a Priory of Benedictines, subject to the abbey of Tewkesbury. It was made a parish church before 1200.

NUNNERY OF ST. MARY MAGDALEN,— founded in 1170 by Eva, widow of Robert Fitzharding. It stood at the bottom of St. Michael's Hill.

MONASTERY OF DOMINICAN OR BLACK FRIARS, founded 1229; stood between Rosemary street, and the Weir. Some considerable and very interesting remains are left.

MONASTERY OF CARMELITE OR WHITE FRIARS, founded 1267. Stood on St. Augustine's back.

Monastery of Franciscan or Grey Friars. Founded 1274. Stood in Lewin's Mead, on the spot where Lewin's Mead Chapel now stands.

Monastery of Augustine or Austin Friars, founded 1310, stood near Temple Gate.

CURIOUS EPITAPH IN BERKELEY CHURCHYARD.

The following inscription, which is supposed to have been composed by Dean Swift, may be seen on a stone in the churchyard of Berkeley.

" Here lies the Earl of Suffolk's fool,
  Some call him Dicky Pearce ;
His folly served to make folks laugh,
  When wit and mirth were scarce.

Alas ! poor Dicky 's dead and gone,
  What signifies to cry ;
Dickys enough are still behind
  To laugh at bye and bye."

On the other side of the stone :—

" My Lord that's gone, made himself much sport of him.

" Buried XVIII June, MDCCXXVIII :
" Aged, LXIII."

Notes and Queries on Local Matters.

BLACK JOHN.

On the 17th February 1758, John Watkins, usually called Black John, died in Bristol. He had entirely supported himself by begging and usually lodged in a Glass-house, notwithstanding that he had a room in Temple-street, where, after his death, was found upwards of two hundred-weight of half-pence and silver, together with a good deal of gold, which he had amassed by public begging. He came of a respectable family in Gloucestershire, and was said to have been heir to a considerable estate, but, the possession of it having been denied him, he vowed he would never shave till he enjoyed it, and he kept to this determination to the day of his death.

THE DROWN-BOY OF BRISTOL.

In St. James's week, 1638, a ship was launched here, and having suddenly capsized when entering the water, eleven boys who were at the time upon the ship were accidentally drowned. In consequence of this melancholy event the vessel was ever afterwards called "the Drown-Boy" of Bristol.

"PLEASE REMEMBER THE GROTTO."

It is by no means an infrequent thing now that oysters are in season, to be accosted in courts and corners of out streets by ragged boys and girls, crying, " Please remember the grotto." Very few of those who are in this manner asked for halfpence for "the grotto," (a grotto formed of oyster shells,) know the origin of this custom. It is supposed to have originated for the following

reason : – Old St. James's day (August 5) is the proper day on which oysters come in ; they are by act of parliament forbidden to be sold before that day. It is said that they were originally erected by poor persons, on the anniversary of St. James, who was of old a very popular saint in England, as an invitation to the pious who were unable to visit Compostella (where was the celebrated shrine of the saint) to show their reverence for him by giving alms to their needy brethren.

THE DUCKING STOOL.

We have received a note from a gentleman who signs himself JUVENIS, calling our attention to the fact that the Ducking, or Cucking stool, (of which we gave an account in our last number,) was used for the correction of cheating bakers, brewers, and other petty offenders, as well as for too talkative women ; also that there is a description of the punishment in Domesday book, from which it is to be inferred that it was not confined to any one locality in England.

We append the following—

In the Museum at Scarbrough, one of these engines is preserved. It is said that there are persons still living in the town who remember its services being employed when it stood upon the old pier. It is a substantial armchair of oak, when in use an iron bar extended from elbow to elbow, just as the wooden one is placed in a child's chair to prevent the occupant from falling forward.—*Notes and Queries.*

NOTES ON STREETS, &c.

Christmas Street was in former times called Knifesmith Street.

Merchant Street anciently styled Marshall Street.

Peter Street formerly called Castle Street, as leading to the Castle. At that time the present Castle Street was occupied by the fortifications of the Castle.

THE ART OF PRINTING.

The art of printing was carried on in Bristol Castle in 1546.

TO CORRESPONDENTS.

" A BIT OF AN ANTIQUARIAN." Received.

** Communications to the Editor to be forwarded to the Office of the BRISTOL DIRECTORY, 9, Narrow Wine-street.

Advertisements to be sent to M. BINGHAM, 9, Broad-street, by the 10th of the month.

A quarto edition of this work, printed on superior paper, price Twopence each. Either edition can be sent, post free, on receipt of an extra stamp.

Published in London, by Houlston & Stoneman, 65, Paternoster Row, and may be obtained through any bookseller in the United Kingdom.

Printed and Published at the Office of the Bristol DIRECTORY, 9, Narrow Wine Street, Bristol, by M. Mathews.—January 1, 1854.

CURIOSITIES OF BRISTOL
AND ITS NEIGHBOURHOOD.

No. 6.   FEBRUARY, 1854.   PRICE ONE PENNY.

CHARLES THE SECOND
AT
ABBOT'S LEIGH.

ON the evening of the day on which the battle of Worcester was fought (September 3rd, 1651.), Charles the Second accompanied by some of his nobility quitted the field and rode to a place called White Ladies in Staffordshire, a distance of twenty-six miles; it was at this place that he found refuge with the Loyal Penderells, five, or as some accounts say, six brothers who lived near together in this district. John Penderell was the owner of White Ladies. It being unsafe for the king to remain here long, he disguised himself as a country fellow and set off in company with a brother of his host, trusty Dick Penderell, hoping to be able to get to London. On many accounts he soon changed his intention as to where he would go and decided on endeavouring to reach the Severn and cross to Wales. This idea he also abandoned upon consideration, thinking it wiser to return to the neighbourhood of White Ladies, to the house of William Penderell who lived at Boscobel where he hoped to hear news from some of his friends. He accordingly did so; there it was that, together with Col. Careless, (properly Carlos) who had joined him, he lay concealed for some hours in the oak tree of which we are annually reminded every 29th of May, the king's birthday and the day on which he entered London at his restoration. He was shortly afterwards joined by Lord Wilmot, with whom he again set out on his travels. Having gone a few miles, Charles sent his companions on to Bentley, the residence of Col. Lane, "to see," said Charles, "what means could be found for my escaping towards London; who told my lord, after some consultation thereon, that he had a sister that had a very fair pretence of going hard by Bristol, to a cousin of hers, that was married to one Mr. Norton, who lived two or three miles towards Bristol on the Somersetshire side, and she might carry me thither as her man; and from Bristol I might find shipping to get out of England."

Approving of this plan the king changed his dress to that of a servant, and the following day set off with Mrs. Lane towards Bristol going past Stratford-on-Avon, and staying a night at Long Marson. From this place they proceeded to Cirencester, where they slept, and the next day reached Bristol. It is related by Lord Clarendon, (whose account is however rather vague and irreconcileable with the state of the Castle of Bristol at that time) that Bristol was "a place and people the king had been so well acquainted with, that he could not but send his eyes abroad, to view the great alterations which had been made there after his departure from thence; and when he rode near the place where the great Fort stood, he could not forbear pulling his horse out of the way, and rode round about it."— By Great Fort the historian means the Castle which Charles would pass in coming into Bristol by the old Gloucester road through Winterbourne, Stapleton, and past Lawford's gate. The present road through Stoke's croft was not then made.

They then proceeded to Leigh. We shall give an account of the king's visit in his own words, dictated to Pepys some years afterwards:—

"Thence to Mr. Norton's house beyond Bristol, where, as soon as ever I came, Mrs. Lane called the butler of the house, a very honest fellow, whose name was Pope, and had served Tom Jermyn, a groom of my bedchamber, when I was a boy at Richmond; she bade him to take care of William Jackson, for that was my name, as having been lately sick of an ague, whereof she said I was still weak, and not quite recovered. And the truth is, my late fatigues, and want of meat, had indeed made me look a little pale; besides this, Pope had been a trooper in the king, my father's army; but I was not to be known in that house for any thing but Mrs. Lane's servant. Memorandum—That one Mr. Lassells a cousin of Mrs. Lane's went all the way with us from Colonel Lane's on horseback, single. I riding before Mrs. Lane.

"Pope the butler took great care of me that night, I not eating as I should have done with the servants, upon account of my not being well.

"The next morning I arose pretty early, having a very good stomach and went to the buttery-hatch to get my breakfast; where I found Pope and two or three other men in the room, and we all fell to eating bread and butter, to which he gave us very good ale and sack. And as I was sitting there, there was one that looked like a country fellow sat just by me, who talking, gave so particular an account of the battle of Worcester to the rest of the company, that I concluded he must be one of Cromwell's soldiers. But I asking him how he came to give so good an account of that battle, he told me he was in the king's regiment; by which I thought he meant one Col. King's regiment. But questioning him further, I perceived that he had been in my regiment of guards, in Major Broughton's company, that was my major in battle. I asked him what kind of man I was? To which he answered by describing exactly both my clothes and my horse; and then looking upon me, he told me that the king was at least three fingers taller than I. Upon which I made what haste I could out of the buttery, for fear he should indeed know me, as being more afraid when I knew he was one of our own soldiers, than when I took him for one of the enemy's.

"So Pope and I went into the hall, and just as we came into it, Mrs. Norton was coming by through it; upon which, I plucking off my hat and standing with my hat in my hand as she passed by, that Pope looked very earnestly in my face. But I took no notice of it, but put on my hat again and went away, walking out of the house into the field.

"I had not been out half an hour, but coming back I went up to the chamber where I lay; and just as I came thither, Mr. Lassells came to me, and in a little trouble said, what shall we do! I am afraid Pope knows you; for he says very positively to me that it is you, but I have denied it. Upon which I presently, without more ado, asked him whether he was a very honest man or no? Whereto he answering me that he knew him to be so honest a fellow that he durst trust him with his life, as having been always on our side, I thought it better to trust him, than go away leaving that suspicion upon him; and thereupon sent for Pope and told him, that I was very glad

to meet him there and would trust him with my life as an old acquaintance. Upon which, being a discreet fellow, he asked me what I intended to do; for, says he, I am extremely happy I knew you, for otherwise you might run great danger in this house. For though my master and mistress are good people, yet there are at this time one or two in it that are very great rogues; and I think I can be useful to you in any thing you will command me. Upon which I told him my design of getting a ship if possible at Bristol, and to that end bade him go that very day immediately to Bristol, to see if there were any ships going either to Spain or France, that I might get a passage away in.

"I told him also that my Lord Wilmot was coming to meet me here; for he and I had agreed at Col. Lane's, and were to meet this very day at Norton's. Upon which, Pope told me that it was most fortunate that he knew me, and had heard this from me; for that if my Lord Wilmot should have come hither, he would have been most certainly known to several people in the house? and therefore he would go. And accordingly went out and met my Lord Wilmot a mile or two off the house, not far off, where he lodged him till it was night and then brought him thither by a back door into my chamber; I still passing for a servant-man, and Lassells and I lay in one chamber, he knowing all the way who I was.

"So after Pope had been at Bristol to inquire for a ship, but could hear of none ready to depart beyond sea sooner than within a month, which was too long for me to stay thereabout, I betook myself to the advising afresh with my Lord Wilmot and Pope what was to be done. And the latter telling me that there lived somewhere in that country, upon the edge of Somersetshire, at Brent, within two miles of Sherborne, Frank Windham, the knight marshal's brother, who being my old acquaintance and a very honest man, I resolved to go to his house.

"But the night before we were to go away, we had a misfortune that might have done us much prejudice; for Mrs. Norton who was big with child, fell into labour and miscarried of a dead child, and was very ill, so that we could not tell how in the world to find an excuse for Mrs. Lane to leave her cousin in that condition, and indeed it was not safe to stay longer there where there was so great resort of disaffected idle people.

"At length consulting with Mr. Lassells, I thought the best way to counterfeit a letter from her father's house, old Mr. Lane's, to tell her that her father was extremely ill, and commanded her to come away immediately for fear that she otherwise should not find him alive; which letter Pope delivered so well while they were at supper, and Mrs. Lane played her part so dexterously, that all believed old Mr. Lane to be indeed in great danger, and gave his daughter the excuse to go away with me the very next morning early.

"Accordingly the next morning we went directly to Trent."

After many hazardous adventures, Charles reached Brighthelmstone, (Brighton) from which place he sailed for France on the 15th October, 1651.

The Leigh Court in which Charles found refuge stood nearer to the road leading to Pill, than the present house. The park belonging to it lay on the opposite side of the road. The king's room continued to be an object of great interest, and was constantly visited by strangers until its destruction, about forty years since. There is a tradition that while at Leigh, the king was employed by the cook to turn the spit; whilst so engaged some soldiers entered, and upon the king's looking up at them the cook gave him a blow in the face, telling him to mind his own business and not trouble himself about the soldiers. The spit or jack which the king is said to have watched on this occasion and also a block of wood on which he stood while performing his culinary duties, were in existence at the time when Mr. Miles purchased the estate. We trust they are still preserved and have not been ruthlessly destroyed, as was the house, consecrated by such interesting historical associations.

We stated in our last number that the old house had been completely destroyed; this statement requires a little modification. A portion of the wall of the laundry and a small window still remain and are incorporated in one of the buildings of the Leigh Court farm which now occupies the site of the old Leigh Court. Access to it is gained through the gate of the lodge nearest to Pill.

Mr. Miles bought the property in 1811, at which time he was living at Naish House, the seat of J. A. Gordon, Esq.

THE BRISTOL RIOTS OF 1831.

(FIFTH ARTICLE.)

THE soldiers finding that their presence was without avail, in consequence of no one giving them orders to use forcible means, almost immediately returned to their quarters, with the exception of a few of them who were ordered to keep guard at the Guildhall and Council House. About this time a troop of Yeomanry, under the command of Captain Codrington, came into the city, but on finding no one to issue orders as to their line of duty they returned homewards.

The destruction of the Bishop's Palace was ere long completed, and nothing remained save a mass of ruins. Some of the more desperate of the rioters then proposed to destroy the Cathedral, and proceeded to take means for this object. A few spirited persons were happily able to prevent the demolition of it. Some gentlemen, among whom may be mentioned Messrs. B. Ralph, J. Livett, and J. Norton, happening to go near the Bishop's Palace late at night, one of them passing through the crowd saw forty or fifty lads collected around a fire, and a man with a pole and flag, surrounded by a number of people, making ready for the destruction of the Cathedral and Chapter House. The floor of the latter being covered with leaves torn from the books, it was considered best to begin with firing that noble apartment. Mr. Norton endeavoured to gain a hearing, but was not listened to. He then went into the cloisters, where he met the other above-named gentlemen, and with them resolved to do whatever they could to preserve the venerable building. Mr. Ralph then went to the mob and seizing the ringleader told him that the Cathedral was public property and that no reformer or friend of the king would destroy it. After a pause, the man shouted, "Reform and *not* burn the College," and then went to his comrades who agreeing with him repeated the cry. Some boys who had anticipated some delight from the destruction of the building, continued near the spot, occasionally throwing pieces of lighted paper into the chapter house. The active precautions of the individuals already alluded to, prevented any damage being done, notwithstanding that they were in the course of their useful efforts assailed with sticks, stones, and brickbats. At length becoming wearied, the crowd gradually diminished and by half-past one in the morning, the place was clear.

The Bishop, Dr. Gray, who had been in town during the week, left in the afternoon of this day, having preached in the Cathedral in the morning, without heeding the stormy and fearful scenes that were raging in the neighbourhood.

Up to this time the rioters in Queen Square and other places had vented their fury only upon public buildings, and after the destruction of the Mansion-house it was hoped that their anger would have been satisfied. This was not to be, and great was the horror and consternation manifested when it was understood that they contemplated destroying the dwelling houses in the Square. The attack commenced, as in former instances, by smashing the windows and forcing the doors, they then plundered or destroyed the valuable articles within, and at last set fire to the premises. At one house, that of the Messrs. Leman, a great number of very valuable books were thrown among the crowd, who soon tore them to pieces and scattered the leaves in all directions. They thus proceeded from house to house, firing one after another, and about twelve o'clock, the whole mass of buildings from the Mansion House to the middle avenue, including

THE CUSTOM HOUSE,

and all the warehouses and other premises in Little King Street, were one mass of blaze. At the Custom House the domestic department was on the second floor: here were collected the inmates, who were assembled round a table eating and drinking. While thus engaged they were thunderstruck—seeing the flames burst in upon them; they immediately rose and rushed about in a state of the utmost terror, hoping to be able to save themselves. Some precipitated themselves from the windows and were much injured by the fall, but others who were up higher, got upon the house-top and throwing themselves down, met with instant death; while others after hesitating what course to persue, threw themselves into the flames and were burned to death. A few escaped by getting upon the balcony and sliding down from thence by means of the pillars.

The demolition of the Custom House was soon finished and the crowd pursued their way, destroying as they went.

(*To be continued.*)

THE BRISTOL FRATRICIDE.

AN ACCOUNT OF THE MURDER OF SIR J. DINELY GOODERE

(*Continued from page 30.*)

WHEN they came alongside the vessel Sir John went on board as well as he could, and the Captain took him down into the Purser's cabin, and staid a little with him, and then left him for a considerable time. He then called Mahony to him and told him he must murder his brother, for that he was mad and should not live till four o'clock in the morning. "I made him reply," says Mahony, "that as he was the next person of kin, he was the properest person to execute the office; and that as for my part, for this ship full of money, I would not do such a thing. He seemed to be much concerned, and told me, if I would not, another would, and made me sit down and drink. He then ordered me to call Elisha Cole; and he being too drunk to undertake such an affair, bid me call one Charles White, a very stout lusty fellow, and the Captain gave him a dram, and bade him sit down, and soon gave other drams and asked him if he could fight, and told him, 'Here is a madman, he must be murdered, and thou shalt have a handsome reward?'"

These two having agreed with the Captain to murder his brother for a large reward, the Captain went down to the purser's cabin, where his brother was confined, and took away the sword from the sentry, and ordered him to go upon deck. Having done that he returned to his accomplices, and proposed the method in which they were to do it, and produced a piece of half inch rope about nine foot long, and Charles White having made a noose in the rope, the Captain said to them, "you must strangle him with this rope,"—he gave them at the same time a handkerchief with which to stop his mouth in case of his crying out; and said, "I will stand sentry

over the door whilst you do it;" he accordingly sent Mahony and White into the cabin, whilst he remained without. The unfortunate Sir John was lying on a bed in his clothes. The Captain, as soon as the men had gone in, fastened the door, and stood without the whole time they were about their dreadful act. White first strangled Sir John with his hands, and then put the rope round his neck, and hauled it tight, the unfortunate man struggling, and endeavouring, without being able, to cry out. Mahony stated, that whilst he was strangling him, he (Mahony) took care to keep him from falling off the bed, and when the end of the rope was loose, he drew it, and held it tight; thus proving that each of these wretches were actually engaged in killing the wretched victim. Finding that he was perfectly dead, they rifled his pockets of his watch and money, and knocked at the door to be let out. The Captain called out, "Have you done?" They replied "Yes." He then opened the door and called again, "Is he dead?" and being answered in the affirmative, and having a light in his hand, swore by G—d he would be sure he was dead; he therefore went into the cabin, and having assured himself that his victim was indeed no more, he came out, locked the door, and put the key in his pocket. They all of them then went into the Captain's cabin, and Mahony delivered to him his brother's watch, and the Captain taking it from him, gave him his own in stead. He then gave them both some money, and White gave his companion in guilt eight guineas, as being part of the money he took out of Sir John's pocket. The Captain then ordered them to be put on shore in his own boat, so that there might be no risk of their confessing to their messmates what had taken place. It appeared on the trial that the Captain intended to keep the body for two or three days, by which time he hoped to be out to sea, and then to throw it overboard. His doing this was, however, prevented; for many persons who had seen the unfortunate baronet carried along by the sailors, spread the tale about in all directions, and as he did not return again to his home, application was made for a warrant, which after some delay was granted. Accordingly the water bailiff, with his silver oar, was sent to Kingroad, where he arrested Captain Goodere, and brought him with him to Bristol. The actual murderers were afterwards taken; Mahony was tried at the same time as the Captain, and White the following day.

The trial took place on the 26th March, 1741, at the Sessions-court of Bristol, before the Mayor, Henry Combe, Esq., and the Recorder, Michael Foster, Serjeant-at-Law. On this day Goodere and Mahony were tried and convicted, the ensuing day White was similarly condemned, and the day following they were all three brought up, and received sentence of death. They all before death confessed the fact. On Wednesday, the 12th of April, they were executed, on the top of St. Michael's hill. The spot where the gallows stood is now covered by Highbury Chapel. The body of Mahony was afterwards hung in chains at the mouth of the river, near the place where the horrid deed was committed.

At the same Court, Charles Morgan, Edward McDaniel, and William Hammon, were indicted, tried, and convicted, for a misdemeanour in forcibly assisting, and seizing Sir John, and carrying him on board the barge belonging to the Ruby man-of-war, and were fined forty shillings each, to be imprisoned for one year, and then each to give security for his good behaviour for one year more.

The two sons of Sir Samuel Goodere (the murderer) successively inherited the baronetcy; the elder son, Sir Edward Dinely Goodere, died unmarried, a lunatic, in 1761; the younger son, Sir John Dinely Goodere, succeeded his brother, and at his decease, also unmarried, in 1776, the baronetcy of Goodere, of such fearful fame, became extinct. Samuel Foote, the dramatist, (Sir John Goodere's nephew) was greatly affected by the frightful tragedy of the death of his relation; in conversation he seldom alluded to it, and never without the deepest emotion. The following singular anecdote respecting it, is related of him:—

On the night the murder was committed, Foote arrived at his father's house at Truro, and described himself as having been kept awake for some time by the sound of the most soothing delightful strains of music he had ever heard. At first he imagined that it was a serenade got up by some of the family in honour of his return home, but on looking out of his window, could see no trace of the musicians, so was compelled to come to the conclusion, that the sounds were merely of his own imagination. When, however, he learned shortly afterwards that the murder had occurred on the same night, and at the same hour when he had been greeted by the mysterious melody, he became, says one of his biographers, persuaded that it was a supernatural warning, and retained this impression to the last moment of his existence. Yet this same man who was thus susceptible of superstitious influences, and could mistake a singing in the head, occasioned, possibly, by convivial indulgence, for a hint direct from heaven, was the same who overwhelmed Dr. Johnson with ridicule for believing in the Cock Lane Ghost.

THE FIRST BANK IN BRISTOL.

On Wednesday, August 4, 1750, the first Bank in Bristol was opened. It was situated in Broad Street, and was styled the Bristol Bank. The following gentlemen composed the company; Messrs. Elton, Lloyd, Miller, Knox, and Hale. This Bank was afterwards removed to Corn Street, and is now appropriately called the Old Bank.—J. D. L.

REMARKS ON DRUIDICAL REMAINS IN THE NEIGHBOURHOOD OF BRISTOL, THEIR ORIGIN, AND THE PURPOSE OF THEIR ERECTION.

BY GEORGE PRYCE.
(Continued from Page 35.)

There are various reasons for believing that all circular Druidical erections may with confidence be assigned to the worship of the Sun or Baal, and it is not improbable they were connected also with the astronomical and mythological notions of the ancients. Like the Persians of antiquity, the Druids constructed their rude but venerable species of temple open to the heavens—rejecting, as that people also did, the idea that Deity could be confined within any space, however magnificent. The properties likewise and the functions of the object adored were also objects of considerable importance in these erections; for besides those raised for the peculiar worship of the Sun, some were constructed in honour of the Moon and the planets—all being built in a circular manner, because those orbs revolve round the Sun, which they believed to be circular also. † Such were the structures at Stanton Drew; I say *were*, because they are now so imperfect that the original position of the stones which composed them, can scarcely be ascertained with sufficient certainty to point out exactly where they were placed. Enough, however, is still left to shew that there were once three circles, the greater denominated by Dr. Stukeley, the solar temple; a second, the lunar temple; and a third, the temple of eight, referring to the number of stones which compose it; there are also sundry stones which are believed by some writers to have referred to other of the planetary orbs designated "the host of heaven." To the northeast of these circles on the side of the road leading to the village in which this monument is situated, is a very large stone called "Hautvill's Coit," from a tradition that it was thrown there by Sir John Hautvill, Knight, a man of prodigious strength, who is said to have lived in the reign of Edward I.

Of this *Stone-town of the Druids,* a brief mention has already been made at page 13 of this work; it is, however, only just enough to raise curiosity in the mind of the inquirer, and to make him wish for further information as to the object, etc., of such erections. This I propose to supply as far as my humble means will enable me to do so, in the observations which follow; and at the same time correct any errors of the writer of that article, yet without referring specially to them.

The great or solar circle consisted originally, according to Mr. Seyer, of twenty-seven

---

† There are however a few exceptions; semicircular stone erections intended to shadow out the lunar phenomena exist in the Isle of Anglesea, the ancient Mona of the Druids; one in Mainland, in the Isle of Orkney; and one, or more, in Wales.

stones; approaching which on the east are five other stones, apparently the remains of an avenue, of which some writers believe there were more than one in the entire structure; and that the stone known as "Hautvill's Coit," formed the portal to, or stood at the extremity of one of them. The lunar circle is said, by the same authority, to have contained eleven or twelve stones; and the smallest of the three circles consisted, as it now does, of eight stones only; with, attached to it on the south-eastern side, seven other stones, which are supposed by Mr. Seyer to have once formed part of an avenue to it. I shall pass unnoticed the absurd statements of other writers on the subject, and confine my remarks chiefly to the opinions of the last named author and Dr. Stukeley, as they appear to be the most plausible; although, as I believe, not quite correct in some, perhaps unimportant, particulars. The notion entertained that the circles at Stanton Drew were intended for astronomical purposes *only* is, I have reason to believe, an error also; for other objects were undoubtedly combined with that science in the minds of those who erected this, as I think, the oldest Druidical structure in Britain.

Circles of stones are generally found on spots naturally elevated above the surrounding country, and one structure frequently consists, as in the present instance, of several circles, so constructed as to suggest the idea of their having been raised with a mathematical attention to regularity of disposition in their arrangement. Very few of them, and these only in minor erections, agree as to the number of stones of which they consist. All are strikingly simple in their character, yet almost all of them differ in many component particulars. Although so little uniformity is observable in these erections, it must not be attributed to accident or chance, for there can be no doubt that the Druids laboured in forming their temples, according to some established rules of construction with which we are unacquainted, but which nevertheless evinced the erudition of the learned few in the profoundest arcana of those sciences for which they were so widely celebrated.

The circles at Stanton Drew are of the most simple design, each consisting of an assemblage of unwrought stones, rude as when first quarried. The number given for the great circle by Mr. Seyer, is, as already stated, 27; but Dr. Musgrave, who wrote more than a century before his time, makes them amount to 32. Stukeley, who saw the monument in 1723, when it had suffered great dilapidation, is altogether silent upon the subject. The first writer observes, (Memoirs of Bristol, vol. 1, p. 93.) "How many there were originally it is impossible to ascertain, for the distances of those which remain are very irregular." He subsequently adds "there were more than 27, without doubt." Between these confused statements I propose to take a

middle course, and consider 30 to be the number of stones which composed this solar circle when in its primitive state; and for this reason, because neither of the numbers before given are at all applicable to the astronomical notions of the ancients. For the same reason I regard the lunar circle as having consisted of twelve stones – that number being supposed by Mr. Seyer, who also thinks it probable some had disappeared from the circle when he saw it in 1821. Of the circle of eight this writer observes, "the workmanship of them is far superior to that of the other circles, so that their appearance cannot fail to surprise."

This superiority of workmanship merely shows that greater care was observed in procuring from the quarry, stones more shapeable than those used in the other circles; and has no reference to their having been chiselled after their removal. All the elder Druidical temples were composed of *unwrought* stones, upon which the tool of the workman was never permitted to be lifted; but in later structures, such as Stonehenge, where tenons have been formed on the tops of the uprights to receive the mortices of the transverse stones composing the trilithons and the outer circle, Druidism may be considered as on the wane, and that it had declined from pure primeval practice. This circle of eight at Stanton Drew not having been polluted by the tool of the workman, may be regarded as devoted—because "the workmanship is far superior to that of the other circles, (or rather because the stones composing it were more regular in shape)—" to some more sacred purpose, than those in its vicinity; and also that it was raised subsequent to them as a finish to the general design. The number of stones of which it is composed clearly indicate that with astronomical teaching it had nothing whatever to do; and it must therefore be designed for some other object.

The simplicity observable in the construction of the solar and lunar circles (I adopt Stukeley's designation of them) evidently shows that they were raised at a very remote period of Britain's history, and when the acquirements of her priests in astronomy were of a very limited character. Their acquaintance with this sublime science was then probably confined to a knowledge of the Druid age, which comprised a period of thirty years—the thirty days which composed their month—the twelve months which made up their year—the twelve signs of the zodiac—and the number of years in which the revolutions of Saturn were performed, of which, multiplied by five, the sexagenary cycle was fabricated. With these numbers the stones comprising the solar and lunar circles at Stanton Drew seem to agree. As the knowledge of astronomy advanced among the Druids, structures much more elaborate were erected, which display a greatly more extended acquaintance with that erudite pursuit. Among these, the most memorable in these islands, was the far-famed temple at

Abury, in Wiltshire, in which the numbers 60, 100, and 180 occur, all referring to the greater periods of astronomical theology, the century, the sexagenary cycle of India, and the last number doubled gives the total amount of the days of the ancient year, in which it was believed that the host of heaven—revolving in vast circles—completed their annual circuit, and the stars their radiant march round the larger orbs, shedding their lustre upon terrestrial things, and blessing the world with their benignant influences for the promotion of the happiness of man.

(*To be continued.*)

RELIGIOUS HOUSES OF BRISTOL, FOUNDED BEFORE THE REFORMATION.

II. THE ANCIENT CHURCHES.

THE CATHEDRAL CHURCH. Formerly the church of the Abbey of St. Augustine.

ST. JAMES, originally the Church of the Priory of St. James.

ST. PETER and ST. PAUL.

ST. PHILIP and ST. JACOB, originally the Church and Priory of St. Jacob.

ALL SAINTS, formerly ALL HALLOWS; very few remains of the old edifice are left.

ST. MARK, now the Mayor's Chapel; originally the Church of the Hospital of the Gaunts.

ST. MARY REDCLIFFE.

St. THOMAS; the tower alone is old.

TEMPLE or HOLY CROSS.

ST. STEPHEN.

ST. JOHN THE BAPTIST.

ST. NICHOLAS; the crypt is the only ancient part.

ST. MARY-LE-PORT.

ST. MICHAEL; the tower is the only old part.

ST. WERBURGH.

ST. AUGUSTINE-THE-LESS.

CHRIST-CHURCH, is built upon the site of an old church, but nothing of the former structure is left.

The following are wholly or almost entirely destroyed.

ST. EWEN, stood on the spot now occupied by the Council House, it was destroyed in 1787; the tower stood as late as 1820.

ST. LEONARD, stood at the bottom of Corn street. Destroyed 1770.

ST. GILES, stood upon St. Giles's gate, at the bottom of Small street. The parish was united to St. Leonard's in 1301. The church was destroyed in 1319.

ST. LAWRENCE,* stood on the West of St. John's. Pulled down 1580.

ST. ANDREW: a church, dedicated to St. Andrew, is supposed to have stood where the Castle Bank now stands; the crypt of it still remains.

* Until within the last few weeks an elegant stoup of the 14th cent., together with an outline of the western window were to be seen in a stable to the west of St. John's Church. Though slight, they were yet interesting remains, being all that was left of this church. We are grieved to say that the stoup, in spite of many urgent efforts made to save it, and to have it preserved, has been filled up with stone and plaster, and the wall levelled; the other remains are in a like manner plastered up. We had hoped that as a better taste for these things now prevails, we should not again have seen such barbarous acts as this; we were, as this last act of desecration shows, mistaken; and the only vestige that were left us of this edifice have been swept from our sight by the hands of a mason, while building upon the site of the church a large tailoring establishment.

Bristol Worthies.

DRAPER Sir William, distinguished as a military officer, and also as the antagonist of "Junius"; born at Bristol; built Manilla Hall, Clifton, where he resided. Died 1787, at Bath, and is buried in the Abbey-Church of that city.

DRAPER, Mrs. Elizabeth, celebrated as the "Eliza," of Sterne. Died 1778, aged 35, buried in the Cathedral.

DAVY, Sir Humphry, the great chemist, resided when a young man, with Dr. Beddoes, No. 3, Rodney Place. Died at Geneva, 1829.

ALDRIDGE John, the original founder of the Infirmary. Died 1739. Buried in Christ Church.

EDGEWORTH Maria, the very distinguished authoress. Born, 1767. Died, 1849. Resided for some time at Ashton. Two of her sisters were married to two eminent medical men of this city: the one to Dr. Beddoes, and the other to John King, Esq.

ESTLIN John Prior, LL.D., author of many valuable theological works. For forty-six years one of the ministers of Lewin's Mead Chapel. Principal of a classical school of celebrity at St. Michael's Hill. Died, 1817.

EVANS John, author of the "Chronological Outline of the History of Bristol," and other works; and editor of the "Bristol Mercury." Born, 1773. Killed by the fall of the Brunswick Theatre, 1828.

EVANS, Rev. John, author of the "History of Bristol," (the first part by John Corry) and many other valuable works. Died, 1831.

ELTON, Bart., Sir C. A., elegant scholar and poet. Born in Bristol, 1778. Died in Bath, 1853. Buried at Clevedon.

FOSTER Nathaniel, D.D., profound scholar and linguist. Born in Bristol, 1717. Died, 1757. Buried in the Cathedral.

FOSTER, Rev. John, author of the well known "Essays" which bear his name. Born in Yorkshire, 1770. Educated at the Baptist College, Stoke's Croft. Minister of the Chapel at Downend. Resided at Stapleton, where he died Oct. 15th, 1843. Buried in Broadmead burying ground.

FREELING, Bart., Sir Francis, Born in the parish of Redcliff, Aug. 25th, 1764. Employed at the Bristol Post Office. Afterwards went to London, and was in time made Secretary to the General Post Office, which post he filled for forty-eight years. Died in London, July 10th, 1835.

Notes and Queries on Local Matters.

BUEOL'S OR BEWELL'S CROSS.

ON the north side of Highbury Chapel a large stone may be seen imbedded in the wall that surrounds the chapel. This has been vulgarly called the Gallows Stone, and we have frequently heard it stated that the gallows pole was fastened into this stone. This is not correct,—the gallows stood a good deal further back, almost close to the large tree which is situated at the ·ast end of the chapel. This stone is the stand.e and only remaining part, of a cross which for a very long period stood here called Bueol's Cross. It is mentioned by Evans, (Chronological Outline of the History of Bristol) under the date 1373, as being one of the boundary marks of the city. He refers to the remains of it as "the stone in the late Gallows Field." It is also mentioned in the Mayor's Kalendar, 1525, as undergoing repair; and is called there, "the cross at the gallows."

CHARLES THE SECOND AT LEIGH.

Since the article on Charles the Second at Leigh was written, we have heard it stated that the block upon which he stood while watching the meat, was some years since cut up into pieces and sold, piece by piece, to the highest bidder. We much wish to discover the truth of this statement, and should be glad if any of our readers would furnish us with any particulars with which they may be acquainted respecting the sale of that interesting relic.

"BRISTOL SOAP."

THE manufacture of soap began in Bristol in 1523. It was carried on with such skill that the London market was supplied with it of the best quality at one penny a pound. It is scarcely necessary to say that Bristol maintains its character as to the quality of her soap.— J. D. L.

ROYAL VISITS TO BRISTOL.

We hope, in some of our ensuing numbers, to give an account of the visits of those of our Sovereigns who have honoured Bristol with their presence. William the Conqueror does not ever appear to have paid this city a visit. William Rufus, too, was never here; in the year 1093, he was in the neighbourhood, at Alveston, where he lay sick of a violent disorder during Lent. His brother and successor, Henry I., spent the Easter of 1121 at Berkeley, together with his bride. There is no record of his having been at Bristol. Stephen, his successor, was the first monarch who visited our city. Like some of his successors, it was in no very friendly way that he came here.

OLIVER CROMWELL'S POST.

WE have received a note from a correspondent asking if the wooden post 'built into the rubble stone wall of the churchyard' of St. Mary-le-Port occupies its original situation. There is, we believe, no satisfactory evidence to prove that it has been moved at all. It was to this post, the existence and history of which is unknown to so many of our fellow citizens, that Mr. Macready made allusion in his beautiful lecture on "The Influence of Poetry," delivered in 1852, for the benefit of our Athenæum. He supposed two men, the one of a poetical, the other of a merely utilitarian frame of mind, passing through the churchyard, and observed, that while one scarcely notices it, "to the other it is an index of grave historical interest, as he remembers the tradition that to it the barge of Oliver Cromwell was moored, after he and the leader, 'whose name in arms through Europe rang,' had taken the city from Prince Rupert; and perhaps, even as he was on his way to write the letter to the parliament, wherein he told them that 'faith and prayers had obtained this city for them,' and that 'God had put the sword into the parliament's hands for the terror of evil doers, and the praise of them that do well.'"

PAY DEMANDED BY MEMBERS FOR BRISTOL.

Sir Richard Hart and Sir John Knight, when members in Parliament (about the year 1693) demanded the usual allowance for citizens in Parliament, and threatened to sue the city for it.

⁎ Communications to the Editor to be forwarded to the Office of the BRISTOL DIRECTORY, 9, Narrow Wine-street.

Advertisements to be sent to M. BINGHAM, 9, Broad-street, by the 10th of the month.

A quarto edition of this work, printed on superior paper, price Twopence each. Either edition can be sent, post free, on receipt of an extra stamp.

Published in London, by Houlston & Stoneman, 65, Paternoster Row, and may be obtained through any bookseller in the United Kingdom.

Printed and Published at the Office of the Bristol DIRECTORY, 9, Narrow Wine Street, Bristol, by M. Mathews.—February 1, 1854.

CURIOSITIES OF BRISTOL
AND ITS NEIGHBOURHOOD.

No. 7.   MARCH, 1854.   PRICE ONE PENNY.

THE BRISTOL THEATRES.

IT appears, from old records and manuscripts, that for a long time previous to the erection of any theatre in this city, companies of players, at different periods, visited Bristol, where they remained for a few days at a time. From the year 1532 and during the subsequent hundred years, our civic archives contain notices of the visits of various companies of players to this city. These visits, with a few exceptions, took place annually, and frequently included two or three companies, nearly always described as pertaining to the nobility. We find but three exceptions to this recorded.

The first, in 1533, when they are styled "the players that came from London;" and in 1536 there is an entry of certain "boys that playd in the Yeld Hall." For the third we are indebted to the late Mr. Tyson, as well as for part of the above information which he communicated in 1847 to the Shakespeare Society. [See Shakespeare Society's Papers, vol. iii.] The principal object of his paper was to mention the interesting fact, that John Heminge, or Hemings, of London—still better known as the coadjutor of Henry Condell, in preparing the first edition of the Works of Shakespeare for the press—had, in the year 1544, visited this city with his players. Every particular connected with the name of Shakespeare or of any of his brother dramatists is of so much interest that we feel sure our readers will be gratified by this statement.

Considerable doubt hangs over the history of the early theatres here, both regarding the exact situation, the time of their erection, and their size and construction, all the accounts referring to them being very vague and unsatisfactory. The first building devoted to the drama of which we have any record was situated in Tucker Street; it was afterwards converted into an Independent Chapel.

We find in the year 1704 (Evans's Chronological Outline), that on "January 17th, the Queen published an order for the regulation of the Play-houses, prohibiting them to act anything contrary to religion and good manners. In Bristol, the acting of stage-plays was prohibited, and the Theatre in Tucker Street, converted into a Meeting-house."

The next theatre of which we possess any record, stood in Stoke's Croft, nearly opposite the Baptist College. A third was built in St. Augustine's Place, the site of which, like that of the Tucker Street Theatre, has since been covered by a chapel. These buildings do not appear to have been occupied by any regular or fixed companies, and were only used when some London "fellows" came down for a short time.

The first theatre in this city conducted in the manner now usual in provincial towns, was situated at Jacob's Wells, and stood on the spot now covered by Cottage Place, and the part behind the Old Malt Shovel Inn. The time of its erection was in the early part of the eighteenth century. It was a very small building, and on nights when there was something particularly attractive to be seen, by way of affording more room for the audience, the back part of the stage was fitted up as an amphi-theatre with benches raised one above another to a considerable height; the doors in the proscenium were also removed and persons were allowed to stand at the sides. No scenery could be employed when this was the case; but as the scenes were few in number and indifferently painted in those days, the loss of that addition was probably not felt to the same extent that we should feel it in the present day, when scene-painting has reached such a state of perfection.

The interior of the Jacob's Wells Theatre formed three sides of a square, consisting of one large front, and four smaller side boxes; front and side galleries, and an upper gallery to which servants were admitted freely, in order that they might be ready to wait upon their masters and mistresses at the close of the performance, and light them to their houses.

The Hotwell Road not being lighted, rendered this last precaution necessary. The custom of admitting servants was very general both in London and other places, until about the close of the last century; as the towns and streets became better watched and lighted, it was gradually discontinued.

The conduct of servants on these occasions, was by no means praiseworthy, for supposing themselves (as indeed they were) privileged persons, they amused themselves with talking, laughing, playing tricks, and not unfrequently fighting among themselves. Occasionally they broke out into a perfect riot, and the play had to be stopped until it pleased them to desist. There was no upper tier of boxes, but one of the side galleries was called the balcony, and over the stage doors in the proscenium, were two small boxes which were called Pigeon-holes.

The mode of lighting the stage at that time was by tallow candles which were stuck round four hoops, and suspended from the roof by ropes. On one occasion when an actor of the name of Winstone was playing, he flourished his sword over his head in rather an unguarded manner, and striking one of the hoops, it fell to the ground and completely encircled him. This happened while he was playing *Richard the Third*, and at the speech where he exclaims, "A horse, a horse," etc., and *Catesby* instead of helping him to a horse, was occupied for some minutes in assisting to free him from his unpleasant encumbrance of tallow.

The prices of admission were three shillings the boxes, two shillings the pit, one shilling and sixpence the balcony and pigeon-holes, and one shilling the gallery. The house when completely filled, and when the stage and the "wings" were fitted up, held about eighty pounds.

Among the most eminent of the actors who visited Bristol in the early seasons of the Jacob's Wells Theatre, were Macklin, so famous for his performance of Shylock, after he was ninety years of age, and also as the author of "The Man of the World"; and "Love à la Mode"; he died in 1797 at the great age of 107. A very favourite actress here, whom we find mentioned in the play-bills of 1743, was Mrs. Pritchard, who frequently acted with Garrick; there is a monument to her memory in Westminster Abbey.

Other very excellent and favourite actors were Woodward and Thomas King; and William Powell, of whom Garrick entertained a very high opinion, and who subsequently became the chief performer at the new theatre in King Street. He died in 1769, and was buried in the Cathedral, where there is a monument to his memory in the north aisle of the choir, with an inscription by George Colman.

In the year 1764 several leading gentlemen here conceived the idea of erecting a new and more handsome theatre, and in a more convenient situation than the one to which we have been adverting. The site chosen was King Street, where a new and elegant theatre was accordingly built, which remains to this day, having, of course, undergone many alterations and improvements; and is now under the intelligent, judicious, and spirited management of Mr. Chute.

It must be remembered that at the time this theatre was built the neighbourhood of King Street was most respectable and fashionable. The wealthiest and most influential of the inhabitants resided in Queen Square, Prince's Street, College Green, &c. Clifton then consisted of a few scattered houses. It could not at that time therefore have been constructed in a more eligible situation.

Great opposition was offered when the scheme was first broached, by the members of the Society of Friends and others, who objected to have the theatre so near their houses; many worthy merchants and shopkeepers were afraid that on play nights they should not be able to keep their clerks and men, at home, at their work and more simple amusements.

In spite of all this, however, great numbers being most anxious for a new place of amusement, the first stone was laid November 30, 1764. In about a year and a half it was completed, and was declared by Garrick to be the most complete of its dimensions in Europe.

The architect of the theatre was Mr. James Paty. It was painted by Mr. Michael Edkins, under the superintendence of John Simmons, of whom we gave a memoir in our second number. The cost of its erection was upwards of £5000.

Under the management of Messrs. Powell, Arthur, and Clarke, it was opened on the 30th May, 1766; the entertainments consisting of a concert; "The Conscious Lovers," by Sir Richard Steele; and Murphy's farce of "The Citizen." A prologue and epilogue were written for the occasion by David Garrick.

THE CONSTRUCTION OF ANCIENT HOUSES.

MR. DALLAWAY gives the following notice of the manner in which the old houses in our ancient city were usually constructed. It may be acceptable to those of our readers who do not possess his works.

An ancient tenement or house, during the early centuries, as inhabited by the Burgesses of Bristow, was thus constructed. The souterrain was a very large cellar (cellarium) with a groined and ribbed roof of stone, and when extending under the street, (as was not unfrequently the case,) divided by arches and pillars. Such instances are not so frequent as those covered by timber beams. In these were deposited the heavier goods. The ground floor was divided into narrow shops (shopæ) three or four upon the same ground plan, with stalls or bulk heads, and open to the street. They were for daily traffic with the inhabitants, and numerous frequenters of the town. In the houses of the chief merchants there was built behind these shops, a hall (aula), with a high arched roof of timber frame. It served commonly to hold linen, woollen, and spices, and the more valuable goods, and at set times for their feasts. The first floor contained the habitable house, (camera) bed-rooms, parlour (parlatorium,) kitchen (coquina,) all of which are mentioned in deeds and wills. And lastly (Solaria) garrets, which had two projecting stories under the roof.

We wish that some of these very interesting dwellings were left us entire; parts of many remain and are well worth examination; the cellars (some on the East side of High street are the most interesting) remain in a few places, and display very good stone workmanship.

SINGULAR RIOT.

IN the reign of Henry the Eighth, a very curious contention or riot, and since styled the brass-kettle riot, took place here. We find it thus related in Adams's Calendar:—

In the days of King Henry VIII., here was a fifteenth or King's silver to be levied, unto which the Clergy being tributary, two of the singing men, dwelling within that Diocese, being taxed, one at fourpence and the other at five-pence (or thereabout,) denying to pay, said they were privileged and exempted; whereupon the collectors for the King came into their houses to distrain for the same: from one they took a pottinger, and from the other a brass pan or kettle, whereupon John, the last Abbot of that place, taking part with the Clergy, arrested our townsmen that came within his diocese, and kept them in hold. The city likewise arrested and imprisoned their men, as they came within our liberties. Abbot John got a riotous company, intending by force of arms, to break open Newgate, to have out his men. The citizens beat them out again, whereupon they went to law, and

after the expense of a thousand pounds and better between them, the King would have them to be friends, and the matter was referred unto two men:. for the Clergy was appointed Cardinal Wolsey, and I think the Lord Cromwell was for the city. But, howsoever, between them it was agreed that the singing men should pay their duties, and redeem their pledges; each party to deliver up their prisoners; the Mayor and Council only by request intreated to resort to the College on Sabbath and festival days, as they were used to do, and the weather fair; and the Abbot, Bishop, Dean, and whole Clergy, in token of submission for their contempt, were commanded and enjoined for ever and whatsoever weather should fall out upon Easter-day in the afternoon, and Easter-Monday in the forenoon, they should all come and meet or stay for the Mayor and Council at the Grammar-school door, at Froom-gate, and so accompany them to the College; which order I have noted them to observe above forty years since, when I knew not the reason of it.

RELIGIOUS HOUSES OF BRISTOL FOUNDED
BEFORE THE REFORMATION.

III. THE ANCIENT CHAPELS.

HOLY VIRGIN. It stood on the centre of Bristol Bridge; completed 1360.

ST. AUSTIN near the Cathedral.

ST. BRENDAN. A Chapel and hermitage on the summit of Brandon hill.

ST. CLEMENT. Near the Merchants' Hall, 1445.

ST. GEORGE. In the former Guild-hall.

HOLY GHOST. In Redcliffe Churchyard.

ST. JOHN. Connected with Spicer's Hospital, Back Hall.

ST. JORDAN. Near the Cathedral.

ST. MARY MAGDALEN. In the Castle.

ST. MARTIN. Also in the Castle.

ST. MATHIAS. In Bridge Street.

THREE KINGS OF COLOGNE. Attached to Foster's Almshouse at the top of Christmas steps. It is still standing, and service is performed in it.

TRINITY. Attached to Barstaple's hospital, in the Old Market. The Brasses of the Founder and his wife are still in existence in the present chapel, but nothing of the old building remains. Service is conducted here also.

CHAPEL IN CANYNGE'S HOUSE. Redcliffe Street. The roof and a few other remains still exist. Mr. Jefferies, the inhabitant of the house, freely allows any one to inspect the chapel.

CHAPEL IN THE ABBOT'S HOUSE; Afterwards the Bishop's Palace. Destroyed at the Riots of 1831.

ST. VINCENT. Clifton Down.

HOLY CROSS. Durdham Down.

ST. ANN. Near Brislington.

HERMITAGE OF ST. JOHN. On the side of the river, near Redcliffe Church.

THE PRINCESS CARABOO.

The latter portion of the last century, and the early part of the present, were periods in which many impostors, some distinguished for their literary abilities, some for their great personal peculiarities and eccentricities started into being, some to make an enduring name for themselves through all posterity; while others in all probability will ere long be forgotten. Three individuals, in or near this city, were among the class of people (if such a name can be applied to them) to whom we have above referred. Of one of them we now purpose to give an account. The subject of our notice was known when she first attracted attention as the Princess Caraboo, the Wonder of the West.

One evening in the early part of the year 1817 some of the inhabitants of the village of Almondsbury near this city were greatly surprised and interested on seeing a young woman dressed in a manner totally different from any thing they were at all accustomed to, enter their pretty village. She was clad in a black stuff gown with a muslin frill at the neck, round her shoulders she wore a red and black cotton shawl; and a black shawl, instead of a cap or bonnet, covered her head; on her feet she had black worsted stockings and leather shoes. In height she was about five feet two inches, her eyes and hair were black, her forehead low, her nose short, her mouth wide, her teeth white, her lips large and full, the under lip rather projecting, her chin small and round; her hands were clean and did not appear as if used to labour. She seemed about twenty-five years of age. When she reached Almondsbury she carried on her arm a small bundle, which contained a few necessaries. She walked with difficulty, as if much fatigued, and when accosted spoke in a language no one could understand, and signified her desire to sleep the night in the village. This request the inhabitants of the spot did not much like to grant, and were in truth somewhat afraid of the stranger; they therefore went to consult Mr. Worrall, a magistrate, at Knowle, what steps should be taken. The lady of the magistrate taking pity on her forlorn condition, sent her maid with her to the public house in the village, desiring that she should have a supper and a bed prepared for her, which was accordingly provided.

The following morning Mrs. Worrall came to her and found her looking somewhat sad; she took her with her to her house at Knowle; the girl appeared not to like going with her.

It was Good Friday and upon seeing a cross bun on the table at the house where she was taken, she cut off the cross and put it in her bosom.

Finding that nothing could be made out as to who she was and whence she came, as no one could understand her speech;—pen and ink were given to her to see if she could write her name; she shook her head; but seeming at last to comprehend what was desired of her, she pointed to herself and cried "Caraboo."

On the following day she was taken into Bristol and examined before the magistrates at the Council-house. Nothing could be made of her and she was committed as a vagrant to St. Peter's Hospital, to which place crowds of people thronged to see her. Mrs. Worrall after this, again removed her to Knowle. Here a gentleman came to see her who had been for some time in the Indies, and by means of signs, gestures, and articulations, he found that she was (according to her own account) a daughter of a man of rank, of Chinese origin at Javasu; and that whilst walking in her garden attended by three women, she was gagged and bound, and carried off by a pirate-crew, and sold to the captain of a brig, from whence she was transferred to another ship, which anchored at a port for two days, where four other females were taken in, who, after a voyage of five weeks were landed at some town; sailing for eleven weeks longer, and being near land she jumped over-board, in consequence of ill usage, and swimming ashore found herself on the Gloucestershire coast whence she wandered about for six weeks, till she arrived at Almondsbury. She described herself at her father's, to have been carried on men's shoulders in a kind of palanquin, and to have been adorned with seven peacock's feathers on her head, open sandals with wooden soles on her feet. Mrs. Worrall gave her some calico, and with it she made a dress in the form of her own, which had been embroidered. The late Edward Bird, R.A. sketched her in her eastern costume, of which many engravings were made. Other particulars of her history as well as her behaviour were singular in the extreme.

At the end of two months she disappeared; and in a short time it was discovered,—to the astonishment and disappointment of numerous friends who had been greatly interested in her;—that the Princess Caraboo "of Chinese Origin," who had been borne on the shoulders of obedient slaves, and dressed in all the fullness of oriental fashion—was nothing more than the daughter of a shoemaker, at Witheridge in Devonshire! A "Narrative" of her strange imposition, very fully told, was written and published by J. M. Gutch, Esq., F.S.A. formerly of this city, now of Worcester; to it we are indebted for some of these particulars.

After the exposure of her fraud, "Caraboo" left this country and went to America.

On her return in 1824, she went to London and took lodgings in New Bond Street, where she exhibited at the charge of one shilling each person. Very few persons availed themselves of the opportunity; and she relapsed into the sphere of life to which she was born, having made as much of herself as she was able. Nothing more was ever heard of her as the Princess Caraboo.

We have been given to understand that she is still living, and resides in this city.

THE EVIL WEDDING.

The following tradition is frequently told at and near Stanton Drew in explanation of the origin of the Druidical stones:—

"Many hundred years ago, on a Saturday evening, a newly-married couple, with relations and friends, assembled on the ground now covered by the Druidical remains, for the purpose of joyously celebrating their nuptials. Here they feasted and danced right merrily, until the clock tolled the hour of midnight, when the piper (a pious man) refused to play any longer: this was very much against the wish of the guests, and it so exasperated the bride, who was fond of dancing, that she swore with an oath, she would not be baulked in her enjoyment by a beggarly piper, but would manage to find a substitute, if she went to h--ll to fetch one. She had scarcely uttered these words, when a venerable man, with a long beard, made his appearance, and having listened to their request, proffered his services, which they most gladly accepted. The old gentleman (who was no other than the Arch-fiend himself) having taken the seat vacated by the godly piper, commenced playing a slow and solemn air, which on the guests remonstrating he changed into one more lively and rapid. The company now began to dance, but soon found themselves impelled round the performer so rapidly and mysteriously, that they would all fain have rested. But when they essayed to retire, they found to their consternation, that they were moving faster and faster round their diabolical musician, who had now resumed his original shape. Their cries for mercy were unheeded, until the first glimmering of day warned the foul fiend that he must retire. With such rapidity had they moved that the gay and festive company were now reduced to a ghastly troop of skeletons. "I leave you" exclaimed the fiend, "a monument of my power and your wickedness to the end of time." Having so said, he vanished. The villagers, on rising the following morning, found the meadow strewn with large pieces of stone, and the pious piper lying under a hedge, half dead with fright, he having been a witness to the whole transaction."

A CURIOUS RING.

Barrett in his "History" (page 511) states that in the year 1398, John Vyel gave to the Church of St. Stephen one Ring, in which was set a stone, part of the very pillar to which Christ was bound at the scourging, *to be kept among the relics for ever.* Query—is this ring to be seen now?

REMARKS ON DRUIDICAL REMAINS IN THE NEIGHBOURHOOD OF BRISTOL, THEIR ORIGIN, AND THE PURPOSE OF THEIR ERECTION.

BY GEORGE PRYCE.

(Continued from Page 43.)

Mr. Seyer regards Stanton Drew as "in some sense the metropolis, or seat of government, of the Hædui (a tribe of ancient Britons inhabiting parts of the counties of Somerset and Gloucester), and that it, and perhaps others in its immediate neighbourhood, were inhabited exclusively by the Druids, some of whom went every day and sat in the cove (not yet referred to), or within the circles, to decide the suits and complaints brought before them; others instructed the youth, and others offered up the daily sacrifices. On stated days probably there was an assembly within the circles, of all the men of property belonging to the tribe (the Hædui), where peace and war, taxation, succession to the lands, and to the throne, and other national affairs, were settled, still under the superintendence of the Druids; and the circles being placed on an easy and pleasant knoll, in a valley surrounded by hills, whatever was done might be seen by the whole assembled tribe." (Memoirs, vol. i. pp. 100, 101.) Now the circle of Eight could not have been that in which a whole tribe assembled, because it was the smallest of the three, the diameter being less than 100 feet. We may rather consider it as appropriated to religious and judicial purposes,—in other words, as the circle to which the Druids repaired "to decide the suits and complaints brought before them," and that in which they "instructed the youth" in the mysteries of their fanciful theology; for, politically forbidding the use of letters, they had no more permanent method of teaching their disciples, or handing down their knowledge to posterity. The circle of Eight, too, was probably that in which were "offered up the daily sacrifices;" whilst in the Great or Solar circle assembled "all the men of property belonging the tribe," to decide upon "peace and war, taxation, succession to the lands and to the throne," and to conduct "other national affairs" to a settlement.

The religious destination of circles of stone will be sufficiently noticed as the subject proceeds; and a few observations only are necessary to show their application to judicial purposes, which it is evident from history, was practised in remote antiquity. A circle in Denmark is still denominated Dom, or Doom—ring, the ring of Doom, or judgment; and another in Oxfordshire is called Roll-right, the circle of justice, equivalent to hall of justice. Martin, in his "Description of the Western Isles," also notices a place where the officers of justice sat on stones in a circular manner, to administer the law. "In the Holm," he says, "as they call it in Shetland, there are four great stones, upon which sat the judge, clerk, and other officers of the court."

As a place of meeting for a concourse of people, Stanton Drew appears to have been admirably adapted, being situated about the centre of the tribe, to which it seems to have formed a place of general rendezvous. Although not surrounded by a lofty embankment, like its more gigantic neighbour at Abury, it was well suited to the purpose of an assembly of the people of the Hædui. The hills around formed an amphitheatre, upon which the assembled thousands of the tribe could overlook the area below, and witness whatever was transacted within the circuit embraced by this natural rampart. Here, when assemblies for council, judicature, and election were convened, the principal persons or chiefs, stood each by a pillar—a custom spoken of as prevalent among the Jews before the Babylonish Captivity; for, when Jehoash was anointed king by Jehoida, he *"stood by a pillar*, as the manner was; "— (2 Kings xi. 14.) evidently referring to its known antiquity even in those early times. King Josiah also when ."he read to all the people the words of the book of the covenant which was found in the house of the Lord, *stood by a pillar*." Wormius tells us that it was customary among the northern nations, so late as the time of Charles IV., and the Golden Bull,* in the year 1356, to

choose their princes in the same manner, the nobles standing in a circle upon or against, rocks or stones. So also Ericus was chosen King of Sweden so late as the year 1396; the electors being placed round a circular monument near Upsal, and himself on a stone in the midst of them. At Stanton Drew also, under the eye of their priests the chiefs assembled and constituting a kind of parliament, they deliberated on affairs connected with the well-being of their tribe, or the people at large, whilst the commonalty occupied the elevated ground on every hand, as spectators of the scene before them. Here we can imagine their anxious councellings when the report of a threatened invasion by the all-conquering legions of mighty Rome was echoed from tribe to tribe throughout the land, calling them to arms in defence of their hereditary independence as a nation. Yet the distress of that generation of Britons, proved the source of innumerable blessings to after ages. By their partial loss of liberty the way to the attainment of knowledge, freedom, virtue, and happiness, was opened up in succeeding times; the Roman eagle introduced the banner of the cross; the pride and ambition of a haughty conqueror, marched as the vanguard of the Prince of Peace; and the iron-handed oppression of the imperial Cæsar, prepared for the reception of the gentleness of Christ. Britain was humanized and civilized in order to be christianized; was nursed for future empire in the bosom of tyranny and despotism; received with slavery the germ of emancipation; learned from the victor the path that led to conquest, derived strength from weakness;

principalities of the empire; the brothers reigning jointly and residing together. A similar observance prevails in the county of Kent to this day, for by the law of Gavelkind—Give all kind—land is divided among all the children of a proprietor at his death, instead of descending to the eldest son.—This law it has been conjectured was introduced into Kent by the Jutes, a branch of the Teutonic conquerors of Britain, who established themselves there in the fifth century. As the joint rule in Germany referred to above, was frequently inconvenient and caused disputes, the custom which more usually prevailed, was to divide the territory, and so create numerous small principalities of the same house or family, but independent of each other as to their governance. From these partitions, many of the reigning princes of Germany still existing, date their origin. In these various petty sovereigns, it would appear, was vested the right of election to the imperial throne during the empire; but the Golden Bull of Charles IV. introduced a different system; for by its provisions, "the electoral territory, that is, the particular district to which the electoral suffrage was inseparably attached, became incapable of partition, and was to descend to the eldest son"; thus establishing by law, the right of primogeniture, which had not before existed in Germany; and investing the possession of all th edominions of the family, exclusively in the reigning elector, who also alone enjoyed the right of voting for an emperor.

* "The reign of Charles IV. (emperor of Germany), is distinguished in the constitutional history of the empire, by his Golden Bull; an instrument which finally ascertained the prerogatives of the electoral college." It owes its origin to the practice which existed in Germany, previous to its introduction or establishment, of partitioning the inheritance or patrimony of a prince among the whole of his children, so that the eldest son claimed or held no more because of priority of birth than his brothers, which seems to have been the general law of the

as it were in one eventful moment into public notice, conscious native importance, and the capability of exertion which has since astonished, over-awed, and blessed the world!

On the introduction of Christianity into Britain, the early Catholic missionaries found the devotional feelings of the people so wedded to their ancient temples, that artifice was required to accommodate the new faith to the superstitious spirit of the age. Thence Pope Gregory advised Augustine, in order to reconcile the pagan converts to its formularies, to celebrate its rites in places which the people had invested with a sacred character. Unable to persuade the pagan Britons from regarding the shapeless objects of their former devotion, as deserving reverence, they first achieved the remarkable triumph over their prejudices of transforming such of the Druids and Bards as had embraced the new religion, into Christian Priests, and then to conciliate the homage of the people to its demands they so far compounded with their scrupulous objections as to embellish the rude mass of stone, before which they had been accustomed to pay their adoration, with the emblem of the Christian Faith; and thus they piously diverted their religious worship into a channel more pure and sacred. In like manner churches were erected in the midst of their circular temples, and the very stones of their most holy places were employed in their construction; as at Abury, the parish church of which was built with, and the village itself stands within the boundary of the exterior circle of that wonderful monument of Druidic contrivance. So attached also were the old Britons to Stanton Drew, that it became necessary to consecrate it to the religion of Christ by erecting a church and nunnery upon its site, not far from which still stands the *Cove* belonging to the pagan temple, and on which it is believed " the Druids sat and administered justice to the neighbouring tribe." (Seyer.)

Circular stone monuments like that at Stanton Drew, and approached by serpentine avenues, are supposed to represent, not only the sun in its circuit in the heavens, but also the Deity, by a serpent and circle—or an amalgamation of Good and Evil—the former being pourtrayed by the circle, an emblem of eternity, and the latter by the serpent. Under this combined symbol, the Deity was worshipped by most nations of antiquity; and their temples constructed in a serpentine form, were, for this reason, denominated Dracontia;—that is, uniting, or originating the worship of the Sun with that of the Serpent. Sometimes these temples were of prodigious dimensions; the largest in Britain being that formerly existing at Abury in Wiltshire, which extended over hill and dale in a double line of stones of enormous size, a mile in length from the head of the serpent near the village of Kennet, towards the South-east, to the circle, which embraced within its ample circumference, a space of twenty acres. From it another double line or avenue of stones reached a mile Westward to Beckhampton, terminating the tail of this monstrous representation of a serpent, with a single stone of large dimensions, like that of "Hautvill's Coit" at Stanton Drew. The temple at Abury including the circle, extended from end to end 15,313 feet, or nearly three miles, and consisted altogether of six hundred and fifty stones, each from twelve to fourteen feet in height, and forty feet in circumference; it was, however, completely eclipsed by that at Carnac in Brittany which reached the amazing distance of eight miles, and of which, upwards of four thousand stones are still computed to remain.

(To be continued.)

Bristol Worthies.

FRAMPTON Walter. Four wealthy inhabitants of Bristol bore this name; one of whom founded the church of St. John the Baptist; probably the second Walter whose will is dated 1388.

GUY —. a member of the corporation settled a colony of Bristol men in Newfoundland, 1609.

GROCYN William, a great reviver and encourager of literature, was born here in 1442. Rector of Newton Longueville, Bucks; Prebendary of Lincoln. He was one of the earliest students of the Greek language, which until his time had been very little cultivated in England; he was also the first who introduced a better pronunciation of that language than had before been known. He resided for some time at Oxford, and while there received the great Erasmus as his guest; who always spoke of Grocyn with great commendation.—He was in 1506, made master of Allhallows College, Maidstone, where he died in 1519. He was the author of many works, several of which are not extant.

HAZARD Dorothy, the wife of a clergyman, a woman of great piety and courage. She was the earliest member of the first dissenting church in Bristol. Died March 14th, 1675, aged 84.

HARDING Robert, founder of the Berkeley family, said to be a son of one of the kings of Denmark; chief magistrate of Bristol in the reign of William the Conqueror. Lived in Baldwin Street. Died 1115. His descendants took the name of Fitz-Harding.

HUME David, the Historian. Born 1711. Died 1776. When a young man he was for some months in 1734, a clerk to Mr. Miller, a merchant here.

HALL Robert, M.A., the celebrated Baptist preacher, was born at Arnsby, Leicestershire, in 1764. He was educated at Northampton; Baptist College, Bristol; and King's College, Aberdeen; at the latter he became acquainted with Sir James Mackintosh, who was also a student there; and their warm friendship lasted while they both lived. He officiated as minister at Broadmead with Dr. Caleb Evans, in 1784. In 1785 he was elected classical tutor to the College in Stoke's Croft. He quitted Bristol in 1791 for Cambridge, and after preaching there and at Leicester, he returned to his congregation in Broadmead; and remained till his death, which occurred February 21, 1831. He was buried in the burial-ground of Broadmead chapel. His published works consist chiefly of sermons, tracts, reviews, and contributions to periodical works.

HESKETH Lady, the valued and attached friend of the poet Cowper. Born July, 1733. Died, Jan. 15, 1807. Buried in the Cathedral.

HOBHOUSE, Sir Benjamin, Bart., F.R.S., F.S.A. Resided for some time in this neighbourhood. Secretary to the Board of Control, in Mr. Addington's administration and afterwards held other important posts. Died, Aug. 15, 1831.

THE CANDELABRUM IN TEMPLE CHURCH.

"THE most beautiful Church of Temple," as it is justly termed by William Wycestre, contains a relic of so singular and interesting a character, and of so high antiquity, that it is really surprising it should not have attracted far more notice than it has hitherto done; I allude to the extraordinary and rare candelabrum, which adorns the chancel of the church. It has been supposed that there is a similar one in the chapel on St. Michael's Mount, in Cornwall, but this is a mistake, that is only a modern copy taken from this, which is perfectly unique. The following description of it was communicated by the late Mr. George Catcott, to the Rev. S. Seyer:—

"There is in this church, a sconce, or chandelier, of curious workmanship, without name, or date, but apparently of very high antiquity. It has two tiers of branches, four in the upper, and eight in the lower tier. The top is ornamented with a brazen image of the Virgin Mary, with the infant Saviour in her arms. The two tiers are joined together by a Knight Templar, in a coat of mail, armed with a spear, and trampling on a dragon. The lowest part is a lion's head of brass, it is suspended by an iron spindle. In the year 1788, Sir John St. Aubyn, Baronet, visiting Temple Church, and struck with the antique appearance of this chandelier, procured another exactly similar to be made by Mr. William Wasbrough, a brass-founder, (now Thomas Hale and Co.) of this City, for the use of his Chapel, at St. Michael's Mount, Cornwall, where it now remains."—F. L.

[This beautiful piece of workmanship has been by some supposed to have belonged to the Knights Templars, and used by them in this church while it was in their possession. But judging from the workmanship, and comparing it with other relics, the period of the construction of which is known, it was most probably made in the reign of Edward the Third, (1321 - 1377) during which period the workmanship in metal was much carried on, and attained a high pitch of excellence.—ED.]

CURIOUS INSCRIPTIONS.

IN the churchyard of Moreton-in-the-Marsh, (usually pronounced Moreton-inmash) the following singular monumental inscription is to be seen:—

" Here lie the bones of Richard Lawton,
Whose death, alas, was strangely brought on;
Trying one day his corns to mow off,
The razor slipped and cut his toe off;
His toe, or rather what it grew to,
An inflammation quickly flew to,
Which took, alas, to mortifying,
And was the cause of Richard's dying."

The following we have seen at Portbury, St. Arvan's near Chepstow, and in two other churchyards:—

" Farewell, vain world, I've seen enough of thee,
And now I care not what thou say'st of me;
Thy time I prize not, nor thy frown don't fear
My days are spent, my head lies quiet here:
The fault thou'st seen in me, strive to shun,
Look at home, enough is to be done."

TO CORRESPONDENTS.

We have reserved the continuation of our notice of the Bristol Riots for a future occasion, as we have been kindly promised some valuable and interesting particulars which have never appeared in print, and which refer to some portions of what has already appeared in our columns.

A third edition of our first number has just been printed, and may now be had of all booksellers.

The first five numbers may now be had stitched in a neat wrapper, price 6d. Quarto edition, 1s.

Printed and Published at the Office of the Bristol DIRECTORY, 9 Narrow Wine Street, Bristol, by M. Mathews,—March 1, 1854.

CURIOSITIES OF BRISTOL

AND ITS NEIGHBOURHOOD.

No. 8.   APRIL, 1854.   Price One Penny.

THE RIOT OF BRISTOL BRIDGE.

The following is an account of the Riot of Bristol Bridge, a very serious disturbance which took place in the year 1723, in which thirty-six persons were killed or wounded. It was occasioned by the re-imposition of a toll which the citizens considered ought to be discontinued, as the surplus from the tolls was very large. The determination of the Bridge Commissioners was however adhered to. A new toll-gate was erected and the tolls demanded as before. The consequence of this will be seen in the following narrative, with the manuscript of which we have been favoured by a correspondent, who informs us that it was formerly in the possession of the late Mr. W. Tyson, F.S.A.

Bristol, Tuesday, 1st Oct. 1793.

A PLAIN CIRCUMSTANTIAL

NARRATIVE OF FACTS of the Proceedings of Yesterday, in the City of Bristol.

At nine o'clock in the morning of yesterday the Toll-Gatherers attended to receive the toll under the direction of the Bridge Commissioners, Mr. Harris having given up the lease which he had taken of the tolls for one year. They continued to do their duty for some time, but with considerable interruption from the people assembled; some persons paid, others refused and forced their way, incited thereto by the by-standers. The clerk of the commissioners came to the Council-House to complain that they could not do their duty without the assistance of the civil power.

The constables being summoned were ordered to attend to support the toll-gatherers in their duty, and one of the magistrates attended to give countenance to the constables, and see that they did their duty. By this means the toll was collected with some difficulty, till about half-past ten o'clock, some persons who refused to pay and attempted to force their way, were taken into custody and committed, and the persons so taken were attempted to be rescued as they were conveying to Bridewell.

In consequence of this violent proceeding of the multitude, it became necessary to make the proclamation in the Riot Act. It was accordingly read three times distinctly by one of the magistrates, the last reading being ended precisely as the clock struck eleven.

Mr. Symons (clerk to the commissioners), addressed the multitude and assured them that an account of the bridge toll should be immediately printed and dispersed, and that the toll was now collected by the trustees, and would be continued to be collected no longer than the sum authorized by parliament should be received. The account is accordingly published this day.

After the reading of the riot act, the multitude were informed of the consequences of their continuing in a tumultuous state, and in any greater number than twelve persons; they were exhorted and implored to consider the consequences, to be assured that the magistrates did only their duty, which duty, however painful it might be to them, would assuredly be fulfilled. They were told, that as in one hour after the last reading of the riot act, which hour would be completed at twelve o'clock, the magistrates would return to do their duty with the civil power, but if that was not sufficient, they should be obliged to call in the military, and those that would not be advised, must take the consequences, and that if they received any injury, it must lie upon their own heads. The magistrates did return and endeavoured by persuasion, and every other temperate means, to prevail on them to disperse, some who refused were taken into custody, but at length from the increased number of the people, and their turbulent conduct, a detachment of military were ordered down. They were drawn up in two lines on the bridge, and there remained on duty until half-past six o'clock, to be aiding if necessary.

A magistrate attended, and by means of the civil power only, supported the toll-gatherer in the receipt of the tolls; another magistrate relieved the first; a third came sometime after to relieve the second, and continued till the said hour of half-past six o'clock, at which time it was that the magistrates had, in humane consideration of the lives of their fellow citizens, prevailed on the bridge commissioners to shut up the toll-houses for the night, from an apprehension that some mischievous persons, who are certainly at the bottom of this business, and who must undoubtedly have been all along inciting the common people —who, in fact, have no cause of complaint about the toll, because they pay it not, but only the substantial citizens, householders, manufacturers, and merchants, and the gentry, who travel over the bridge—to acts of violence, should, under cover of the night, be guilty of outrages, and draw destruction upon themselves and others who might be culpably looking on, though not with any evil intention of their own.

At the withdrawing of the guard, and shutting up the toll-houses, the multitude became very noisy and riotous, hissing and abusing the officers. The commanding officer, in attempting to seize one of the multitude, received a blow from some other man. The soldiers of course would have been ready, upon the word of command, to have charged the mob. The civil magistrate then present interfered, and prevailed on the military to march off. The post and chain were removed, and the magistrates retired, with their peace officers, in the rear of the military, persuading the people to be quiet, and retire to their respective homes. The magistrates repaired to the Council-house, and there met the mayor and other magistrates assembled. In confidence that, now the toll was abandoned for the night, there could be no further occasion for the military, they were permitted to depart. The magistrates had not been at the Council-house more than half an hour, before intelligence was brought that the mob was in great force, and preparing to burn down the toll-house. They despatched two of their peace officers, to inquire into the truth of the report; they presently returned with an account that the mob had broken into the toll-house, and were then burning the wood-work, with the posts, &c. A messenger was despatched for the military aid: an officer, with a small number of men, who remained at the guard-room, proceeded down, to attempt to disperse the mob; they were insulted, and compelled to retire; being unaccompanied by any magistrate, they did not attempt to fire, although the officer had been wounded in two places. Very soon after, a company of the military, with an officer, marched off to the Council-house, and the mayor, and five of the aldermen, who were present, with one of the sheriffs, and their peace officers, preceded the military, and commanded the mob to disperse; but before they had reached half over the bridge, they were assailed by stones, oyster-shells, &c., and some of the military were wounded thereby. The magistrates were in consequence compelled to direct the military to do their duty: the front rank had no sooner discharged their pieces than they were assailed by stones, &c. from a larger mob, that had collected in the rear, upon which a division faced about and fired up High-street. The consequence (much to be lamented as it most undoubtedly is,) has been that several persons have been killed and wounded, several of whom, it is very probable, may have been innocent, without any evil intention themselves, but certainly indiscreet and blameable in adding to the multitude by their individual presence, after having been forewarned by printed hand-bills, distributed about the town by direction of the magistrates, which hand-bills informed the citizens that the riot act had been read, and that the military would be desired to fire, if the rioters did not disperse.—Published by order of the Mayor and Aldermen. Worrall, Town Clerk.

THE RECORDERS OF BRISTOL.

WE are enabled by the kind assistance of THOMAS GARRARD, Esq., Chamberlain of Bristol, to present our readers with what we believe to be as complete a list as can be compiled of the Recorders of this city. Many were men most highly distinguished in their profession, who rose to some of the highest legal offices in England. To the names of the more eminent we have appended a few biographical notices. Such a list, therefore, cannot fail, we think, to be found both valuable and interesting. We must remark in passing that the list given by Barrett is very incorrect both in names and dates.

The first on record is—

1344 : William de Coleford, who is also noted for having drawn up an account of the customs of the city, and for having preserved the forms of the oaths to be administered to the members and officers of the corporation.

1394: Simon Oliver.

1430: Sir Richard [Newton] Cradock. A member of the very ancient family of Newton. He dropped the name of Newton in the later part of his life, on taking the name of Cradock. He was made a Justice of the Court of Common Pleas, 1439; and was raised to the Chief Justiceship of the same Court, 1440. He resigned the Recordership in 1439; died 1444, and was buried in the Cathedral Church of this city.

1439 : Sir John Inyn. He was, successively, Chief Baron, 1423 ; Chief Justice of the Court of Common Pleas, 1427 ; and lastly Chief Justice of the Court of King's Bench, 1439; in which year he died, and was buried in the chancel of Redcliffe Church, where a handsome brass is placed over his remains.

1463 : Thomas Young. In 1468 he was made a justice of the Court of Common Pleas ; in the same year he resigned the Recordership. He was M.P. for this city many years.

1468: Michael Harvey.

1483: John Twynyho. He was M.P. for this city in 1472, and again in 1484.

1486: Thomas Treymayle. In 1488 he was made a Justice of the Court of King's

Bench. On the visit of Henry VII to Bristol in 1486, the mayor, sheriff, and others met him on his way, in whose names the Recorder "right cunningly welcomed him."

1500: John Greville.

1505: William Glenville.

1517: Sir John Fitz-James. In 1522 he was made a Justice of the Court of King's Bench; in the same year, Lord Chief Baron; and in 1526, Chief Justice of the Court of King's Bench.

1522: Thomas Jubbes.

15—: Thomas Cromwell, Earl of Essex, Lord High Chamberlain of England.

No document has been discovered by which we can fix the time when this distinguished statesman was appointed to this office. Indeed his having filled the post at all is only known from the following extract from one of the audits in the possession of the Corporation. It is found in the account book of the Chamberlain, Gilbert Cogan, under date of the year 1540:—

" For so much the £20 charged in this side paid to the Lord of Essex, late Recorder of this Town, for his fee due to him at the feast of the nativity of our Lord God, in anno 1540, which customary used to be paid at one time. and for that the said Lord of Essex was beheaded before that feast, in the said year, anno 1540, we the auditors find that the £20 ought not to be allowed in this account."

The king insisting on having the money due to the late Earl of Essex, it was paid under protest of the auditors. The following refers to it : " Paid unto the Lord Privy Seal, by the hands of Mr. Davye Brook, Recorder, £20."

This noted man, so instrumental in the suppression of monastic houses in England, fell under the displeasure of Henry VIII, from having been very active in bringing about his marriage with Ann of Cleves. He was beheaded on the 24th July, 1540.

1541: David Brook. From the foregoing notice it is evident that Serjeant Brook succeeded the Earl of Essex. The first payment recorded as made to him was on the 25th March, 1541, when he received the sum of £3 6s. 8d. being the amount of a quarter's salary.

—: Robert Kelway.

—: John Welsh. In 1562 he was made a Justice of the Court of Common Pleas. He was for many years M.P. for this city.

1574: Sir John Popham. This eminent man was the eldest son of Edward Popham, Esq., of Huntworth, Somersetshire, and was born in 1531. He was made a Serjeant-at law about 1570; Solicitor General, 1579; Attorney General, 1581; and in 1591, Chief Justice of the Court of Queen's Bench, when he was knighted. He resided at Wellington, Somerset, (of which place he was a native,) when not engaged in his judicial duties. As a judge he was extremely severe, especially in cases of highway robbery ; which happily were in some measure checked by his severity. He died June 10, 1607, aged 76, at Wellington, in the church of which place he is interred, beneath a very handsome monument. He resigned the Recordership of Bristol soon after he became Solicitor General, and was succeeded by—

—: Thomas Hannam, M.P. for this city, 1585—1597.

(To be Continued.)

Bristol Worthies.

HOBHOUSE, Sir John Cam, now Lord Broughton. Author of "Travels through Albania," the "Historical Notes to the Fourth Canto of 'Childe Harold,'" &c. Born at Westbury-upon Trym. Educated at Dr. Estlin's school on St. Michael's Hill. In the administrations of Earl Grey he filled the office of Secretary-at-War. In that of Viscount Melbourne, 1834, Chief Commissioner of Woods and Forests. In Lord Melbourne's second administration, 1835, he was president of the Board of Control; which office he also filled under Lord John Russell, from 1846 until 1852. In 1851 he was raised to the peerage by the title of Baron Broughton.

JAY John, a very intrepid navigator, of Bristol, who made a voyage of discovery to Brazil in 1480, without however meeting with the success he had anticipated.

JAMES THOMAS, captain of an expedition which was sent out in search of the North-West passage, by the Society of Merchant-Venturers of Bristol, 1531. He explored a large tract of the coast of Labrador, and Hudson's Bay.

JENNER EDWARD, M.D., the discoverer of vaccination. Born at Berkeley.
   [We shall give a notice of the life and labours of this great benefactor to the human race on a future occasion.]

JERRARD, J. H. D.C.L., formerly principal of the Bristol College; afterwards Examiner in the Classics at the University of London. Died 1853.

KENTISH, Edward, M.D., author of many valuable medical works. Resided here many years and died here.

KNIBB, Rev. William, an eminent missionary to Jamaica, and distinguished for his exertions in the cause of the abolition of slavery. Served his apprenticeship, as a printer, in Bristol. Died in Jamaica 1845, aged 49.

LAVINGHAM, Richard, Prior of the Carmelite Monastery, which stood on St. Augustine's Back, in the 14th century. Author of many works in divinity and philosophy which attracted great notice at the time of their publication; also of an abridgment of Bede's History.

LEWIS REV. John, scholar, literary man, and antiquary. Born in Bristol, in 1675. Vicar of Minster, Kent; and Master of Eastbridge Hospital, Canterbury; died at Margate, in 1749. He was the author of "The History and Antiquities of the Isle of Thanet," "History of the Abbey and Church of Feversham," Lives of Caxton; Wickliffe; and other works.

LOCKE John, the Philosopher. Born at Wrington, in a house adjoining the church-yard, (which is still standing), 1632; died at Oates, in Essex, 1704.

LAWRENCE, Sir Thomas, President of the Royal Academy, the very eminent portrait painter. Born, No. 6, Redcross Street, Bristol, April 13, 1796. Died, No. 65, Russell Square, London, Jan. 13, 1830. Buried in St. Paul's Cathedral.

LEE, Rev. Samuel, D.D. Canon of Bristol Cathedral. Eminent Hebrew Scholar. Died, 1853.

THE BRISTOL RIOTS OF 1831.

DEFENCE OF THE COUNCIL HOUSE.

THE substance of the following account of the defence of the Council House, has been kindly supplied us by one who assisted in its defence, and in preserving the valuable archives and other municipal treasures which were there deposited.

Expecting an attack upon the Council House from the assaults which had already been made on other buildings, the Chamberlain, with about forty men, most of them sailors, took measures for the defence of the same. All the valuable muniments and plate were removed into the cellar of the adjoining house in hampers.

During the night, (Sunday) the house was twice attacked by the mob; previous to the first onset, the Chamberlain addressed the men in the hall, who promised to support him in its defence. At the first attack the rioters were headed by a man with a large fur cap on; he was speedily cut down, and the cap was recognised as the official cap worn on state occasions by the Sword Bearer.

The men who assisted the Chamberlain acted with much bravery, and ere long compelled the mob to fly. Two men were seriously hurt, and were carried into the Council House; no surgeon unfortunately was then to be found to render them any assistance.

Though defeated, the mob after a while proceeded to make a second attack upon the building; they were rendered desperate by the loss and repulse they had sustained; and advancing with caution commenced with shouts and yells. The Chamberlain formed the men in front of the building ready to receive them. As on the first attack, these men fought with the most determined courage, and succeeded in driving the rioters back, and taking several of them prisoners. One man they seized was entirely naked, except his shirt; he was one of those who had escaped from the Gaol, and having divested himself of the prison dress was too eager in search of spoil and destruction to get more clothing. They were also successful in securing a quantity of stolen goods, which the mob had seized. Not having sufficient means to detain the prisoners in close custody they were released.

After this second attack application was made to the inhabitants of the neighbouring houses to join the brave defenders of the Council House, but the request was not complied with; a large majority of the people were terrified, and would not move from their houses, considering themselves better employed in guarding their families and their property; it being night time too, added much to their fear. As day dawned, however, they made their appearance, but they were too late to be of any assistance then.

Great credit is due to those who were thus able to save the Council House and its valuable contents. Some of the defenders were severely wounded, and the Chamberlain was twice thrown to the ground by a violent blow; upon his leading on the men he was greeted with curses and execrations, some crying out "Here comes again the b—y Chamberlain," &c. Soon after the second attack Captain Gage arrived at the Council House with a troop of Dragoons. The mob still remained there, and the soldiers in dispersing them cut down several. They then stationed themselves at the Council House, and remained with its defenders until morning, and then left.

The men who defended the Council House were armed with cutlasses and oaken staves, but the former were so light as to be of comparatively little use; they therefore laid them aside, using only the sturdy oak bludgeons, with which, as we have shown, they did great execution.

One man was shot in Wine Street, and fell a few yards off from the place where the Chamberlain and his party were standing. He was shot through the back and never spoke again. On the Chamberlain's turning him on his back and scanning his features with the aid of a lantern, he recognized him as one of the leaders of the party who was most active in the attack upon the Council House.

NOTICE OF THE LIFE OF THE RAJAH RAMMOHUN ROY.

THIS interesting and very enlightened man having spent some time in and near this city, and having been known and respected by many of our fellow citizens, a sketch of his life may not be unacceptable to our readers.

His paternal ancestors were Brahmins of very high standing, and were devoted to the religious duties of their race, until about the beginning of the seventeenth century, when they relinquished their spiritual for worldly pursuits. His maternal ancestors, also of high Brahminical rank, and priests by birth and by profession, devoted their whole time to religious observances.

The subject of our notice was born in the district of Burdwar, in Bengal, about the year 1774, and was a Brahmin by birth; his father, Ram Hant Roy, trained him early in the doctrines and ceremonies of his sect; under the paternal roof he learnt the Persian language, he afterwards went to Patna to study Arabic, and subsequently he was sent to Benares to acquire a knowledge of Sanscrit. He afterwards learnt seven other languages: Hindustanee, Bengalee, English, French, Hebrew, Latin, and Greek; most of which he could speak and write with fluency.

In spite of all the anxious religious training which he received from his father, it appears that he became heretical in his opinions at an early age.

"When about the age of sixteen," he says in a letter to a friend, " I composed a manuscript calling in question the validity of the idolatrous system of the Hindoos. This, together with my known sentiments on the subject, having produced a coolness between me and my immediate kindred, I proceeded on my travels, and passed through different countries, chiefly within, but some beyond the bounds of Hindostan. When I reached the age of twenty, my father recalled me, and restored me to his favour."

He had in early life taken a dislike to the character of the Europeans, but about this time becoming acquainted with several natives of Europe, he found reason to change his opinion, and took great interest in gaining information respecting our mode of life, government, laws, etc. His continued controversies with the Brahmins, in which he inveighed against many of their superstitious rites, in particular the barbarous custom of burning widows, greatly increased their dislike to him, and in consequence of their influence over his father, he was again deprived of the paternal favour; his father, however, still allowed him what pecuniary assistance he could afford.

His father died in 1803, and he soon afterwards published several books and pamphlets on the abuse of the Brahminical rites and forms of government. This so incensed them, that a suit was commenced against him to deprive him of caste, which after the delay of some years was decided in his favour. He was rewarded for all his trouble and anxiety, by seeing many of his friends, some of whom were very influential persons, adopt his sentiments.

Of the several works which he published about this time, the most important was a translation of the " Vedat," a compilation in Sanscrit of the rules and principles of the religion of the Hindoos into Bengalee and Hindoo. He also published an abridgement of it for gratuitous circulation, which he afterwards translated into English, in 1816. Soon after this he began to direct his attention to the Christian religion, but found himself greatly perplexed by the multiplicity of doctrines, which he found insisted upon by various authors, and by the different Christian teachers with whom he became acquainted. He resolved therefore to study the scriptures for himself, and for this purpose he learnt the Hebrew and Greek languages. Becoming strongly impressed with the excellence and importance of the Christian system of morality, he published in 1820, in English, Sanscrit, and Bengalee, a series of selections principally from the first three gospels, which he entitled, "The Precepts of Jesus, the guide to Peace and Happiness." For writing this work he met with great opposition and was styled a heathen by many of his religious opponents. He soon afterwards published a defence of it, in which he stated that he believed, not only in one God, whose nature and essence is beyond human comprehension, but in the truths revealed in the Christian system. This led him into other controversies in which he displayed great and sound knowledge of the scriptures, great judiciousness of arrangement, and much acuteness and skill in controverting the assertions of his opponents. To be able the better to bring out his several works, he established a printing-press, solely for the use of his own productions. Many were the struggles he underwent in the loss of old and faithful friends, who considered it unfit to associate with one who held such doctrines. He always said, however, that he could not wish he had pursued a different course, and declared that " whatever may be the opinion of the world, my own conscience fully approves of my past endeavours to defend what I esteem the cause of truth."

He had for a length of time, ardently

desired to visit Europe, and in particular, England; at last in the year 1830, he embarked for this country, having been engaged by the King of Delhi to make a representation of grievances to the British Government. Before his departure, the king conferred on him the title of Rajah, when giving him the appointment of Ambassador to this country. So well did he discharge his mission for his employer, that he succeeded in obtaining an additional stipend of about £30,000 per annum for the king of Delhi, for which his own reward was to be between £3,000 and £4,000 per annum.

He arrived in London in April 1831, accompanied by the youngest of his three sons, and his coming created much interest, not only in the metropolis, but in this country generally. After being a short time in England, he went to Paris for a few weeks, where he was taken much notice of by the late king Louis Philippe. On his return to London, he attended many public meetings and anniversary dinners, and repeatedly attended divine worship at some of the Unitarian chapels in and near London. It was, however, his system to avoid identifying himself with any religious body, and he was also desirous of hearing preachers of other denominations who had acquired a just celebrity. The church in London and the service there performed which seems to have most interested him, was St. Olave's, Southwark, where the Rev. Dr. Kenney officiated.

He subsequently visited several provincial towns, but in none did he stay longer, nor in any other town was he more esteemed than in Bristol. While in this city he attended worship at Lewin's Mead Chapel, having been on terms of intimacy with the late Rev. Dr. Carpenter, one of the ministers.

In the autumn of 1833, he was the guest of Miss Castle of Stapleton Grove, near Bristol. Unhappily, in a short time after his arrival there, he was taken seriously ill of a severe disorder, which in a few days terminated his valuable life, on the 27th September.

His body was submitted to an anatomical examination; when the distinctive thread of his caste, was observed passing round him, over his left shoulder, and under his right.

Fearing more attacks upon the property and the caste of his children by his bigoted countrymen, in case his body should be interred in a Christian cemetery, it was buried in the grounds of Stapleton Grove, where it remained several years, until it was removed to the cemetery at Arno's Vale, where a handsome monument has been placed over it. His name and the year of his death is the only inscription engraven upon it.

The amiability of his character, his great acquirements, and the kindness and benevolence which he always manifested, had attached him to a large number of people, by whom his sudden and unexpected removal was deeply felt and lamented.

REMARKS ON DRUIDICAL REMAINS IN THE NEIGHBOURHOOD OF BRISTOL, THEIR ORIGIN, AND THE PURPOSE OF THEIR ERECTION.

BY GEORGE PRYCE.

(Continued from Page 51.)

There is, perhaps, no ancient people into whose mythological system the mysteries of serpent worship were not largely infused, and in which they did not constitute an important ingredient. Nearly every temple, erected among nations of antiquity, was not only consecrated to the worship of this idol in some way or other, but most of them symbolized that particular deity, either alone, or in connexion with some equally abhorred divinity. Nor was this superstition confined to the heavens, where Baal, his compeer, was supposed to reign supreme, as the Lord of Light, the Father God, &c.; and upon the earth, where he was portrayed in long undulating lines of unwrought stones upon the wide expanse of unbounded plains, or in the bosom of deeply receding vallies—but he was despotic also in the realms of everlasting sorrow. Scripture refers this universal prevalence of the dominion of the Serpent under the figure of Sin, to the Tempter in the book of Genesis; and tradition points to his worship as the result of the Fall of Adam,—the writings of Moses directing us to the very infancy of time as the period of its birth. To the Serpent the ancient Egyptians rendered their homage, as to the emblem of the Divine Nature, and the symbol of Eternity. To it the Israelites burnt incense in Palestine, and offered idolatrous worhip in the land of their fathers. It was elevated to the lofty temples of Tyre and Sidon; and it was sculptured, in a thousand modifications of its sinuous body, upon the pagodas of Hindostan. It is found in Persia and Java; is wrought on the monuments of Athens, and depicted in the sanctuary of Minerva at Tegra. We recognise it in the great dragon of China, find it preserved in Mexico, and we examine, in our own day and in our own country, the relics of a superstition which once spread over the beautiful hills and dales of Britain, in the waving folds of Serpent idolatry and Baal worship—a portraiture of the debasing influence of a corrupt theology, in the stone erections of the ancient Druids.

I have already intimated that the ancients, when erecting temples to their divinities, did so with a due regard to the properties and functions of the deity to be adored within the sacred edifice to whose peculiar honour it was constructed. This practice not only prevailed in oriental nations of great antiquity, and was ultimately introduced into Britain, but it obtained also in old Greece. The lofty eminences of that classic land were graced with the temple of Jupiter, Juno, and Minerva, the supreme deities, as at Athens, Corinth, the promontory of Sunium, and other places, where these tutelary gods, overlooking the almost boundless space within which stood the object of their peculiar guardianship, presided over its destinies. To Mercury, temples were built in the spacious forums both of Greece and Rome, because he was the god of traffic, and these, emporiums of commerce. The sanctuaries of Apollo, the god of poetry, and those of the festive Bacchus, were erected near the theatre, the dwelling-place of mirth and song. Hercules—the robust and hardy Hercules—had his temple near the circus or amphitheatre, because there athletic exercises and mortal combats were decided ; and so in the British isles ; and many have argued that Diodorus Siculus alludes specifically to the circular temple at Stonehenge, because, in speaking of the adoration paid to Apollo, or the Sun, among the aborigines of this country, he refers to such homage being paid to that divinity in a circular temple, by a race of people inhabiting an island beyond Gaul.

That superstitious veneration in which the Sun was held by those inhabiting the plains of Ur, in Chaldea, in the first ages after the flood, soon spread itself throughout all the Asiatic world, and ultimately reaching the shores of Britain, is a marked and characteristic feature in the religion of our ancestors. The devotions of mankind had been kindled by this luminary from age; and throughout the world it had been the great source of idolatry. Sometimes represented under one form, and sometimes under another, it had exacted the tribute of devotion from every generation since the days of the patriarchs of Holy Writ.

The appellation of Baal—the name by which the sun was generally known among the ancients—originated in Phœnicia. It is the same as the Bel of the Babylonians ; and it was imported into the kingdom of Israel by Jezebel the wife of king Ahab, who was herself a native of that country—her father being Ethbaal, king of the Lidonians,—and Baal the special divinity worshipped by that people. Besides the instances just given in the case of Ethbaal and his daughter, we find the name of this deity appended to those of illustrious persons in many countries where homage was paid to this idol—as in the case of Hannibal, Asdrubal, Adherbal, and others which might be mentioned—the terminating syllable having an undoubted reference to the object of their veneration.

As a proof that this custom of affixing the name of the god to that of men, did not result from accident, we find it recorded that Nebuchadnezzar changed the name of Daniel to Belteshazzar, because he said it was according to the name of his god. In like manner the designation was applied to Britain after it was inhabited, for in the archæology of the Welsh it is called the island of Bel.

I have said that the idolatrous homage paid by the Asiatics to the Sun, as the great object of their worship, was early brought into Britain. The great corruptors of religion soon after the days of Noah were the descendants of Belus, who introduced among the inhabitants of the Greater Asia subject to them, an admixture of the Solar worship with pure patriarchal observances ; and this corrupt theology was subsequently adopted by the Phœnicians or Canaanites, who ultimately spread it among the descendants of Jacob in their newly acquired possessions in that country. Now as the Phœnicians, who inhabited the north-west coast of Palestine, were eminent traders at a very remote period, and the introduction of their deities, together with the method of constructing temples, in which to pay their adorations, were also imported into Britain at a very early date, I shall endeavour to trace the progressive steps by which this was accomplished, for there can be no doubt that wherever the merchants of Tyre and Sidon established a settlement, there also they worshipped Baal or the Sun as the supreme God of their adoration.

Although we cannot with any degree of certainty, fix the time when the Phœnicians first visited Britain, yet we know it was as early as the time of Moses—1500 years before the Christian era—for tin, which in ancient as well as in modern times, abounded chiefly in the county of Cornwall and the Scilly Isles, as it is distinctly mentioned by the great Jewish lawgiver; among whose people it must have been introduced by their neighbours, the Phœnician merchants. (Numbers, xxxi. 22.) * No other nation that we read of, traded in this metal so extensively as the Tyrians, and as their commercial dealings extended over the then known world, it was introduced into every country with which they became acquainted. Hence it may be reasonably inferred without any very great stretch of probability, that a colony of Phœnicians was settled at the western extremity of Britain, who worked the tin mines in that quarter, in the time of Moses. With the establishment of this colony, was introduced also their customs, manners, and theology; and as the trade with Britain soon proved a lucrative monopoly, the Tyrians fixed upon a place where to settle another colony of their people, as an intermediate station between these islands and their own land. This was Gades, the modern Cadiz, in Spain, which limited the travels of Hercules westward. There, as well as in Britain, the Phœnicians established their religious observances ;—engrafting upon the mysteries of Chaldean idolatry in which they had been primarily educated, the worship of the Hercules of Tyre and Sidon—the Bel of Babylon, and the Baal of Scripture.

* See Notes and Queries, vol. viii. p. 344, for some remarks on this subject.

(To be continued.)

Pl. III

Drawn by J. Willis

Engraved by J. Skelton

*The High Cross, formerly standing on College Green, Bristol, now placed in
the grounds of Sir Richard Colt Hoare, Bar.* *Stourhead, Wilts.*

Drawn & Engraved by J. Skelton

Peter's Pump, which stood formerly in Peter Street,
now placed at the source of the river Stour in Wiltshire.

Pl. V

N.E. Portion of the Cloisters of the Cathedral, and back of Minster House.

Drawn by J. Willis

Monuments of Canynge in South Transept of Redcliff Church.

Engraved by J. Skelton

Pl. VII

Drawn by J. Willis

Engraved by J. Skelton

The Chapel of S.ᵗ Mark, commonly called The Mayor's Chapel.

Pl. VIII

Drawn by J. Willis

Engraved by J. Skelton

South Aisle of Bristol Cathedral.

Pl. IX

Singular Buildings in Lewin's Mead.

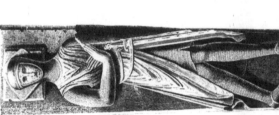

Maurice de Gaunt,
ob. 1230.

Robert de Gournay,
ob. 1260.

Henry de Gaunt,
ob. 1266.

PL. X.

Drawn by J. Willis.

Engraved by J. Skelton.

Effigies in the South Aisle of the Chapel of St. Mark.

PL. XVIII.

Drawn by J. Willis.

Engraved by J. Skelton.

Stone Effigies in the Cathedral of Bristol.

Pl. XI

Drawn by J. Willis

Engraved by J. Skelton

North Porch of Redcliff Church, looking Westward.

Back of an Old Mansion in Small Street.

Pl. XIII

Drawn by J. Willis

Engraved by J. Skelton

The Great Hall of the Mansion House in Small Street.

Pl. XIV

Drawn by J. Willis

Engraved by Joseph. Skelton

The Sacristy of Bristol Cathedral.

Pl. XV

Engraved by Joseph Skelton, from a drawing in the Bodleian Library, Oxford.

South View of part of Bristol Castle.

Built Anno 1110. Demolished in a fortnight by an order from Oliver Cromwell, dated Whitehall, 28 Dec.ʳ 1654.

Pl. XVI

West End of St. James's Church. 1820.

Pl. XVII

Drawn by J. Willis

Engraved by J. Skelton

The Mint, now St Peter's Hospital.

Pl. XVIII

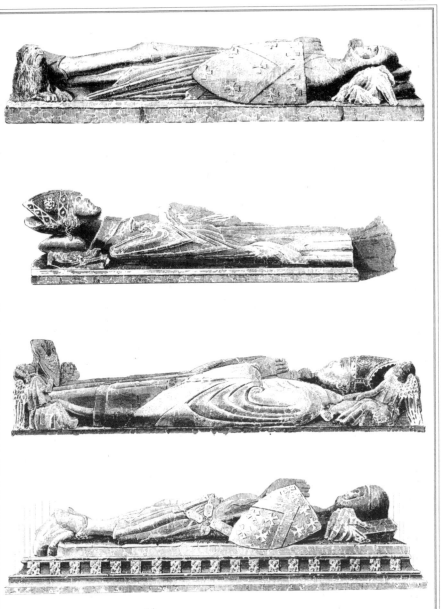

Drawn by J. Willis

Engraved by J. Skelton

Stone Effigies in the Cathedral of Bristol.

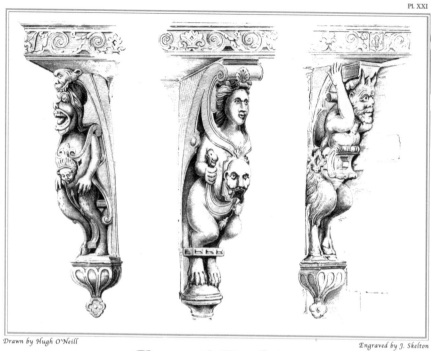

Brackets at St Peter's Hospital.

Specimens of Decorations in the Mint, now St Peter's Hospital.

Pl. XXII

Drawn by J. Willis

Engraved by J. Skelton

Staircase in the house of Mess.ʳˢ Franklyn on the Back.

Pl. XXIII

Castle Bank, &c.

Pl. XXIV

Bank premises of the Keepers Compartment, &c.

in Newgate Prison, now destroy'd.

(In the second story died Savage the Poet.)

Drawn by J. Willis

Engraved by J. Skelton

The Lady Chapel in Radcliffe Church.

Now used as the Free grammar School of Queen Elizabeth.

PL. XXV

Engraved by J. Skelton, from an original drawing in the Bodleian Library.

South Front of the Abbey Gatehouse.

Entrance to the Crypt of St. Nicholas Church.

Drawn during the alterations in 1822.

Engraved by J. Skelton, from an original drawing in the Bodleian Library, taken in the year 1751.

The North View of Temple Gate, now demolished.

Pl. XXIX

A Bastion and Wall — works of the Castle,
belonging to & adjoining Newgate in 1819.

Drawn by J. Willis

South East View of Bristol Cathedral.

Engraved by J. Skelton

Pl. XXXI

Drawn by J. Willis

Engraved by J. Skelton

Doorcase, &c. of the North Porch of Redcliffe Church.

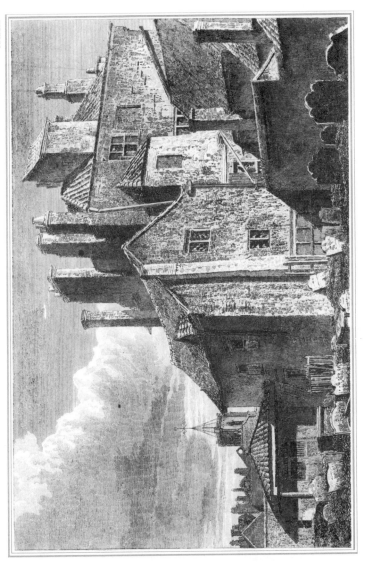

Old Custom House from St. Nicholas Burial Ground.

Pl. XXXIII

Drawn by J. Willis

Engraved by J. Skelton

East end of the North Aisle of Redcliffe Church.

Pl. XXXV

Tailors Hall and part of a Monastery,
Cyder House Passage.

Pl. XXXVI

Drawn by J. Willis

Engraved by J. Skelton

Interior of the North Porch of Redcliffe Church.

Pl. XXXVII

Engraved by J. Skelton, from a drawing in the Bodleian Library, Oxford.

South View of Redcliffe Gate.

Taken down in the year 1772.

Pl. XXXVIII

Drawn by J. Willis

Engraved by J. Skelton

East Aisle of St. Mark's, or Mayor's, Chapel.

Old House in Temple Street with part of the Church Tower.

Pl. XL.

The Poyntz Chapel,

on the south side of that of S.ᵗ Mark's.

Pl. XLII

Drawn by J. Willis.

Engraved by J. Skelton.

Apartment in Red Lodge, Park Row.

Pl. XLIII

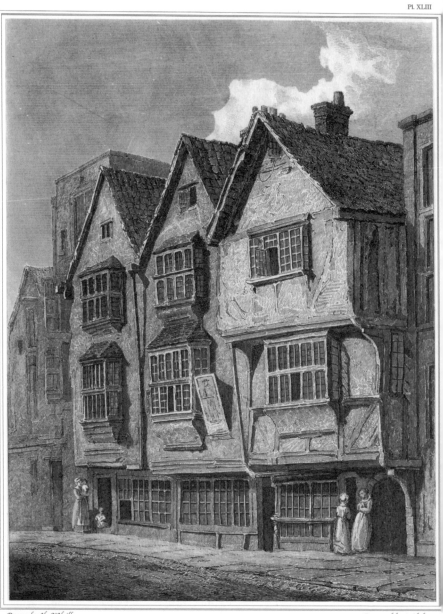

Drawn by H. O'Neill   Engraved by J. Skelton

The Jolly Sailor, and other Lodging Houses
which stood formerly in Marsh Street.

Pl. XLIV

West End of Redcliff Church, from the Wharf on Redcliff Back.

Pl. XLV

Drawn by J. Willis

Engraved by J. Skelton

Chimney Piece.

in the House of Mess.ʳˢ Franklyn & C.ᵒ on the Back.

Pl. XLVI

Drawn by J. Willis

Engraved by J. Skelton

State Swords of the City of Bristol.

Pl. XLVII

Demolished house standing formerly on the south side of Wine Street.

Pl. XLVIII

Canynge's Chapel, or Masonic Hall, Redcliff Street.

Pl. XLIX

Drawn by J. Willis   Engraved by J. Skelton

The Transepts of Redcliffe Church.

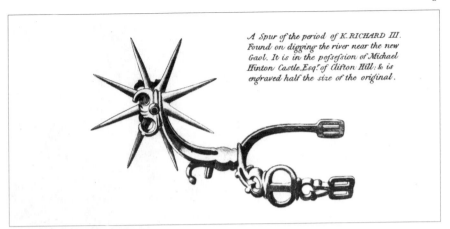

A Spur of the period of K. RICHARD III.
Found on digging the river near the new
Gaol. It is in the possession of Michael
Hinton Castle, Esq.r of Clifton Hill: & is
engraved half the size of the original.

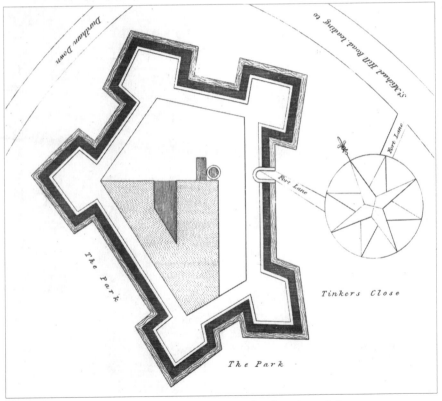

Engraved by Joseph Skelton, from a drawing in the Bodleian Library, Oxford.

Plan of the Royal Pentagonal Fort built on the North West
side of Bristol by Prince Rupert, and the City in 1643-4.

Pl. LI

Bastion of the City Wall,
leading from Union Street to the Pithay.

Pl. LII

Drawn by J. Willis

Engraved by J. Skelton

Entrance door of the Drawing Room at Mess.ʳˢ Franklyn's on the Back.

Pl. LIII

Drawn by J. Willis

Engraved by J. Skelton

Altar Screen in the North Aisle of Bristol Cathedral.

View on the Froom near Lewin's Mead.

R. Rowbotham, Bristol, del.

J. Skelton, Oxford, sculp.

VIEW OF THE BIRTH PLACE (IN RED CROSS STREET BRISTOL) OF

SIR THOMAS LAWRENCE, P.R.A.

Born 13th April 1769

Died 7th January 1830

Pl. LVI

Drawn by J. Willis Engraved by J. Skelton

Chapter House in Bristol Cathedral.

Notes on Local Matters.

THE PORTER FAMILY.

In the churchyard of St. Paul's church, Portland Square, a plain gravestone, bearing the following inscription, covers the remains of some members of a family long connected with this city, and by whom the literature of England is much enriched :—

"Here lies the body of
Charles Lempriere Porter,
Departed this life 14th February, 1831.
Æt. 31.

"Here sleeps in Christ,
ANNA MARIA PORTER,
(late of Esher, in Surrey,)
Born, Dec. 1779.   Died, June, 1832.
She was blessed with high mental endowments.
Her pen indited a good matter.
She was still more blessed :
She sat at the feet of Jesus.
May they from whom thou art taken,
Blessed and beloved sister,
Be so found in the Lord."

"Also, PHŒBE, aged 79, wife of Dr. Porter, Portland Square, who departed this life, 20th February, 1845.

"Also, her grandson, John Augustus Marlin, aged 18, who died on the 11th of November, in the same year.

"MISS JANE PORTER, a celebrated writer, died on the 24th May, 1850. Aged 74 years.

"W. O. PORTER, M.D. Surgeon in the Royal Navy, died 15th August, 1850. Aged 76 years.
He practised as a physician in this city for nearly forty years,
And wrote many Medical and other works."

"PART OF A MONASTERY IN CIDER HOUSE PASSAGE."

In Skelton's "Etchings of the Antiquities of Bristol," Plate xxxv., is a view of part of Tailors'-hall, and a late Perpendicular English window in an old house in Cider-house passage, which he styles "part of a monastery." As this may mislead visitors and strangers into whose hands Skelton's book may fall, we take this opportunity of stating, that there never was any monastery at all on that site, or any ancient religious house. Most probably the window, which is the only part that would attract the attention of the antiquary, was inserted in the house as an elegant addition to it at the time when that style of building was by no means uncommon in civic and domestic, as well as in ecclesiastical, edifices.

THE BLOCK AT LEIGH COURT.

We have been favoured with some particulars of the history of this interesting relic. It appears that it remained at the old Leigh Court until the removal of Mrs. Trenchard, who took it with her to her new residence, in the village of Abbot's Leigh, which stood almost close to the Inn. After the death of Mrs. Trenchard her effects were sold, and among them was this block, which was in appearance like a butcher's block, being part of the trunk of a tree. It was about two feet and a half high, and two feet in diameter. Instead of selling it entire at the auction, it was cut up into small pieces, for each of which there was great competition, and the fragments accordingly fetched very good prices. We have never seen any of these pieces of King Charles's log, and are ignorant if any remain in or near this city; we trust that this may be the case, and if so we should be glad to be informed of it.

Folk Lore.

"SHOW SILVER TO THE NEW MOON."

When you expect the new moon—and you may know the exact time by consulting "Old Moore's Almanack," (say our Bristol conservators of folk-lore)—never look at it through the window, or you will most assuredly be unlucky ; but go to the door, and there jingle your money, in sight of the moon, and you will be lucky all through the month. This custom still prevails extensively, among the lower classes in this city and neighbourhood.

THE STRAY EYE-LASH.

If ever you find a stray eye-lash upon your cheek, you must put it on the back of your left hand, and *wish*, and you shall get what you want the next morning ; but if not, you will have to wait seven years.

THE WISHING STEPS ON REDLAND GREEN.

You must stand on the top of these steps, and wish for what you most desire, and you will find it under your pillow the next morning ; but if not, you will not get it for seven years. You must be sure to go up the steps on one side and down on the other.

TO CORRESPONDENTS.

FILIUS ECCLESIÆ.—We have received a kind communication from a gentleman signing himself as above. We regret not being able to answer his query respecting what member of the Poyntz family Poyntz-Pool was named after. We have not been able to discover whether any of the family had property near that locality ; we should be glad of any information on the subject which some of our correspondents may be able to furnish.
Received with thanks :—J. D. L.—F. L.

A quarto edition of this work, printed on superior paper, price Twopence each. Either edition can be sent, post free, on receipt of an extra stamp.

. Communications to the Editor to be forwarded to the Office of the BRISTOL DIRECTORY, 9, Narrow Wine-street.

Printed and Published at the Office of the Bristol DIRECTORY, 9 Narrow Wine Street, Bristol, by M. Mathews,—April 1, 1854.

CURIOSITIES OF BRISTOL

AND ITS NEIGHBOURHOOD.

No. 9.   MAY, 1854.   PRICE ONE PENNY.

ROYAL VISITS TO BRISTOL.

IN the year 1138 the contest between Stephen and the Empress Matilda arose. Bristol Castle was defended by a son of the great Earl of Gloucester. Stephen, after having seized the Castle of Gloucester, came to Bristol, which he besieged and conquered. Sir Bartholomew de Courcill, or de Chirchil, a distinguished soldier and ancestor of the Duke of Marlborough, was placed in command of the castle. In the following year the fortune of war changed, and the castle was taken by Matilda's party. Matilda after this spent two months in this city. Her gallant brother at the battle of Lincoln, in 1141, took Stephen prisoner and brought him to his Castle of Bristol, where he was imprisoned, says the chronicler Fabyan, "from the sayde time of Candlemasse unto the Holy Rodde day next ensuing."

Matilda was now sovereign of this country, and ought, if right were done her, to be included as Queen of England among our sovereigns as such. The Archbishop of Canterbury, and all the Bishops gave in their adherence to her at Winchester, and a deputation from the citizens of London after a little vacillation, acknowledged her also. Had she used her power with discretion, she might have held the sovereignty with which she was invested; but becoming intoxicated by triumph, she took injudicious measures, which, instead of consolidating her power as she had hoped, only produced the contrary effect, and Stephen's Queen with a large force, again changed the fortune of the war, and Stephen was set at liberty, while the Earl of Gloucester was consigned to imprisonment. He was afterwards released by Stephen, who again endeavoured to take the Castle of Bristol, but without success, and after making many plans for the destruction of the city, none of which proved feasible, he at last gave up the dsign altogether.

Henry II. when a youth was brought to Bristol by his uncle Robert, to be educated here in company "with other—the chiefest men's sons of the city," * The house inhabited by the young prince, was situated in Baldwin Street, and was in after years, pointed out to strangers, as the place where the future conqueror of Ireland received his early education. Mr. Seyer mentions being shown, in the year 1813, the house and the room where his tutor Matthews instructed him. It was situated two or three doors from Blind Steps, going towards Clare Street, adjacent to it, formerly stood a chapel dedicated to St. John.

The young Prince remained at his studies in this city, from 1142 to 1146, when he returned to Anjou, where he remained for eight years, when by the death of Stephen, he became king of England.

THE LORD HIGH STEWARDS
OF BRISTOL.

THE recent interesting ceremony of installing His Grace the Duke of Beaufort into the office of Lord High Steward of our ancient city, has suggested to us the propriety of presenting our readers with a list of the names of those who have filled that office. Many of them were among the most distinguished men of the time in which they lived, and are well known to posterity by the achievements which they performed in the court, in the camp, and on the bench.

The Duke of Beaufort, the third of that name who has been Lord High Steward of Bristol, was installed on the 16th of March, 1854.

The Mayor, attended by the majority of the Corporation, wearing their robes of office,

---

* "To be instructed," says Gervase of Canterbury, a writer of that period, "in letters and trained up in correct behaviour as became a boy of his parts and quality."

arrived at the Council House shortly before two. At two o'clock His Grace arrived, in company with the Sword-Bearer, and on alighting from the Mayor's carriage, was met on the steps by the Town Clerk, the Treasurer, the Deputy-Treasurer, and other official personages. Preceded by them he ascended to the Council Chamber, where the Mayor and Corporation were assembled. The Mayor having addressed the Duke in a speech worthy of the occasion, presented him with his appointment engrossed on vellum. His Grace suitably replied, and after taking the oath of allegiance adjourned with the Mayor and Corporation to an adjoining room, where an elegant *Déjeuner* was provided; after partaking of which, and drinking a few toasts, the Duke and most of the company took their departure.

——o——

1540 : EDWARD SEYMOUR, Duke of Somerset, generally known as the Protector Somerset.

1546 : EDWARD, Earl of Hertford.

1549 : SIR WILLIAM HERBERT.

1570 : ROBERT DUDLEY, Earl of Leicester.

1588 : WILLIAM CECIL, Baron Burleigh. Died August 4th, 1598, having been Prime Minister of England for upwards of half a century.

1598 : ROBERT DEVEREUX, second Earl of Essex, the unhappy favourite of Queen Elizabeth.

1600 : THOMAS SACKVILLE, Earl of Dorset.

1608 : ROBERT CECIL, Earl of Salisbury.

1613 : WILLIAM HERBERT, third Earl of Pembroke.

1630 : RICHARD WESTON, first Earl of Portland. Lord High Treasurer of England.

1635 : PHILIP HERBERT, fourth Earl of Pembroke, and first Earl of Montgomery. Lord Chamberlain of the Household to Charles I.

1650 : SIR HENRY VANE. Beheaded as a Regicide, June 14th 1662.

1651 : OLIVER CROMWELL.

1661 : JAMES BUTLER, second Duke of Ormonde. The very distinguished military officer.

1715 : JAMES, third Earl of Berkeley.

1738 : PHILIP YORKE, first Earl of Hardwicke. Lord High Chancellor of Great Britain.

1756 : WILLIAM HENRY CAVENDISH : third Duke of Portland.

1810 : WILLIAM WYNDHAM GRENVILLE, first Baron Grenville.

1834 : HENRY CHARLES SOMERSET, sixth Duke of Beaufort.

1836 : HENRY SOMERSET, seventh Duke of Beaufort.

1854 : HENRY SOMERSET, eighth Duke of Beaufort.

REMARKS ON DRUIDICAL REMAINS IN THE NEIGHBOURHOOD OF BRISTOL, THEIR ORIGIN, AND THE PURPOSE OF THEIR ERECTION.

BY GEORGE PRYCE.

(Continued from Page 59.)

With the worship of Baal, the Sun, or, as he is sometimes designated, Molech, the Phœnicians also introduced that of Amalcta or Astarte, the Moon—the Ashtaroth of the Old Testament. The symbol of the former was fire, and this emblem from age to age had kindled the devotions of mankind throughout all the Asiatic world; at length this great fountain of idolatry extended, as we have seen, as far as the British Isles. Here blazed in succeeding ages the Bealtine, or fires in honor of that deity, and both Baal and Astarte were worshipped in the circular stone monuments of the Druids, the relics of which still remain in Britain; and within them the Bards chaunted their hymn of praise to the harmonious strains of the harp, in honor of the supreme gods of their adoration, the Sun and Moon and the Host of Heaven.

There can scarcely be required a greater proof that the monuments of Druidism were introduced into this country from Phœnicia, than the fact that the adytum, sanctum sanctorum, or inner circle of many of these temples, bears so strong a resemblance or analogy to the Holy of Holies in Solomon's temple, as to incline to the belief that they were constructed after the manner of the sanctuary in that memorable building. Moreover, Solomon himself, when he forsook the God of his fathers, erected a temple on the Mount of Olives in honor of Baal or Molech, and many of his successors followed in his steps. The city of the house of Baal, mentioned in the tenth chapter of the second Book of Kings, most probably means a sort of Holy of Holies, where the most sacred images of Baal were kept;—a place separated from the *temple* of Baal, as the *Holy of Holies* in the temple of Jehovah was separated from what was called the *Holy Place*. With the erection of Solomon's temple the workmen of Hiram king of Tyre, were, as we know, well acquainted; and to them doubtless were the ancient Britons indebted for the erection of those stupendous circular temples once scattered over the face of the country, and which now lie in confused heaps upon its surface. By them too, the superstitions of Canaan were brought over, and which the untaught native seems to have universally adopted; these rites were identified with the religion of Britain until its invasion by Julius Cæsar fifty two years before the Christian era; soon after which, by the introduction of the Gospel, it gradually dwindled away before the light of a pure faith, until its final extinction, which may be dated at a period not far distant from the age of the great Augustine, who was recommended by the Pope to assimilate the worship of Christian institution to that of Pagan prejudices, with a view to the establishment of the former upon the decaying existence of the latter.

The first time mention is made of a circular stone erection in all antiquity, is in the fourth chapter of the Book of Joshua, where that leader of the people of Israel was commanded to select twelve men from among the congregation, and these on passing the river Jordan to take possession of the Promised Land, were each to take up a stone out of the river, and leave the whole in the place where they should lodge that night;—we subsequently read that the twelve stones "which they took out of Jordan, did Joshua pitch in Gilgal."

From this narrative it is evident the circle of unhewn stones was of divine origin, and that Joshua arranged them in a circle is manifest from the name given to this group, viz., Gilgal.—Gal, in Hebrew signifying *to roll*; and the doubling of the root gal-gal or gil-gal, means rolling *round* and *round*, or rolling off completely, the reproach of Egypt from Israel. It also means a circle or wheel; the reduplication giving importance, as much as to say, *the circle*, by way of distinction. This wheel-like arrangement is no doubt alluded to where we find that "The Lord said unto Joshua, this day have *I rolled* away the reproach of Egypt from off you; wherefore," it is added, "the name of the place is called Gilgal unto this day."

The circle of stones set up by divine command in Gilgal is distinguished from the similar works of idolatrous Canaanites by the fact that the former referred to the twelve tribes of Israel—each tribe being represented by a stone—and the latter to the idolatrous worship paid to the Sun and Moon and the Host of Heaven. Roll-right, the name of a circle in Oxfordshire, means the Druids' *wheel* or *circle* (as well as place of judgment), which was equally a sacred symbol in India as with the Druids; the wheel being, in all probability, an ancient emblem of astronomical cycles; or rather, it was the *rota solis*, or orb of the sun, to which their peculiar superstition led those infatuated idolaters continually to allude.

The rites and ceremonies observed in connection with these circular stone monuments of the Druids were various—that of the worship of the Sun—symbolized by fire—has been already noticed. Within the adyta, or sanctum sanctorum, the ancients preserved the sacred fire perpetually blazing; as did the Jews in their Holy of Holies, and the Druids of Britain in their rude unwrought temples of stone. On May-eve—one of Baal's great festivals, all the fires in the country were put out, that only upon the altar of the priests remaining unextinguished. From it alone the people were supplied, but no criminal could obtain of the sacred fire until he had undergone the punishment to which he had been sentenced by the Druids; nor was any one permitted to assist him under the severest penalties. This excommunication shut out the delinquent from all society, and closed every social avenue against him, even the family associations which were dearest to him—none daring to aid him in his utmost need. Most eastern nations in which the Sun and the Host of Heaven were adored as eternal fires, observed the same custom of preserving the symbol of the deity worshipped always blazing upon their altars in living flame; and, as an emblem of Jupiter—the Sun—Quintus Curtius tells us the wise men of ancient Persia kept a perpetual fire burning upon altars of silver in honor of that deity. Elementary fire, too, was the medium through which the goddess Vesta - the Earth—was worshipped; because it was believed that an eternal fire continually burned in its centre, and it was the only image by which that divinity could be represented. This idea of eternal fire seems to have originated in Troy, from whence it was brought into Rome by Æneas together with the ceremonies pertaining to its worship. The Holy Fire was anxiously watched both by the Vestal Virgins and the Pontifex Maximus, to whose special care it was consigned; and if permitted to expire, the most severe penalties were inflicted upon them for their negligence, as it was believed that the duration of the empire depended upon the perpetuity of that fire. Among the Greeks too, although, like the Romans, they were not much addicted to the worship of the heavenly bodies, yet they had a place denominated the Prytanuim, where the consecrated fire of Vesta was perpetually burning; and these sacred altars existed in every town in that classic land. The purity of the Holy Fire of the ancients, was preserved in all its integrity; the means to restore it in case it went out by accident or negligence, being by the aid of lightning, burning-glasses, or by friction. These fires were continually fed by means of the most precious woods, oils, and perfumes; like that which Moses commanded to keep always burning upon the altar in the wilderness, and upon which Aaron was to burn sweet incense "a perpetual incense before the Lord." It is not improbable that the heavy judgment which befel the two sons of Aaron was inflicted because they attempted to rekindle the fire upon the altar with an unholy flame—the holy fire having been extinguished through their want of care.

(To be continued.)

THE BRISTOL RIOTS OF 1831.

(CONCLUDING ARTICLE.)

THE next objects of destruction after the Custom House had been burnt, were the North and West sides of Queen Square, which where besieged, pillaged, and afterwards set on fire in a wonderfully short space of time. Some of the old houses in King Street, which were chiefly composed of wood, were set on fire by the wind taking the flames in that direction, and were totally destroyed. On the West side of Queen Square stood the excise office, which was the first of the buildings attacked on that side; some of the scenes witnessed about that part were most dreadful. Women were seen endeavouring to force their way through the flames, in doing which their clothes were set on fire, and but for the speedy and most praiseworthy exertions of some sailors who observed the dangerous situation in which they were, many of them would have been burnt to death; after doing all in their power to rescue the human beings who were in danger, they employed themselves in staying, as much as possible, the fury of the flames.

On the morning of Monday, the rage and strength of the multitude seemed to have spent itself in some measure; and about five o'clock A.M., a detachment of the 23rd dragoons arrived in Prince's Street. The inhabitants of some of the houses there accosted them, and were told in reply by the officer in command, that if assisted by a number of the citizens they would be able to restore order in that neighbourhood, and to prevent the destruction of more property. Several men volunteered their aid, and they set forward with the troops in prosecution of their good work. At an earlier stage of the disturbances, the late Rev. Mr. Edgworth, a catholic priest, then resident in this city, had in company with his colleague, the

Rev. P. O'Farrell, gone to the Council House and promised immediately to find two hundred and fifty able men, ready to do their utmost in quelling any further tumult. Singularly enough, this offer was disregarded, one of the aldermen thinking that the civil and military force were not of sufficient number to stay the tumult. Mr. Edgeworth on the Monday again went to proffer the same assistance, which, incredible as it may seem, met with a similar response.

A small number of the rioters seemed inclined to proceed with more outrages, but they were speedily dispersed by the military under the command of Col. Brereton, the soldiers for the most part, using merely the flat of their swords; consequently none were killed, and very few wounded. After seeing the mob retire, the troops returned to their quarters; an officer, Major Mackworth, riding off to Keynsham to order the 14th to return, so as to effectually quell any further assault that might be made. Though the violence of the mob was not manifested at this time, the same plundering was continued by women and lads, as well as men, and the same scenes of drunkenness and debauchery were still to be witnessed in the Square. Here and there knots of men collected together, while one among them addressed the rest on the subject of their recent success, and the very effectual gaol delivery they had been the means of accomplishing in the morning.

About ten o'clock, the 14th returned to Bristol, and the magistrates issued an order for the streets to be cleared. This accordingly was done; the military, some of whom had been injured on the previous day, were glad of being able to perform their duty which they ought to have been ordered to do by the Mayor when they first came into the city. Now the mob was so much diminished in numbers as well as in strength, that there was scarcely any occasion for this act of severity. Many were killed, and others most severely wounded by the soldiers. Orders were given for all the inhabitants, except those who had been sworn in as special constables, to remain within their houses.

The constables walked about the streets in companies consisting of from sixty to a hundred individuals; and used their utmost to send the people to their homes, and to save as much property as possible. They also succeeded in taking a great many of the rioters prisoners; and in the course of a day or two, as many as two hundred were in custody.

The list of killed and wounded, as subsequently made out, was-killed twelve, wounded ninety-six; this list, however, included only those who were taken to the hospitals, many more were killed and burnt while engaged in plundering the houses.

The total loss of property has been estimated at £200,000.

On Tuesday morning, November 1st, 1831,

the city was restored to order; but it was many days before the terror and excitement of the people was diminished.

A special commission for the trial of the rioters was opened at the Guildhall on January 2nd, 1832, before the Lord Chief Justice Tyndal, and Mr. Justices Taunton and Bosanquet; 114 persons were indicted for various offences committed during these disturbances. Against 12 no bill was found; 21 were acquitted, and 81 convicted. Of those convicted, 5 were condemned to death, one of whom was spared on account of insanity; against 26 the sentence of death was recorded, 1 was transported for fourteen years, 6 for seven years, and 23 were sentenced to various terms of imprisonment.

Courts-Martial were held on Col. Brereton, the military commander of the district, and upon the second in command, Captain Warrington. Col. Brereton finding that the trial was going against him, and that he would in all probability be cashiered, put an end to himself by blowing out his brains. Captain Warrington was ordered to be cashiered, but was allowed to sell his commission. Ex officio informations were also filed against several of the magistrates for neglect of duty, and against the Mayor, Mr. Pinney, whose trial took place before the Court of King's Bench. His defence was that the citizens refused to confide in, or assist the magistrates, and that consequently, deserted as they were by their fellow citizens, they could not have acted more efficiently. Upon these grounds a verdict of acquittal was given; and the other informations were withdrawn.

THE RECORDERS OF BRISTOL.

(Continued.)

1593: Sir George Snigge. In 1604 he was made one of the Barons of the Court of Exchequer; he resigned the Recordership. He was M P. for this city from 1597 to 1605. He was the son of George Snigge, an alderman of this city, who with his wife Margery, are interred in St. Stephen's Church. Sir George died November 11th, 1607. His body having laid in state for six weeks at Merchant Tailors' Hall, was buried in St. Stephen's Church, at the upper end of the chancel, where the communion table now stands. A monument was erected over it, which, on the re-paving of the church in 1733 was removed to the east end of the south aisle, where it now remains. It bears a long Latin inscription.

1615: Sir Nicholas Hyde. In 1626 he was made Lord Chief Justice of the Court of King's Bench. He was M.P. for this city in 1625.

1630: William Noy. A Lawyer of much eminence; he was born about 1577. "He was," says Fuller, "for many years the stoutest champion of the subjects' liberty,

until King Charles I. entertained him to be his attorney." He was made Attorney General in 1631. He has gained an "imperishable infamy" for having been the inventor of the odious impost styled Ship-money. He did not live long enough to witness the disastrous effects of which that measure was the cause. He died August 6th, 1634. He wrote several works on points of law, many of which were published posthumously.

1630: Sir John Glanville, the second son of John Glanvile, or Glanville, of Tavistock, a puisne Justice of the Court of Common Pleas, who died in 1600.— John Glanville was made a Serjeant 1637. M.P. for Totness. In the parliament of 1640 he was elected its Speaker; and was knighted the year following. He was during the civil wars imprisoned for some years. Several of his parliamentary speeches were printed, and also some charges made against the Duke of Buckingham in 1626. He died October 2nd, 1661, and was buried in the Church of Broad-Hinton, Wiltshire, the manor of which he had purchased.

1646: Edmund Prideaux.

Sir Henry Vane.

1651: Serjeant Bulstrode Whitelocke, M.P. for Marlow, Buckinghamshire. In 1648 he was made one of the Parliamentary keepers of the Great Seal, which office he retained for some years. He was also summoned to Parliament as a Peer of the Commonwealth; and held the situation of High Steward and Recorder of Oxford. In 1654 he was sent to Sweden as Ambassador to Queen Christiana, and displayed much diplomatic talent in the discharge of his duties. He resigned the Recordership of Bristol in 1655; and died January 26th, 1676. His father, Sir James Whitelocke, was a Justice of the Court of King's Bench.

1655: John Doddridge. He was elected M.P. for this city in 1656; but a petition against his return being presented by Desborough, the distinguished Parliamentary officer, he was unseated and Desborough accordingly represented the city. Doddridge gave to the city the two elegant flagons preserved in the Council House.

1658: John Stephens.

1662: Sir Robert Atkyns was the son of Sir Edward Atkyns, a Justice of the Court of Common Pleas during the Commonwealth, and was a co-adjutor with Hall, Rolle, Wyndham, and others, in effecting various law reforms. He was one of the Judges appointed to try the Regicides at the Restoration; he also then received the appointment of a Baron of the Exchequer, which he held until his death, 1669.—Sir Robert was born in the year 1621, and after an early education at home, was sent to Oxford, where he remained some years. He was M.P. for East Looe in the parliament of 1660. His first legal appointment, after receiving the Recordership of this city, was Solicitor General to the Queen. In 1672 he was made a Justice of the Court of Common Pleas. He resigned this appointment in 1680, and the Recordership two years afterwards, having been compelled to do so by unfortunate disputes. He gave up all interest and concern in public affairs on leaving the bench, but in 1683 on the approaching trial of the unfortunate William, Lord Russell, he at the request of some of the family of the accused, interested himself in the case, and assisted Lord Russell in preparing his defence. After the revolution he published two pamphlets entitled "A defence of Lord Russell's Innocency." He subsequently published other judicial works. He represented Gloucestershire in the only Parliament called by James the Second. He was made Lord Chief Baron by William the Third in 1689; and in the latter part of the same year was appointed speaker to the House of Lords, which office he held until the year 1693, when the great seal was given to Lord Somers. He finally retired from public life in 1694, and went to spend the remainder of his days at Saperton Hall near Cirencester. Here he died in 1709, at the advanced age of eighty-eight years. In early life he had married Anne, daughter of Sir Thomas Dacres, and by whom he left a son Robert, who was knighted by Charles the Second, when he visited this city, but who is better known as the author of the "History of Gloucestershire."

1682: Sir John Churchill. He was appointed Master of the Rolls, January 12th, 1685. M.P. for Bristol the same year.

1685: Hon. Roger North, the youngest son of Dudley, fourth Baron North.

1688: William Powlett.

1704: Sir Robert Eyre. In 1708 he was made Master of the Rolls. In 1710 a Justice of the Court of Queen's Bench. In 1723 Lord Chief Baron; and in 1725 Chief Justice of the Court of Common Pleas.

1728: John Scrope. M.P. for this city from 1727 to 1734. He was also one of the Secretaries of the Treasury. Resigned the Recordership in 1735.

1735: Sir Michael Foster. This eminent lawyer was born at Marlborough, December 16th, 1689. After a preliminary education, he was entered at Exeter College, Oxford. In 1725 he married Martha, eldest daughter of James Lyde, Esq., of Stantonwick, Somersetshire; soon after which he removed to Bristol. In 1745, he was appointed a Justice of the Court of King's Bench, which office he held until his death, which took place November 7, 1763. His remains were interred in the church of Stanton-Drew. He was the author of some legal works.

NOTICE OF THE LIFE OF EDWARD JENNER, M.D.

THIS very able physician and great benefactor to his race was born at Berkeley, of which place his father was vicar, in 1749. After receiving his education at Cirencester, he was placed with Mr. Ludlow, a surgeon, at Sudbury. After having been with him for the usual time, he went to London, and became a pupil of the celebrated John Hunter, with whom he resided for two years, while studying medicine at St. George's Hospital. A friendship sprung up between them, which lasted during their lives. Jenner always spoke of the advantages he derived from this connection, as at Dr. Hunter's he was accustomed to meet some of the most learned and scientific men of the time. In 1773, he returned to his native village, and practised as a surgeon and apothecary till 1792, when he resolved on devoting himself entirely to medicine; he accordingly took the degree of M.D. at the University of St. Andrew's.

But it was not by his success in the old line of practice that Jenner was alone to distinguish himself, he had the happiness of making a discovery which has been the means of saving many lives, and which will long keep his memory in grateful remembrance. The circumstances of this discovery are as follow:—

One day at Sudbury, he was struck by hearing a country-woman say that she could not take the small-pox, because she had the cowpox; on making inquiry into this—to him, at that time—remarkable assertion, he found that it was a general notion in that district, that milkers who had been attacked with a peculiar eruption which sometimes occurred in the udder of the cow, were completely secure from small-pox. On inquiry among the medical men in the neighbourhood, he was told that this could not be depended upon, that they had long known of it, and had communicated it to Sir George Baker, who neglected it as a popular error. After this Jenner mentioned it to his friend Hunter, but he did not take any interest in it, thinking it a piece of superstition or folk-lore.

Notwithstanding these rebuffs, he diligently pursued the subject at Berkeley. He found that there were some to whom it was impossible to give small-pox by inoculation, all these had had cow-pox. He also found however, that there were others who had had cow-pox, and who in spite of the remedy took small-pox. This at first gave gave him much trouble and anxiety, but at last he discovered that the cow was subject to a variety of eruptions, one of which only was efficacious in preventing small-pox, and this, which he called the true cow-pox, he found, could only be given effectually to the milkers at one period of its course.

About 1780, the thought was suggested to him of propagating cow-pox, and with it the security from small-pox, first from the cow to the human being, and thence from one man to another.

In 1788, he carried a drawing of the eruption as seen in the hands of the country-people, to London, and showed it to his friend Hunter, and other scientific persons; they were yet unconvinced, and would neither give aid nor hope of success to their friend; every one smiled at him, ridiculed him for such an idea, as has so often been the fate of other valuable and important discoveries, before and since the time of Jenner. But let a thing only be good, it will succeed in the end, though the learned and the sceptics may sneer and throw discredit upon it. Such happily was in time, the fate of Vaccination; but an arduous task it was for Jenner to go striving on with a discovery which he knew would benefit and save the lives of numbers of his species, and yet to meet with none, or very few to give him encouragement, or to offer him assistance.

In 1796, he first made the decisive experiment; on the 14th of May (a day which is still commemorated by an annual festival in Berlin), a boy of eight years of age was vaccinated with matter taken from the hands of a milkmaid; the boy passed through the disorder in a highly satisfactory way, and in the following July was inoculated for small-pox without the least effect. After the success of this most valuable and interesting trial, Jenner made many extensive experiments of the same nature, and in 1798, published his first work on the subject, "An Enquiry into the causes and effects of the Variolæ Vaccinæ.'

—This work created great interest, and the conclusiveness of the evidence convinced many; among the physicians however, the same distrust was shown as before, until after the lapse of about a year, when upwards of seventy of the principal physicians and surgeons in London, signed a declaration of confidence in it. Some now tried to take away the honor of the discovery from Jenner, but without the slightest success, and honors of a scientific nature were given to him from various learned and scientific bodies. He always as much as possible resided at Berkeley, to which place he was deeply attached, and nothing could induce him to go any where else for any length of time. To the end of his days, he continued to study and urge forward his great discovery, and had the happiness of witnessing how generally it was becoming employed, not only in England, but in several other countries. He expired suddenly in the year 1823, at Berkeley, where he is buried.

He was the author of some other valuable treatises on objects connected with science and natural history, the most important and interesting of the latter class, was a paper "On the Natural History of the Cuckoo."

In the years 1802 and 1807, two grants, the one of £10,000, and the other of £20,000, were voted to him by the House of Commons.

The only son of Dr. Jenner,—Lieut. Col. Robert Fitzhardinge Jenner, of the Royal South Gloucestershire Militia, also a magistrate and Deputy-Lieutenant of the County, died at Berkeley, on the 16th of March, 1854; aged 56.

THE MISSES LEE, THE NOVELISTS.

In the parish church of Clifton, an elegant marble tablet has been erected to the memory of the authors of the well known works of fiction, "The Canterbury Tales," "The Recess," etc. It bears the following inscription :—

Sacred to the memory of
Two sisters,
Sophia Priscilla Lee and Harriet Lee,
Authors of the Canterbury Tales and other literary works.
Sophia Priscilla Lee, born May, 1750.
Died, March 13, 1824.
Harriet Lee, born, April 11, 1766.
Died, August 1, 1851.
The rest is in the hearts
Of those who knew and loved them.
The dust of each lies beneath.
"The spirit has returned
To Him who gave it."

O'BRIEN, THE GIANT.

PATRICK COTTER O'BRIEN, a well-known giant who resided for some time in this city, was a native of Kinsale in Ireland. He was eight feet three inches in height, very largely made altogether, and of very great strength. He died at Mardyke, Hotwell Road, on the 8th of September, 1816, in the 46th year of his age. His remains were interred in the Roman Catholic Chapel, in Trenchard Street.

At the sale of the effects of the late Captain George Bailey, of the Hotwells, which took place in March, 1854, a large arm chair was sold which was once the property of O'Brien, and the one in which he usually sat. Another relic of the giant was exhibited a few months since in the shop window of Mr. James, Bath Street, dealer in antiquities;—this was a well worn shoe of very large dimensions, which had evidently been in his use a very long time.

J. D. L.

[A tablet bearing the following inscription, is placed in the vestibule of the Catholic Chapel in Trenchard Street :—

Here lie
the remains of
Mr. Patrick Cotter O'Brien,
a native of Kinsale,
in the kingdom of Ireland.
He was a man of gigantic stature,
exceeding 8 feet 3 inches in height,
and proportionably large.
His manners were amiable and unoffending,
and the inflexible integrity of his conduct
through life,
united to the calm resignation
with which he awaited the approach of death,
proved that his principles
were strictly virtuous.
He died at the Hotwells
on the 8 of September, 1806,
in the 46th year of his age.
Requiescat in Pace.

O'Brien having a great horror of his body getting into the hands of the surgeons, gave directions for his funeral, so as to insure that his body should "rest in peace;" His coffin was lowered into a vault cut in the sandstone rock, and above it was placed upwards of a ton of iron bars, imbedded in cemented masonry. Whether the body was removed from the coffin immediately before the funeral; or whether the coffin with its unresisting inmate, was slid from beneath the mass above, through a tunnel into the cellar of the adjoining dwelling house, we cannot say, certain it is that a skeleton 8 feet, 3 inches in height, and stated to be that of O'Brien, is preserved in a niche in the museum of the Royal College of Surgeons.]

WINE STREET IN 1643.

On the 30th May, 1643, one George Boucher, merchant, was hanged, drawn, and quartered upon a gibbett against a tavern, called the Nagg's Head in Wine Street.

OLD NICK'S ENTRY.

"Old Nick's Entry," was the name of a passage, situated near the Steam Packet Tavern, and nearly opposite the Drawbridge, which led from the Quay into Marsh street. It was so called because one Nicholson there kept an alehouse, celebrated for "Bristol Home Brewed," for a long series of years. This entry remained till a few years since. When the Sedan Chair Tavern and houses adjacent were rebuilt, [1840] it was done away with.

J. D. L.

CURIOSITIES OF BRISTOL
AND ITS NEIGHBOURHOOD.

No. 10.   JUNE, 1854.   PRICE ONE PENNY.

THE MARTYRS OF THE TIME OF QUEEN MARY.

FEW people think when standing at the top of St. Michael's Hill, and looking at the tasteful and elegant chapel erected there, what dreadful scenes were witnessed on that spot in the years 1555, 1556, and 1557. In the time of Queen Mary, Bristol was not spared the pain of seeing five of her citizens brought to the stake for their religious opinions. Though the persecutions in the ensuing reign were very great in other parts of England, we do not find any instances recorded as having taken place in this city. The following extracts from various calendars refer to the martyrs of the time of Queen Mary :—

"1555. On the 17th of October, one William Shepton (or Shapton), a weaver, was burnt for religion."

"1556. This year two men, one a weaver, the other a cobbler, were burnt at St. Michael's Hill for religion; and a sheerman was burnt for denying the sacrament of the altar to be the very body and blood of Christ, really and substantially."

"1556. In this year two men suffered the fire for the profession of the Gospel of Jesus Christ in Bristoll. One was Edward Sharpe, an ancient man of threescore, a Wiltshire man born; and the other a young man, by trade a carpenter."

"Three men suffered here as martyrs :— 1st, Richard Sharpe, a weaver of Temple parish; who being examined by Dalby, the chauncellor, March 9th 1556, was by him persuaded to recant; of which he sorely and openly repented, and shortly after was brought to the flames. The 2nd, was Thomas Hale, who shook hands with the said Richard Sharpe at the fire, May 7th, 1557; he was a shoemaker. He was, by David Harris, alderman, and John Stone, one of the Common-council, caused to arise out of his bed, and committed to the watch, and by them charged to be conveyed to Newgate, and shortly after he suffered. The 3rd was Thomas Benion, who was burned, August 27th, 1556. More were questioned, but escaped."

Fox says that R. Sharpe and Hale were burnt in the same fire, fastened back to back to the stake.

Another calendar refers to the year 1558;

though we find it in the record under the year—

"1555. This Mr. John Griffiths, (one of the sheriffs) was a very forward man in apprehending the martyrs; and with David Harris, and Dalby, the Chancellor, deserve to be enrolled. Three suffered in Bristoll, and more had done, had not Queen Elizabeth's coming to the crown hindered; which brought back again from banishment Mr. Pacy and Mr. Huntingdon, two preachers of this city. The said Mr. Huntingdon, after his return, preaching at the Cross in the Colledge-green, charged those men there present with ill-using both those that suffered, and those that escaped, in these or like words :—

"Oh, cruelty without mercy! that a man should act so laboriously that, which without repentance, shall hasten his damnation! know ye not who made the strict search for Mr. Pacy? whom if God had not hid, as Jeremiah, you had burned stump and all," he being lame, "yet you had no pity. And who you know, went to Redland to buy green wood for the execution of those blessed saints that suffered; when near home at the Back or the Key, he might have had dry. Take heed: a little sorrow will not serve—God may cast you into unquenchable fire, worse than the soultering of green wood."

It was with great pleasure that we saw, a few years since, a monument erected in Highbury Chapel to the memory of the five noble men who perished in the flames, rather than renounce their religious views. It is a simple marble monument, and bears the following inscription :—

In memory
of the undersigned
Martyrs,

who, during the reign of Queen Mary, for the avowal of their Christian faith, were burnt to death on the ground upon which this chapel is erected.

William Shapton, suffered Oct. 17, 1555.	Richard Sharpe, May 17, 1557.
Edward Sharp, September 8, 1556.	Thomas Hale, May 17, 1557.

Thomas Banion, August 17, 1557.

"Be not afraid of them that kill the body, and after that have no more that they can do."

This spot was afterwards chosen as the place of public execution in Bristol, and so continued until the new drop was erected in front of the gaol on the new cut.

THE TOLZEY COURT.

A VERY interesting account of this ancient court, drawn up by the late Arthur Palmer, Esq., for many years Prothonotary of the Court, has been kindly placed in our hands by J. M. Gutch, Esq., F. S. A., of Worcester, for many years a well known and much respected resident in this city.

We extract from it the following paragraphs :—

"The Court of the Tolzey, or the Tolzey Court, of the city of Bristol, is a most ancient Court of Record, by prescription, which has existed time immemorial, and, as understood traditionally, in the time of the Saxons. It is held in the Guildhall, before the two bailiffs, who are, in later ages, also the sheriffs of the city for the time being ; and the Court sits every Monday throughout the year. This Court existed long prior to the creation of a sheriff of Bristol, which was not till the year 1372, by charter, 47 Edward III.

"The hundred, or bailiwick of Bristol, was in former times part of the honour of Gloucester, and having been held by some of the great Barons, as tenants in capite, it became again the property of the crown, by union of possession, in the reign of King John, who had been possessed of it when Earl of Morton. John, when Earl of Morton, married Avisa, the daughter and heiress of William Earl of Gloucester, who was possessed of the honour of Gloucester, and thereupon the honour became vested in the crown. Bristol was, no doubt, originally, like other bailiwicks, under the administration of the lord's bailiff.

"When the castle of Bristol became a royal residence, the appendages and appointments of a regal palace became of course annexed to it ; and accordingly mention is made in the charters, and other authentic documents, of the King's marshal, constable of the castle, seneschal,* or steward of the household, who was judge of the Palace Court, justices of the forest of Kingswood, &c. When this establishment took place, the Old Court of the hundred became united to the Palace Court, in which the King's seneschal was assisted by the bailiff.

"The Court was held at the Tolzey, or place where the King's tolls and duties were collected ; and it was called the Court of the Tolzey, or Tolzey Court.†

* A judicial officer ; Co. Lit. 61 ; Croke's Jurisdic. 102 ; Kitch. 83.

† Tollsed, Tolsey, from the Saxon word " Toll," i.e. Tributum, Tollsend, Geld, Yeld, Zeld, denotes a payment, as to yield is to pay ; hence the Tollseld, or as it was afterwards written Tolsey, signified at first the payment of Toll, and the place or house where such payment was made.

"The steward of this Court being the seneschal of the castle of Bristol, held his appointment immediately from the Crown.— The privileges and authority of the Court have always been saved and kept distinct from those granted by charters to the corporation of the city ; and the sheriffs sit with the steward, not as sheriffs of the county of Bristol, but as bailiffs of the hundred ; for as sheriffs they have no authority as to this Court under the charters, as the King's court of the Tolzey was long antecedent to, and is independently of, all charters ; and, as above-stated, existed for ages prior to the creation of sheriffs of Bristol.

"In this Court of Tolzey, all actions of debt, assumpsit, covenant, trespass, trover, and other civil actions, to an unlimited amount, in cases where the cause of action arises within the city, may be prosecuted by action, or by foreign attachment, where, in the latter process, the ground of action is for debt,—and it also holds pleas of ejectment. And its jurisdiction extends to the whole of the county of the city, on land and by water, and down to the Flat and Steep Holmes, below Kingroad, where the Severn ends ; which Holmes are thirty miles below the city ; and law process is executed on the water down to the Holmes.

"The sheriffs of the city, but in character of bailiffs, (the two offices being united in the same persons ever since the creation of two sheriffs by the charter of 15 Henry VII.) preside in the Court, and are judges. All process is tested in their names, and one of them must be present at every sitting Court, which is held on every Monday throughout the year, and oftener if occasion require. They are assisted by a steward who is a barrister, and who tries all causes, by jury, in the presence of the sheriffs, or one of them. There are also a prothonotary and four sergeants at mace, who execute all process issued by the Court. The steward is appointed by the common council of the city, by charter, 9 Anne, 1710. The prothonotary is by usage appointed by the steward.

"Prior to the charter 47th Edward III. (1373,) that part of Bristol, which lies on the Somersetshire side of the river Avon, was in the county of Somerset ; and that part of the town which stands on the Gloucestershire side of the river, was in the county of Gloucester. The charter 47th Edw. III. separated the town of Bristol, with its suburbs and precincts, in all respects from the counties of Gloucester and Somerset, both by land and by water, and declared it to be a county by itself, by the name of " The County of Bristol," and appointed one sheriff. By a subsequent charter two sheriffs were appointed. The town was afterwards made a city, and county of the city of Bristol, by charter 34th Henry VIII. in the year 1543.

"Upon the creation of two sheriffs, by the charter of Henry VII. the persons who were chosen bailiffs were also thenceforth to be sheriffs ; and the office of sheriffs being superior in name and dignity to the office of bailiffs, the Tolzey Court has ever since been more commonly called the Sheriff's Court, though this is improper, as the ancient as well as modern, and continuing name in all the records and proceedings, is, "The Tolzey Court." The real Sheriffs' Court is the county court of the sheriffs, in their official character, as sheriffs of the county of the city of Bristol; the well known county court incident to the office of all sheriffs of counties; and Bristol is a county of itself.

"In the charter of Edward III. the antiquity of the Tolzey Court is shown; for after giving power to the mayor and sheriffs to have cognizance of all pleas, and also of assizes of novel disseizen, and mort d'auncestre, and of all trespasses, covenants, &c., such cognizance to be holden in the Guildhall, in the said city, there is the following saving clause :—

"Salvo semper quod placita, quæ in curia nostra in dicta villa Bristol *vocata Tollsed coram senescallo* et aliis ministris nostris ibidem teneri, consuevere in eadem curia coram senescallo et aliis ministris nostris et hæredum nostrorum ibidem de cetero teneantur ; nobisque et hæredibus nostris de proficuis inde provenientibus per ministros ipsos aut alios qui eadem proficua nostro et hæredum nostrorum nomine perceperint, prout justum fuerit et antea fieri consuevit respondeatur."

The still more ancient Court of Pie Poudre (which is said to have been instituted by Alfred the Great) is a branch of the Tolzey Court. The office of Prothonotary, or Registrar, of each, is at present filled by Henry A. Palmer, Esq. We must defer a notice of the Pie Poudre Court to a future number.

THE RECORDERS OF BRISTOL.

(Concluded.)

1763 : Hon. Daines Barrington, third son of John Shute, first Viscount Barrington. He was a King's Council, and also held the office of second justice of Chester. He was the author of "Observations on the Statutes" and some papers contributed to the Royal Society, and the Society of Antiquaries. He died in 1800.

1766 : Dunning, Lord Ashburton. He was born at Ashburton, October 18, 1731 ; and attained in early life a very high rank in his profession. In 1768 he was made Solicitor General ; in the same year he was made M.P. for Calne. He resigned the Solicitor-Generalship in 1770. On the 8th April, 1782, he was raised to the peerage as Baron Ashburton ; and on the 13th of the same month was made Chancellor of the Duchy of Lancaster. He married in 1780, Elizabeth, the daughter of John Baring, Esq., by whom he had two sons, John, who

died young ; and Richard Barre, who succeeded his father as Lord Ashburton, he died without issue in 1823, and the title became extinct. Lord Ashburton died 1783.

1783 : Richard Burke, a brother of the celebrated Edmund Burke, and a man of considerable ability. He was one of the Secretaries to the Treasury in 1783. He died February 4, 1794 ; and is immortalized by Goldsmith in his poem entitled "Retaliation."

1794 : Sir Vicary Gibbs ; so frequently called "Vinegar Gibbs" on account of his severity. In 1795 he was Solicitor-General to the Prince of Wales, and was knighted in 1805. In 1807, M.P. for Cambridge, and Attorney-General. In 1812, a Justice of the Court of Common Pleas. In 1813, Lord Chief Baron ; and the following year Chief Justice of the Court of Common Pleas, which office he resigned in 1818.

1818 : Sir Robert Gifford, afterwards Lord Gifford. He was born in 1779. Was appointed Solicitor-General 1817; Attorney-General 1819 ; Chief Justice of the Court of Common Pleas 1824. He was created a Peer in the same year by the title of Baron Gifford. He resigned the Chief Justiceship, and received the appointment of Master of the Rolls, also in 1824. He died September 4, 1826.

1826 : Sir John Singleton Copley, afterwards Lord Lyndhurst, was born May 21, 1772. He is the son of the late John Singleton Copley, R.A., the eminent painter of the well known picture in the National Gallery, "The Death of Chatham," and other works. Lord Lyndhurst was made Solicitor-General 1819 ; Attorney-General 1824 ; Master of the Rolls 1826 ; and on the retirement of Lord Eldon, in the following year, Lord Chancellor, when he was raised to the Peerage as Baron Lyndhurst. He resigned the Great Seal in 1830, and in the following year was made Lord Chief Baron. In 1834 he was again Lord Chancellor ; and filled the office a third time in 1841. He finally resigned it in 1846.

1827 : Sir Charles Wetherell who will always be remembered in this city for his intimate connection with the riots of 1831. He was the third son of Dr. Nathan Wetherell, Dean of Hereford, who was a friend of Dr. Johnson. In 1816 he was made a K. C. and a bencher of the Inner Temple. In 1825 he filled the office of Treasurer of the Temple. From 1820 to to 1826 he was M.P. for Oxford, and in 1830 and 1832 for Boroughbridge. On 31st January, 1824, he was made Solicitor-General, and was knighted. In September, 1826, he was made Attorney-General—he resigned the office in the following April. In February, 1828, he was again Attorney-General and held the appointment until June, 1829, when he finally relinquished it. Sir Charles married, in 1826, his cousin, Jane Sarah Elizabeth, second daughter of Sir Alexander Croke; she died April 21, 1831. He subsequently, in 1838, married Harriet Elizabeth, second daughter of Col. Warneford, who survived him. Sir Charles's death was caused by the fright occasioned by the upsetting of a vehicle in which he was travelling, near Maidstone. He was removed to Preston Hall, the residence of C. Milner, Esq., where he expired a few days afterwards, on the 17th August, 1846.

1846: Sir Richard Budden Crowder, Q. C.; Counsel to the Admiralty, and M.P. for Liskeard from 1849 to 1854, when upon the sudden and deeply lamented death of Sir Thomas Noon Talfourd, he was raised to the Bench as a puisne Justice of the Court of Common Pleas. He was knighted on the 3rd May, 1854.

1854: Sir Alexander James Edmund Cockburn, Q. C., M.P. for Southampton. Solicitor General from July, 1850, until March, 1851, when he was made Attorney-General; he held the latter office until the change of ministry in February, 1852. In December of the same year, when the Aberdeen Administration came into office, he was again appointed Attorney-General. Sir Alexander is the son of the late Alexander Cockburn, Esq., Ambassador to the Hanse Towns, Lower Saxony, Wurtemberg, and Columbia. He is nephew to the last two possessors of the baronetcy which was granted to a member of this ancient family in 1627. He is also nephew to the present baronet, Sir William Cockburn, Dean of York; and is presumptive heir to the title.

THE MURDER OF MRS. RUSCOMBE AND HER MAID.

The following account of a murder perpetrated in this city in 1764, and marked by features of peculiar atrocity as well as mystery, was drawn up by the late Richard Smith, Esq., a gentleman who took much trouble and interest in collecting and preserving accounts of such occurrences, and of other matters connected with the history of Bristol.—It has been forwarded to us by J. D. L., who mentions that a branch of the family of the unfortunate Mrs. Ruscombe has long been settled at Bridgewater. One of the family filled the office of Mayor of that town, about twelve or fourteen years ago.

MURDER OF MRS. FRANCES RUSCOMBE AND HER MAID, IN COLLEGE GREEN, A.D., 1764.

The above "barbarous, bloody, cruel, and inhuman murder," is not forgotten to this day. Our grandfathers and grandmothers handed it down to their children as a wonderment, and from them it has reached the present inhabitants of Bristol; in fact there is scarcely a family which can reckon back

two generations, where the occurrence is unknown: even Barrett thought it an event worthy of mention in his History of Bristol, nevertheless there has not, I believe, been any continuous record, so that the oft-told tale has been obscured and mutilated by tradition, through a lapse of 78 years in such a manner, that I am induced to leave a correct memorandum relating to the occurrence, for the benefit of the future, and perhaps yet unborn, historiographers of Brightstowe. On the 28th of September, 1764, the dwelling house of a Mrs. Frances Ruscombe was entered by some person or persons, between the hours of ten in the forenoon and one. At the first period, all was well, and at the latter, a relative went to the house with the intention of taking her dinner there. Finding the door upon the latch, she opened it, and was horror-struck at the spectacle. Upon the stairs, close to the door, lay the body of Mrs. Ruscombe, her throat was dreadfully cut, there was a large wound in the mouth, one of her eyes was beaten out, and upon her head was an injury inflicted with such violence (it was thought by a hammer), that the skull was shattered and driven in upon the brain. In the back parlour was the body of Mary Champness, alias Sweet, with her head nearly severed from the trunk, her lower jaw broken, a heavy blow had been inflicted upon her forehead, and her skull cleaved as with a wedge or hatchet. The bodies were quite warm, and all the windows and back entrances were secure, so that the murderer must have gone quietly out at the front street door after this horrible butchery. The bloody footsteps were traced to a closet in the old lady's bedchamber, but they were not sufficiently distinct to ascertain the important fact, whether one person only, or more had perpetrated the crime. A portmanteau box had been forced, and from it had been taken fifty-seven guineas, tied up in a bag, and also a purse containing seven thirty-six shilling gold pieces, and twenty-one guineas: this was ascertained by a memorandum of the deposit in the writing of the deceased, thrown out and scattered upon the floor, with letters and other papers. The sensation produced in Bristol may be readily conceived, and the crowds of people who went to see "the sight," were incessant. These we shall leave to the discretion of Mr. John Wraxall, the coroner, and his jury, whilst we take a look at the locality of the murders. It happens that we have an engraving upon a sheet, nineteen inches, by fifteen wide, so that here we are quite at home. This engraving is headed,— "The North-west view of Bristol High Cross, with a prospect of the Cathedral and the parish Church of St. Augustine." The drawing is by R. West, and the engraving by W. H. Toms; there is no date, but the probability is, that it was published about 1737. The Cross, is a copy of Buck's picture, drawn 30 years before, but the rest. I should consider to be original, and no doubt correct. In those days there were six straggling irregular houses between the Church and Cathedral. At about where No. 2 or 3 now stands, was the dwelling house of Mr. Jarret Smith, an attorney, who to reconcile Captain Goodere and Sir J. Dinely, his brother, invited them to dine together on the day of "*that*" murder; being in sight of the White Hart Public-house, now No. 41. The house of Mrs. Ruscombe, which was a low pointed structure, with two slopes of common tiles, occupied the site of the present end house, of the now No. 7. Here I lived during 1803-4-5; and I must say that neither the ghosts of the murderer, or murdered, ever gave me the least trouble whatsoever; nor did I ever hear that they molested Mr. Frank Gold, apothecary; or Mr. Hanson, the surgeon; or the Rev. Mr. Millner, my successors. In the engraving there seems to be a wall running between the Cathedral and the house which was probably cleared away to make the access of Trinity Street. The following is a copy of a handbill which has reached me :— " Bristol, October 2nd, 1764.—If the woman that called early Thursday morning last, at the house of Mr. Thompson, in College Green, and asked the servant if she was not to wash there, and was answered in the negative, and was seen to go into the court of the house of the late Mrs. Ruscombe, adjoining, will call upon Mr. John Lambert, attorney, at Foster's coffee-house, and inform him who she saw and spoke to, at the said Mrs. Ruscombe's, or any other particulars which by that means may have come to her knowledge, she shall be amply rewarded for her trouble, by the said I. Lambert. Printed by E. Ward, adjoining the Council-house, in Corn Street." It may be well just to inform the reader, that Mr. Lambert was the master of the talented, but unhappy Chatterton, and Foster's coffee-house was next door to the present Council-house. In Felix Farley's Journal, published three days after the occurrence, there is a paragraph respecting the murder, and also an advertisement from "Elizabeth and Sarah Jefferies, relatives of the deceased," offering upon the usual terms and exceptions, 50 guineas for discovery. To this the Rt. Hon. Robert Nugent added £100, and James Ruscombe, the husband of the deceased, £10. His Majesty likewise, was graciously pleased to grant a conditional pardon to any but the actual murderer; neither was this all; for Mr. Elton, the town-clerk, promised in the name of his worship, Henry Swymmer, and the aldermen, another £100. Here there were impunity and £262, for a confederate : a bait quite tempting enough to induce a companion to peach and hang a comrade, yet as Macbeth expresses it, "the deed" seems to have "trammelled up the consequences." The officers of justice were, however, every where upon the alert. "*Felix*" announces the next week, "that several persons had been charged."

Amongst the persons so apprehended, were two sailors who had been recently in Newgate; they were traced to Hungerford, and thence brought to this city. It was known that they were two infamous scoundrels, but the blood of Mrs. Ruscombe was not upon their hands. Search was upon the rack on all sides, in the hope of fathoming this strange and mysterious affair, but all was darkness.

(To be Continued.)

REMARKS ON DRUIDICAL REMAINS IN THE NEIGHBOURHOOD OF BRISTOL, THEIR ORIGIN, AND THE PURPOSE OF THEIR ERECTION.
BY GEORGE PRYCE.
(Concluded from Page 59.)

It has been previously remarked that Baal or Molech, were names synonymous, both meaning the Sun, as the prime object of idolatrous worship throughout the ancient world, and that consecrated fires blazed to his honour from the earliest antiquity. Repeated mention is made of both these idols in Scripture. The prophet Jeremiah referring to the rites performed by the Israelites on the east of Jerusalem says, "They (the Jews) built the high places of Baal, which are in the valley of the son of Hinnom, and cause their sons and their daughters to pass through the fire unto Molech." The coincidence between the practice of the Israelites in thus exposing their children to the fire in honor of Baal, and that of the ancient Britons, is very striking, for Quintus Cicero, one of Cæsar's confidential officers in Gaul, writing to his brother Marcus Tullius, the Roman Orator, says, "The time when the Sun enters Cancer, is the great festival of the god (Baal); and on all high mountains and eminences of the country, they (the Britons) light fires at the approach of that day, and make their *wives*, their *children*, and their *cattle*, to *pass through the fire*, or to present themselves before the fire, in honor of the deity. Deep and profound is the silence of the multitude during the ceremony, until the appearance of the sun above the horizon, when with loud and continued exclamations and songs of joy, they hail the utmost exaltation of that luminary, as the supreme triumph of the symbol of the god of their adoration."

The fires thus kindled in honor of Baal were supposed to confer a sanctity upon those who passed through them; and it is not a little remarkable that the practice should have descended even to modern times; for so late as the year 1826, a wealthy old farmer residing a few miles from Perth, in Scotland, having lost several of his cattle by some disease then prevalent, and being able to account for it in no way so rationally as by witchcraft, had recourse to the following remedy, recommended to him by a weird sister in his neighbourhood, as an effectual protection from the attacks of the foul fiend. A few stones were piled together in the barn-yard, and wood and other fuel having been laid thereon, it was ignited by will-fire, that is, fire obtained by friction. The neighbours being called in to witness the solemnity, the cattle were made to pass through the flames, in the order of their dignity and age, commencing with the horses and ending with the swine. The ceremony having been duly and decorously gone through, a neighbouring farmer observed to the enlightened owner of the herd, that *he*, along with *his family*, ought to have followed the example of the cattle, and " the *sacrifice to Baal* would have been complete !"

Circles of stone were sometimes, but not necessarily so, situated amidst the seclusion of embowering forests of oak trees. In these recesses the Brahmin temple of Asia, and the Druid structures of Europe were always to be found—a fact which forms another decided feature of affinity in the religion of Britain, and that of eastern nations, and is an additional evidence of the Asiatic descent of both. The oak was an object of profound veneration at a very early period, for we read that before the time of Abraham, covenants, solemn and binding, were made beneath their consecrated shadow. That patriarch himself " passed through the land of the place of Sichem, and to the *oak-grove* of Moreh, where the Lord appeared unto him, and where he built an *altar* unto the Lord." This was evidently the prototype of the sacred groves of succeeding ages, and in every quarter of the globe. In process of time, groves were *planted* and hallowed to purposes of the basest superstition ; and we find that Manasseh " reared up altars for Baal (the Sun), and made a grove ;" or, as Dr. Adam Clarke translates this passage, he " made Asherah, the Babylonian *Melitta* or *Roman Venus*, and worshipped all the host of heaven and served them."—" Asherah," says this learned commentator, " which we translate *grove* means a *tree*, which was worshipped by the gentiles (of the East), like as the oak was worshipped by the ancient Druids of Britain."

Within the hallowed bounds of the consecrated grove, the impious oblation was offered by the priests of these islands to the false gods of Phœnicia. The deep shade of these sylvan retreats, their solemn stillness, and profound solitude, inspired the contemplative mind with a kind of holy horror. Here the most awful rites of the religion of the Druids were celebrated, the bare recital of which makes one shudder. The impressive relation given by Lucan of those performed in the Massilian grove of Gaul, is sufficient to convey an idea of the sanguinary deeds which abounded in these secluded retreats. " It was gloomy, damp, and scarcely penetrable ; a grove in which no sylvan deity ever resided, no bird ever sang, no beast ever slumbered, no gentle zephyr ever played, nor even the lightning could rend a passage. It was a

place of blood and horror, abounding with altars reeking with the gore of human victims, by which all the trunks of the lofty and majestic oaks which composed it, were crimsoned, dyed with blood, and foul with putrefaction. No soul ever entered the forlorn abode except the priest, who went thither to celebrate the horrible mysteries of this tremendous species of superstition, which revelled in savage ferocity of soul, and boundless lust of sacrificial blood."—" The pen of History," says Maurice, " trembles to relate the baleful orgies, which their frantic superstition celebrated in these gloomy recesses ; and, however incredible the imputation, it is not without reason, suspected that they sometimes proceeded to even more criminal lengths, than immolating human victims, by finishing their horrid sacrifice with a still more horrid banquet !" Such was the religion of the Druids, and to such guilty excesses did its rites compel its votaries. Happily for Britain, civilization and a purer faith have swept the barbarous customs and sanguinary rites of heathen times from her soil, and her sons are taught to value the free institutions of a religion which brings peace on earth and goodwill towards men, instead of demanding the immolation of our fellows as a sacrifice to imaginary deities.

At Druid's Stoke near this city, in a field on the road to Shirehampton, is a large stone and three smaller ones, evidently Druidical ; others are found at Wick and Abson, Gloucestershire, but as the remarks already offered are considered sufficient for popular reading, further description of them is regarded as unnecessary. Their origin, with that of all such erections, may with certainty be traced to a remote antiquity, when the adventurous Phœnicians traded with the rude untutored native of these islands ; and those primæval navigators visited the shores of Britain to bear away its products to that great mart of nations—ancient Tyre. But where now are the cities and peoples with whom this island of the sea was once associated in the idolatries of Druidism ? Tyre is emphatically " the top of a rock, a place for fishers to spread their nets upon." Babylon is " a possession for the bittern and pools of water ;" and India sits tributary at our feet ! The glory has long departed from their once populous shores, and the busy hum of commerce no more awakens the energies of the enterprising mariner as of old. Dimmed by the mists which float in the low atmosphere of human folly, they sought to perpetuate the mysteries of a dark idolatry ; whilst Britain, no longer the idolater, spreads truth and liberty throughout every portion of the civilized world. In power and strength ; in wealth, resources, and industry ; in arts and sciences ; in commerce and agriculture, she is the greatest empire that ever existed upon earth ; and in knowledge, moral character and worth, she far surpasses all that ancient and modern history can boast of! Her empire is yet to be extended, but not by conquest, nor is the power towards which she is advancing to be steeped in blood. Her destiny is to promote happiness and peace; and it is by making savage man familiar with the blessings which the utmost reach of mind has discovered ; by helping youthful nations into maturity ; by introducing comforts into uncultivated regions ; and by extending the pale of social intercourse, that the wisest, the most moral, and the freest of nations is to fill up the career which is now before her. If she makes distant shores resound with her great artillery, she blesses them with the produce of her still greater engines of peace ; and her triumphs shall be illuminated, not by flaming cities, but by the nightly blaze which issues from her mighty fabrics of prosperity and happiness.

(*Conclusion.*)

RELIGIOUS HOUSES OF BRISTOL, FOUNDED
BEFORE THE REFORMATION.

IV. HOSPITALS AND ELEEMOSYNARY HOUSES.

THE GAUNTS. The Church of the Hospital is now the Mayor's Chapel. In a house at the corner of Pipe Lane, is a niche and the fragment of a winged lion sadly mutilated, which marks the boundary wall of the hospital in that direction.

ST. BARTHOLOMEW, situated in Christmas Street. Founded early in the 13th century. Some remains are yet to be seen in Christmas Street; the entrance gateway is a very interesting specimen of early English architecture.

ST. CATHERINE, Brightbow, Bedminster. Founded in the 13th century. Nothing remains as ancient as that period, but some late Perpendicular English windows, and part of a doorway, are left in a very dilapidated condition in a mean house.

ST. MARY MAGDALEN, situated between Redcliffe Church and the Hospital of St. Catherine, Brightbow.

ST. LAURENCE. A Hospital for Lepers, in the parish of St. Philip. Founded ante 1223.

WEAVERS' HOSPITAL, Temple Street. Some Perpendicular English remains are left under the Weavers' Hall.

TRINITY OR BARSTAPLE'S HOSPITAL, stands on the right hand side, at the top of the Old Market, and was founded by John Barstaple ; the almshouse on the opposite side of the street, is said to have been founded by his wife Isabella. He died 1411. His wife in 1404. The hospital has been rebuilt since his time, and the only ancient remains, are the brasses in memory of the founder and his wife, bearing short Latin inscriptions.

BURTON'S ALMSHOUSE, Long Row.

TRINITY OR SPENCER'S ALMSHOUSE, Lewin's Mead, Founded 1493. It is now rapidly falling to decay. Notwithstanding its great dilapidation, it is a very picturesque looking building.

RICHARD SPICER'S HOSPITAL, Back Hall. The Chapel in it founded by Thomas Knappe. Some considerable portions remain.

JOHN SPICER'S HOSPITAL, Temple Street. Mentioned under date of 1393 by Evans, who says the "site is now marked by the Swan public-house, etc."

ST. JOHN THE BAPTIST'S HOSPITAL, Redcliffe Pit.

ST. JOHN'S OR STRANGE'S HOSPITAL, St. John's Steps. Founded by Robert Strange, 1489.

FOSTER'S ALMSHOUSE, top of Christmas steps. Founded by John Foster, in 1504, who was Mayor in 1481. To it is attached the Chapel dedicated to the Three Kings of Cologne.

RICHARD FOSTER'S ALMSHOUSE, near Redcliffe Gate.

TUCKER'S HOSPITAL, Temple Street.

CANYNGES' ALMSHOUSE, Redcliffe Hill.

Notes on Streets.

The ground now styled Great Garden, in the parish of Temple, was in ancient times called The Military Garden. When the Castle was in existence, the soldiers who were quartered here used this part as a place for military exercises. In a room adjoining the garden a council of war was held during the siege of Bristol, when the members of it were urged by Fiennes to surrender the city to Prince Rupert.

In the year 1635 the following discourse was printed :—" Bristol's Military Garden: a Sermon, preached unto the worthy company of Practisers in the Military Garden of the well-governed City of Bristol, by Thomas Palmer, Master of Arts and Vicar of St. Thomas and St. Mary Redcliffe, in the same City. London : Imprinted by Felix Kyngston."—4to.

CURIOUS INSCRIPTION.

The following inscription, in memory of a country blacksmith, is copied from a tomb in Cambridge churchyard, Gloucestershire :

My sledge and anvil is declined,
My bellows pipe has lost its wind,
My fire is quench'd, my forge decay'd,
And in the dust my *vice* is laid ;
My coal is spent, my fire is gone,
My nails are driven, my work is done!"

TRELAWNEY, BISHOP OF BRISTOL.

SIR JONATHAN TRELAWNEY, Bart., Bishop of Bristol, 1685; of Exeter, after the Revolution, 1688; and lastly of Winchester, 1707, was one of the seven bishops committed to the Tower by James II. for protesting against the declaration that the king ordered to be read in every church in England.

The following letter was addressed by Trelawney to Hyde, Earl of Rochester, soliciting promotion. It is a good specimen of the manner in which that kind of epistolatory correspondence was carried on.

"*The Rev. Jonathan Trelawney, to Lawrence Hyde, Earl of Rochester.*"

"My lord,

"Give me leave to throw myself at your lordship's feet, humbly imploring your patronage if not for the bishopric of Peterborough, at least for Chichester, if the bishop of Exeter cannot be prevailed on to accept that now vacant see. Let me beseech your lordship to fix him there, and advance your creature *(meaning himself)* to Exeter, where I can serve the king (James II.) and your lordship. My estate must break to pieces if I find no better prop than the income of Bristol, not greater than 300*l.* If Peterborough and Chichester shall be both refused me, I shall not deny Bristol. But I hope the king (James II.) will have some tender compassion on *his slave.*

"July 10, 1685.   "J. TRELAWNEY."

A very spirited ballad, with the chorus— "And shall Trelawney die for this?" etc., composed in reference to the arrest of the Bishop, is no doubt familiar to many of our readers. The original verses sung in the western counties at the time of the Revolution are lost, with the exception of the burden, upon which the Rev. R. S. Hawker, of Morwenstow, Cornwall, has founded the very excellent stanzas to which we have adverted.

So generally was this ballad sung at that turbulent period, and so great was the enthusiasm it occasioned, that Mr. Macaulay has deemed the circumstance and the ballad worthy of mention in his "History of England."

Sir Jonathan Trelawney died while Bishop of Winchester, in the 1721.

A PAINTING IN THE DUKE OF YORK INN.

ON a panel over the fire place in a room in the Duke of York Inn, Thomas street, there is a painting of a musical party very much in the manner of some of Hogarth's works. It was until lately too dirty to be at all distinctly seen; the landlord has very properly had it cleaned, and it is now worth looking at. We heard it stated some time since that when Hogarth was here he had got into debt with a former proprietor of the inn, and not being quite able to pay it, he painted this picture, in lieu of discharging the debt in money. This we believe however to be but a tale; and we should be glad if any of our readers could throw any light on the subject.

It has also been attributed to Simmons the celebrated Bristol sign-painter.

ERRATA.

P. 53, col. 1, line 7; for 1723, read 1793.
P. 68, col. 2, line 17; for 1840 read 1850.

CURIOSITIES OF BRISTOL

AND ITS NEIGHBOURHOOD.

No. 11.   JULY, 1854.   PRICE ONE PENNY.

THE MURDER OF MRS. RUSCOMBE AND HER MAID.

(Concluded from p. 73.)

On the 20th of October, a great hue and cry were raised after a publican, who had disappeared on the day of the murder. A Post Boy swore that the party hired a chaise at Bedminster, and directed him to avoid the high road, and to "drive him on the bye lanes;" this certainly wore the look of escaping publicity. He was traced to Plymouth, and there apprehended. He did not deny the alleged fact, but his absconding was unconnected with the murder. This was followed on the 27th, by the apprehension of a man who passed for a sweetheart of the servant's. It was deposed that he had a great quarrel a few days before with the girl, and did not deny that he had threatened her with vengeance, but he proved an *alibi*. His employer and others swore, that during the whole time in question he was at work in a garden on Stony hill. Early in November, upon the evidence of a female, a tinker and his trull were apprehended at Gloucester: the latter gave some notices which dovetailed with the previous information. The first informant declared that a tinker was in the habit of coming to Mrs. Ruscombe's, where she had seen him. In order to try her, the tinker was disguised and placed with several prisoners in the yard, but the girl instantly singled him out. The man denied ever having been near Mrs. Ruscombe's, and declared that he did not know even where College Green was. The girl, however, swore so steadily to the fact, that the party was ordered to Bridewell, and a messenger was despatched to Speenhamland to search his lodgings. "*Felix Farley*" next week, says:—"Hucklebridge the Sheriffs' Officer, is returned with a package for the tinker, Kemp, who it appears, had purchased some silver buttons just after the murder, and had paid for them with two 36 shilling gold pieces. This was decisive and poor *Rattchin* was settled in durance vile, under the safeguard and tender mercies of the keeper, James Welsh. The reader has no doubt seen, "The Beggars' Opera," by Gay, and may perhaps remember that Macheath complains when in *quod* that "the charges here are so abominable, extortionate, and endless, that a gentleman is soon reduced to his last guinea." So it was with the tinker; his buttons, one after another slipped away, so that he became buttonless, which was to

him synonymous with pennyless. On the 10th of November, the same newspaper announces "a valuable snuff-box embossed with the story of 'the judgment of Paris,' was amongst the missing valuables, and calls upon pawnbrokers and others to stop it." Nothing new occured until the 27th of April, 1765, when a woman was apprehended who had been already twice tried : first for the murder of a turnpike man, and then for the destruction of her infant child ; as appears by a letter from Sir John Fielding, of the London Police. It did not, however, appear that she was concerned in this horrible affair, and she was discharged. But the unhappy purchaser of the silver buttons was still in close custody, and I have a word to say respecting these said curiosities, which will probably be new to the reader. Know, then, that at this period, the beaux of the day had adopted the strange fashion of converting sixpences, shillings, halfcrowns, and crowns into waistcoat and coat buttons; a silver shank being soldered to the centre of the coin. Of this metamorphosed money, one crown piece was bought by the father of my departed friend, Rd. Rowland, of "*honourable mention*," heretofore. This had been converted into the bowl of a punch ladle, by hammering, the shank being left untouched in the middle to mark its identity ; this Mr. Rowland showed to me just before his death, and it is now in his family as an heir loom. One more victim of suspicion must be added to the list : this was the nephew of the deceased. That he was a profligate, dissipated young man, was not denied ; but he was upon good terms with his aunt, and often visited her. A person, however, deposed that upon the morning of the murder, the nephew was seen near the house, that he was observed to walk the deck of his vessel (for he was a sailor), in a state of great agitation, and that he had changed his clothes. He was apprehended ; but after a strict examination and overhauling of his lockers he was released ; many however, continued to think that he had been the culprit, and he was avoided. It preyed upon his spirits; he became ill,—in fact, his end was fast approaching, he then sent for my uncle, the Rev. Alexander Catcott, vicar of Temple, who took with him the Rev. Dr. Casford, vicar of St. Augustine's, they questioned him closely, but he so solemnly denied all knowledge of, or participation in the crime, that they administered the sacrament to him. The circumstance of clergymen being sent for by him, excited so much curiosity, that they were obliged to publish, in a pamphlet, conjointly, "An Account of the Last Moments of Peaceable Robert Matthews, with a declaration that they both believe the man to have been perfectly innocent." Inquiry had by this time exhausted itself, and the rest was left to chance and time.

Such are the particulars of a murder perpetrated in open day, whilst the people in numbers were passing and repassing the door behind which were the bodies, and that within a few yards of the cathedral and during divine service; and yet, from that moment even to this, the whole matter was, and is involved in total darkness, and so will now probably remain to the Day of Judgment.

Richard Smith, surgeon.
Bristol, Feb. 19th, 1842.

OLD HOUSES.

THE interesting and very picturesque old dwelling-houses in this city are so rapidly disappearing altogether, or yielding to modern improvements, that our readers may be glad to know where those best worthy inspection may be seen. While we are writing, the old Bush Tavern, opposite the Exchange, is hourly disappearing, and in a few days nothing will be left of that well-known house, in front of which such serious disturbances used to take place at the elections of members of Parliament; and from the balcony of which, Edmund Burke delivered his noble speeches to the electors of Bristol. Another house, known to every one, we suppose, in this city,—the Castle-Bank,—until June 5 the banking-house of the Messrs. Stuckey and Co., will we believe be shortly doomed to destruction. This house is one of the three houses which were constructed in Holland, brought over in pieces, and erected here. One of the most curious houses in Bristol is to be seen in Steep Street, it quite hangs over part of the street. A few paces below is Host Street, which contains many most picturesque houses—the exteriors mostly in very good condition. The other streets which are enriched with several houses together—many very interesting on account of their peculiar construction,—are High-Street, Mary-le-port-Street, Wine-Street, the Pithay, Lewin's-Mead, Horse-Fair, Silver-Street, Castle-Street, the Weir, Broad-Street, Small-Street, Thomas-Street, Temple-Street, &c. The White Lion Inn, Thomas-Street, has a gallery running along the side, with doors opening on it from the rooms of the Inn. Single houses that should be seen by lovers of old specimens of domestic architecture, are the Fourteen Stars Tavern, Bath-Street; the Hatchet Inn, Frogmore-Street; the Messrs. Wills' premises, and Canynges' house, Redcliffe-Street. Many others are scattered about in various directions.

THE COURT OF PIE POUDRE.

THIS very ancient court which has in most towns fallen into total disuse, is still held in this city on the 30th of September. It is said to have been established by King Alfred the Great. The court is opened in the open air (under the house with the pillars in front, in the Old Market), by the Registrar of the Tolzey Court, who goes there in procession attended by a body of policemen, bailiffs, etc. After the first day the court is adjourned to the office of the Tolzey Court, and sits there for fourteen days. On the last day the sitting is again held in the open air, as on the day of opening the court, and is then closed until the next 30th of September.

We extract the following sentences from Blackstone, explanatory of the system of the court:—

"The lowest, and at the same time the most expeditious, court of justice known to the law of England is the court of *piepoudre*, *curia pedis pulverizati*; so called from the dusty feet of the suitors; or, according to sir Edward Coke, because justice is there done as speedily as dust can fall from the foot; but the etymology given us by a learned modern writer[*] is much more ingenious and satisfactory; it being derived, according to him, from *pied puldreaux*, (a pedlar, in old French,) and therefore signifying the court of such petty chapmen as resort to fairs or markets. It is a court of record, incident to every fair and market: of which the steward of him, who owns or has the toll of the market, is the judge; and its jurisdiction extends to administer justice for all commercial injuries done in that very fair or market, and not in any preceding one. So that the injury must be done, complained of, heard, and determined, within the compass of one and the same day, unless the fair continues longer. The court hath cognizance of all matters of contract that can possibly arise within the precinct of that fair or market; and the plaintiff must make oath that the cause of an action arose there. From this court a writ of error lies, in the nature of an appeal, to the courts at Westminster; which are now also bound by the statute 19 Geo III. c. 70. to issue writs of execution, in aid of its process, after judgement, where the person or effects of the defendant are not within the limits of this inferior jurisdiction; which may possibly occasion the revival of the practice and proceedings in these courts, which are now in a manner forgotten. The reason of their original institution seems to have been, to do justice expeditiously among the variety of persons that resort from distant places to a

---

[*] Barrington.

fair or market: since it is probable that no other inferior court might be able to serve its process, or execute its judgements, on both, or perhaps either of the parties; and therefore unless this court had been erected, the complaint must necessarily have resorted, even in the first instance, to some superior judicature."

Bristol Worthies.

LEE, Sophia Priscilla, and Harriet Lee. These accomplished sisters,—the authors of the well-known "Canterbury Tales," etc.,—resided long in this city, at St. Vincent's Parade, Hotwells, where the elder sister died. Miss Harriet Lee died at 15, Vyvyan Terrace, Clifton. [See *ante* p. 67.]

LOVELL, Robert, the Poet. The intimate friend of Wordsworth, Southey, and Coleridge. He married Miss Fricker, whose sisters, Edith and Sara were married to Southey and Coleridge. In 1794 he was residing at No. 14, Old Market-Street; he afterwards lived at 16, Berkeley-Square.

MAPES, or Map, Walter, Rector of Westbury-on-Trym, author of many Latin Poems and other works. He was a great favourite of Henry II, who highly esteemed him for his extensive learning and courtly demeanour. His death is supposed to have taken place in 1210.

MATHEWS, William, born at Llandaff, author of a Guide to Bristol. He established in 1791, the " Bristol Directory," which has appeared annually since that year. Died, Oct. 28, 1830, aged 84.

MORE, Hannah, was born at Stapleton, in 1745. Resided for some time at Barley Wood, near Wrington, and afterwards at 4, Windsor Terrace, Clifton, where she died, September 7, 1833. She was interred in Wrington Churchyard, in the same grave with four of her sisters.

MULLER, W. G., the eminent artist. Born in this city. Resided and died at the house at the corner of Park Row and Park Street Avenue. Interred in the burying-ground, belonging to Lewin's Mead Chapel, Brunswick Square.

MANCHEE, T. J., for many years the active, zealous, and intelligent Secretary to the Charity Trustees. From 1819 to 1829, he was the editor of "the Bristol Mercury." In 1831 he published an account of "the Bristol Charities," in 2 vols. 4to. Mr. Manchee, died, June 11, 1853, in his 65th year.

NORTON, Thomas, an eminent philosopher of the 15th century, and author of a poem, entitled "The Ordinall," (which may be found in Ashmole's "Theatrum Chemicum Britannicum," 4to., 1652,) was a native of

Bristol. He lived in the house in St. Peter's Churchyard, now St. Peter's Hospital.

PENN, Admiral Sir William, born 1621. Died 1670, and was buried in Redcliffe Church. His armour and some of the flags which he took in his naval engagements are suspended in the South transept, near his tomb. He was the father of William Penn the founder of Pennsylvania.

POWELL, William, an actor of great merit, one of the patentees of the T. R. Covent Garden. Died, July 3, 1769, aged 33 years, and was interred in Bristol Cathedral.

PRICHARD, James Cowles, M.D. The well known author of the " Physical History of Mankind." He was a resident in this city (at the Red Lodge, Park Row), for thirty-five years. Born at Ross, February 11, 1786. Died in London, December 22, 1848. Buried in Sellack Church, Herefordshire.

PORTER, Jane, author of " The Scottish Chiefs." etc. Born at Durham. Died 29, Portland Square, Bristol, May 24, 1850, aged 74 years. Buried in St. Paul's Churchyard, Portland Square. (See *ante* p. 60.) Her sister, ANNA MARIA PORTER, author of "The Hungarian Brothers," etc. Born, December, 1779. Died at Montpellier, Bristol, June 21, 1832. Buried in the same grave with her sister; where also are interred the remains of her brother, Dr. W. O. Porter, who for many years practised as a physician in this city, he died at his residence, 29, Portland Square, August 15, 1850, aged 76 years.

RICAUT, Robert, Town Clerk of Bristol in the latter part of the 15th century. Author of the Mayor's Calendar.

REDWOOD, Robert, gave the house in King Street, for the Bristol Library.

REYNOLDS, Richard, the great philanthropist, Born at 17, Corn Street, Nov. 12, 1735. Died, September 10, 1816. Buried in the ground adjoining the Friends' Meeting-House, in Rosemary Street.

RICH, Claudius James, the accomplished author of a work on the remains of Babylon. Born in Bristol. Died at Shiraz, October 5, 1821, at the early age of 35.

ROBERTS, William Isaac, a young man of much promise, as a literary man. Born, May 8, 1786. Died, December 26, 1806, and was buried in St. Michael's Churchyard.

ROBINSON, Mary, well remembered for her elegant poems, her beauty, and her misfortunes. Born in the Minster-house, near the Cathedral, November 27, 1758. Died, December 26, 1800. Buried in Old Windsor Churchyard.

SHIPWARD, John, merchant, to whose generosity we are indebted for the very beautiful tower of St. Stephen's Church. He was

Sheriff in 1441, and Mayor in 1455 and 1463. He died 1473, and was interred in the church which owes so much to him.

SECKER, Thomas, D.D. Born, 1693. Died, 1768. This very accomplished and learned divine, was successively Bishop of Bristol, Oxford, and Archbishop of Canterbury. He was buried in an humble grave in Lambeth Churchyard.

SAVAGE, Richard, the ill-fated poet, born in London 1698. Died in Newgate, Bristol, August 11, 1743, and was interred in the adjoining churchyard of St. Peter's; the exact spot where his body rests is unknown, and no monument is erected to his memory.

SOUTHEY, Robert, LL.D., Poet Laureate, born at 11, Wine Street, August 12, 1774. Afterwards resided with his aunt, in Terrell Street; and subsequently on Montague Parade and at Westbury, in a cottage which stood on the spot now occupied by the Convent.

SMITH, Sydney, a Canon of Bristol Cathedral. Editor of the first No. of the " Edinburgh Review." Born at Woodford, Essex, 1768. Died February 23, 1845. Buried in the Kensal Green Cemetery, London.

SHIERCLIFFE, Edward, compiler of the first Bristol Guide. Died Feb. 1, 1798, aged 71. Buried at St. Augustine's.

SEYER, Rev. Samuel, M.A., Rector of Felton. Author of the " Memoirs of Bristol," &c. Born in this city, and died here August 25, 1831.

THORNE, Nicholas, founder of the Grammar School, died 1546. Buried in St. Werburgh's Church.

TYSON, William, F.S.A. This well known antiquary – than whom few were better acquainted with the history of Bristol – died at his residence, Dove Street, Sept. 30, 1851, in his 67th year.

WARBURTON, William, the friend of Pope and many of the greatest literary men of his time. Born 1698. From 1757 to 1759, he was Dean of Bristol. At the end of 1759 he was made Bishop of Gloucester, which bishopric he held till his death, which took place June 7, 1779.

WESLEY, Charles (son of the Rev. Charles Wesley, and nephew of the celebrated John Wesley), for many years organist to George III. and George IV., and composer of some excellent concertos, songs, &c. Born in Bristol, Dec. 11, 1757. Died in London, May 23, 1834.

WORGAN, John Dawes, a young Poet of much ability. Born in Bristol, 1791. Died 1809, and was interred in the Moravian burying ground – the neatest cemetery in Bristol.

WHITELOCKE, Lieut-Gen. Born in 1759. This unfortunate officer, so well remembered on account of his unfortunate expedition to Buenos Ayres and for the investigation fol-

lowing it, lived at Clifton in the latter part of his life, and died in Princes' Buildings.

WYRCESTRE, William. [See ante p. 17.]

WHITSON, John. [See ante p. 32.]

YEARSLEY, Ann, the literary milkwoman. Born in Bristol, 1756. Kept a circulating library in one of the houses under the Piazza, Hotwells. Died at Melksham, 1806.

JOHN WYCLIFFE.

This great man—" The morning star of the Reformation,"—was in 1375 presented with the prebend of Aust, in the collegiate church of Westbury-on-Trym, by Edward III. John Purney, a coadjutor of his, and one of the most zealous of the Lollard preachers, frequently performed service in this city.

JOHN WESLEY.

It was in the neighbourhood of this city that the founder of the Methodists first preached in the open air. This was near the spot where the Wesleyan Chapel, Baptist Mills, now stands. The stone upon which Wesley stood to address his congregation, was preserved and used for the foundation of the above-mentioned chapel. The celebrated Whitfield, the friend and fellow-worker of Wesley, was the first person who in late times preached in the open air; this took place on Saturday afternoon, February 17, 1739, on Hannam Mount, at Rose Green, near this city; the congregation consisting principally of the Kingswood Colliers. Wesley soon followed the example of Whitefield, and preached his first sermon (as above mentioned) shortly afterwards.

NOTICE TO PURCHASERS.

WITH the present issue we conclude the first volume of this work. The four pages of which it is deficient will be added to the number to be issued August 1, and will consist of a title page, table of contents, etc. The August number, it is intended, shall form a prefatory guide book, which will be found of service to strangers and to those desirous of visiting the various objects of interest in this city.

ERRATUM.

P. 76, col. 1, line 51, dele " the."

A quarto edition of this work, printed on stout paper, is also published.

Printed and Published at the Office of the BRISTOL DIRECTORY, 9, Narrow Wine Street, Bristol, by M. Mathews,—July 1, 1854.